Preaching Black Lives (Matter)

Preaching Black Lives (Matter)

EDITED BY GAYLE FISHER-STEWART

CHURCH
PUBLISHING
INCORPORATED

Church Publishing
19 East 34th Street
New York, NY 10016
www.churchpublishing.org

Cover design by Paul Soupiset
Typeset by Rose Design

Library of Congress Cataloging-in-Publication Data

Names: Fisher-Stewart, Gayle, editor.
Title: Preaching Black lives (matter) / edited by Gayle Fisher-Stewart.
Identifiers: LCCN 2020013561 (print) | LCCN 2020013562 (ebook) | ISBN
  9781640652569 (paperback) | ISBN 9781640652576 (epub)
Subjects: LCSH: Preaching. | Racism--Religious
  aspects--Christianity--Sermons. | Race relations--Religious
  aspects--Christianity--Sermons. | Anglican Communion--Sermons. |
  Episcopal Church--Sermons.
Classification: LCC BV4235.S6 P74 2020 (print) | LCC BV4235.S6 (ebook) |
  DDC 241/.675--dc23
LC record available at https://lccn.loc.gov/2020013561
LC ebook record available at https://lccn.loc.gov/2020013562

Contents

PART II. Advocating for Black Lives / 75

Beginning Words

Kwasi Thornell

The Rev. Dr. Kwasi Thornell was ordained an Episcopal priest in 1972. He has always pushed the envelope of what it is to be Black and Episcopalian. We are called to remember our roots, remember our heritage, who God has created us to be, and bring all of that to the Episcopal Church. In his own words . . .

It was a beautiful day on that Saturday morning in Chicago in 1989. People had come from all over the country to St. James Episcopal Cathedral to celebrate the homegoing service for our sister Mattie Hopkins. The Rev. Ed Rodman would say that Mattie Hopkins was the "Mother of the Union." She was there from the beginning of the Union of Black Episcopalians with her quiet and insightful leadership skills. As a member of Trinity Church, she was active in her church, the diocese, and on the national church level, always moving the church to be what it should be and a forceful advocate for the Episcopal members of a darker hue. She often could be seen sporting African clothing and wore a short Afro hairstyle before many of our sisters were ready to make this statement of beauty.

The funeral service was grand in its Episcopal liturgical style. In the procession were several bishops as well as many clergy and lay leaders from the progressive side of the church. The addition of hymns from *Lift Every Voice and Sing*, the Episcopal African American hymnal, gave the service that Black church feel that Mattie would have appreciated. The casket sat on a platform that was covered with a beautiful piece of Kente cloth: bright reds, yellows, and oranges that stood in stark contrast to the traditional heavy pall of gold and white brocade that covered the casket. A statement was being made, one way or another; we just were not sure what it was.

The preacher said all the right things about the witness of Mattie to church and society. A few "amens" could be heard bouncing around the stone columns of the cathedral. The service moved forward in perfect order and, as it was coming to a close, we joined in singing "Lift Every Voice and Sing." During the singing of what many call the Black national anthem, I realized what was wrong with the symbolism of the casket sitting "on" the Kente cloth. Something had to be done. Richard Tolliver, Ed Rodman, Earl Neal, and Jesse Anderson Jr., all priests, were seated with me to the left of the altar. I said to them, "Follow me," and, to my surprise, they all did. As we approached the casket, I said, "Lift it up," and they did. I pulled the Kente cloth out from under the casket and, in an act that would make traditional altar guild members faint, we covered the *Episcopal* white and gold brocade pall with the royal African cloth that a queen of Africa deserved. It truly was an act of the Holy Spirit.

What does it mean to be Black in the Episcopal Church?

Introduction

Gayle Fisher-Stewart

We're still segregated in so many ways. . . . Every Sunday, I look out and, with one or two exceptions, I see all white faces. I bet most of the people in my church don't have any black friends. They know people who are of color, but because they don't associate with them, stereotypes and tensions can flourish.

—*The Rev. Ray Howell*[1]

What is it to be Black and Christian; to be Black and Episcopalian; to be Black and a member of a White denomination? To be unapologetically Black and unashamedly Christian; those words greet you on the website of Trinity United Church of Christ in Chicago, Illinois. Trinity is a Black church in a White denomination. It is a church that is proud of its roots in the Black religious experience. It is a church that claims its African heritage. It is a church that has clung to the values of the original Black churches in this country: a proud people, steeped in their belief in a Jesus who looks like them and knows their suffering; congregations involved in educating and uplifting their people.[2]

To be unapologetically Black and unashamedly Christian, that is also the journey on which we join the Rev. Dr. James Cone as he leads us through the twists and turns as he discovers himself, discovers the self that is the Black theologian. In *Said I Wasn't Gonna Tell Nobody*, his memoir finished shortly before his death in April 2018, Cone challenges us, his Black people, to stop hating who we are. It is time to love the reflection of God we see in the mirror. It is time to stop chasing after Whiteness. I write, as Cone commands, for my people, those who are part of a church—the Episcopal Church—whose roots are in the birthing of slavery. For my people who are witnessing their churches, begun because of the racism in the Episcopal Church, wither away because of gentrification and benign neglect by the Episcopal Church. Cone offers, "When you write, you need to know *who* you are writing for and *what* message you want to deliver to them and *why* you feel the need to say what you've got to say."[3]

---

1. The Rev. Ray Howell, pastor, First Baptist Church, Lexington, NC, "Racial Slur Reveal's a County's Deep Rift," *Washington Post*, October 22, 2019, A-1, 6.

2. Trinity United Church of Christ, accessed July 2, 2019, *https://www.trinitychicago.org/the-history-of-trinity/*.

3. James H. Cone, *Said I Wasn't Gonna Tell Nobody* (New York: Orbis Books, 2018), 22.

And so, I write for my people, my Black siblings who still strive for Whiteness; who shun Black worship, Black religious music; who shun themselves. And I write for my non-Black siblings who see Blackness as less than, something to be feared, something to be avoided at all costs; who believe that to be Episcopalian, we must be like them; like a mold that is all things Anglican; who believe that White theology is the only theology. I also write for my Black siblings who find themselves in other White denominations.

Since the sixteenth century, Christian theology has been implicated in the denial of Black humanity in this country and that denial continues today. Christian theology has defined who was human by exclusion; taking upon itself the power to define who was heathen, who was uncivilized, who was unworthy of God's grace, by using the measuring rod of Whiteness comingled with theology.[4] Anti-Black racism is alive and well in the Church, including the Episcopal Church. Regardless of the Church's claims, our society has never been modeled after the way of Jesus Christ. Rather, as Drew G. I. Hart writes, the White, wealthy, Western male has been the image promoted and adopted. From Constantine, to Thomas Jefferson, to Donald Trump, the White male has been lifted up as the standard against which all people are measured and Jesus has been fashioned into a White man. Hart writes, "With a pseudo-white male Jesus let loose in the church, the boundaries of acceptable theological reflection have neatly aligned with powerful, elite American (white) male interests."[5] Just as to be *American* is to be White, *theology* is White and all who are not White must find themselves in "Black theology," "Womanist theology," "Latin American theology," "Queer theology," and others, to be whole, to be who God created us to be, while Whites just have to be White.

It is time to throw off a colonized mind as it relates to being American and Christian, Christian and Episcopalian. Franz Fanon is correct in his assessment that a colonized people participate in their own oppression by emulating and internalizing the culture and ideas of the oppressor.[6] In *Pedagogy of the Oppressed*, Paulo Freire agrees with Fanon in that he offers that those who are oppressed have been conditioned to fashion themselves after the oppressor,

---

4. Santiago Slabodsky, "It's the Theology, Stupid! Coloniality, Anti-Blackness, and the Bounds of 'Humanity,'" in *Anti-Blackness and Christian Ethics*, ed. Vincent W. Lloyd and Andrew Prevot (New York: Orbis Books, 2017), 32–35.

5. Drew G. I. Hart, *Trouble I've Seen: Changing the Way the Church Views Racism* (Harrisonburg, VA: Herald Press, 2016), 160–61.

6. Peter D-Errico, "What Is a Colonized Mind?" *Indian Country Today*, December 12, 2011, *https:// newsmaven.io/indiancountrytoday/archive/what-is-a-colonized-mind-yMyi0CHjMEO_HV3uM7caRQ*.

the colonizer.[7] This is not to say that those who trace their lineage to various tribes and countries in Africa cannot be Christian and Episcopalian (or members of other White denominations); rather, it means we must, as Freire offers, constantly assess the teachings of the church and decide which are favorable to us. We must make being Christian and Episcopalian (or any other White denomination) our own. Why? Because colonization has contributed to racial self-hatred. The colonizing efforts of the Europeans led to the suppression of indigenous religion, customs, and traditions of those who survived the Middle Passage and their heirs. The veneration of ancestors, "holy dancing and shouting, deity possessions, and drumming"[8] were considered by European colonizers as pagan and savage and were destroyed through torture and other punishments to complete the control over their human chattel. A desire to recover those traditions and customs beaten and bred out of God's people of ebony grace led Teresa P. Mateus to create the Mystic Soul Project, an organization that creates "space for activism, mysticism, and healing by and for people of color."[9] Mateus felt a need to create these spaces for people of color because she didn't see herself reflected in spiritual practices centered in Whiteness. In these spaces—conferences, retreats—people of color gather and have the freedom where they are able to shake off the shackles of suppression and oppression and celebrate all of themselves.

For the Church to reflect Jesus, there must be a White metanoia—a White repentance—because the shame of slavery is not ours; it is the sole property of White people. Colonization has taught us to bear the shame of something that was done to us as opposed to putting it squarely in the laps of those who denied us humanity, in and out of the Church. To be Black is not to be deficient, or defective; we are just different. Say it loud, I'm Black and I'm proud and I want to be me, to see me in whatever Church I may be a member. On occasion, the Episcopal Church will trot out Blackness, usually during Black History Month or other special, read *ethnic*, occasions.

On the other hand, it seems we have a church that is more interested in maintaining the institution than it is in taking a chance, risking it all, as Jesus did, and changing this world into what God created it to be. Jesus, God incarnate, came to earth to show how the world could be if God's people would just

---

7. Paulo Freire, *Pedagogy of the Oppressed*, 20th anniv. ed. (New York: Continuum, 1997), 27.

8. L. H. Whelchel Jr., *The History and Heritage of African-American Churches: A Way Out of No Way* (St. Paul, MN: Paragon House, 2011), 82.

9. Da'Shawn Mosley, "Recentering Spirituality: Creating Space for Activism, Mysticism, and Healing by and for People of Color," *Sojourners* 47, no. 11 (December 2018): 16–18.

get with the program and follow him into the margins where those who have been excluded by a world that commodifies humanness will be found. The presiding bishop of the Episcopal Church, Michael Curry, has stated that we should be challenged to change the world from the nightmare human beings have made it into the dream God wants it to be. That is a rough, a tough pronouncement, certainly not something you want on signboard, that the world, in its current state, is a nightmare. Or perhaps the nightmare should be the truth we proclaim and claim. Perhaps if the truth of what the world has become was on the lips of all who call themselves Christians, the Church could be a place where we come to gird up our loins to get into the battle against the forces that long for a White America and Church.

Since 2017 the Rev. Yolanda Norton[10] has been the inspiration behind the Beyoncé Mass, first held at Christ Episcopal Cathedral in San Francisco. In the promo for the mass, the Rev. Jude Harmon says:

> I think a lot of the people who show up tonight are people of color, LGBT people, people onto whom other people's narratives have been projected and just to be honest, the church hasn't been the best at lifting up those voices. [The service] really began with us saying, how can we actually be the people of God we hope to be in the world. . . . Honestly, I think Beyoncé is a better theologian than many of the pastors and priests in our church today. That is not an exaggeration.[11]

As the Rev. Yolanda Norton offers, using the music of Beyoncé enabled her to have conversations about Black women, their worship, and their spirituality.[12] All too often, particularly in mainstream, dominant culture denominations, the worship culture is White and overseen by men. Those who enter are expected to leave their religious culture(s) at the door and assimilate to the proper way of worship. And while Black women (and men) serve in all capacities in the Episcopal Church, that does not mean that the stained glass ceiling has been forever cracked or dismantled in other denominations. It does not mean that our Black churches, historically and otherwise, and Black denominations, created and maintained by racism, are thriving. Nor does it mean that

---

10. The Rev. Dr. Yolanda Norton is assistant professor of New Testament at San Francisco Theological Seminary.

11. "The Church Service That Worships Beyonce," YouTube, May 17, 2017, *https://www.youtube.com/watch?v=PXci-sRayAQ&t=202s.*

12. "The Church Service That Worships Beyonce," YouTube.

non-Whites and our LGBTQIA+ siblings have found recognition and freedom of worship at all levels of the Church at large.

This book announces from the very top of the mountain that Black people (and others) are created by and in the image of a loving God and the contributors are willing to speak their truth to change the world and the Church. The contributors have the ability to see the great multitude pictured in Revelation 7:9:

> After this I looked, and there a great multitude that no one could count, from every nation, from all tribes and peoples and languages, standing before the throne and before the Lamb. . . .

Life has gotten better for African Americans since the 1950s when our schools were legally segregated, when I watched my cousin's father who looked White go into a country store to purchase ice for our outing after my father had been denied because of his skin color. Things have changed, even from the 1970s, as I patrolled the streets of Washington, DC, as a police officer. In some sections of the city, I would be met with "Can they send a White officer?" or "Would you go to the back door?" Yes, things have changed; however, as more things change, the more things remain the same or get worse.

In *Breathe: A Letter to My Sons*, Imani Perry writes of the fear she has for her two Black sons in a society that denies their humanity.[13] Kelly Brown Douglas writes:

> Every time he [her son] leaves the house I pray, "God please be my eyes, and be my hands, watch over my son and bring him safely home." I am sure that I am not the only black mother who prays such a prayer when her black child, especially a black male child, leaves home. . . . So I tremble at the thought that the world is not safe for our sons because if God cannot protect them who can?[14]

How many Black mothers and fathers sit in our pews wondering if God cares enough to protect our children from White racism? Is there a word from the Church?

On the other side of the coin, as we look at the church, the Diocese of Vermont elected and consecrated its first African American female diocesan

---

13. Imani Perry, *Breathe: A Letter to My Sons* (Boston: Beacon Press, 2019).

14. Kelly Brown Douglas, *Stand Your Ground: Black Bodies and the Justice of God* (New York: Orbis Books, 2015), 130.

bishop, Shannon McVean-Brown, in 2019. Vermont is 95 percent white. In 2016, the Diocese of Indianapolis elected and consecrated the first female African American diocesan bishop in the history of the Episcopal Church, Jennifer Baskerville Burrows. The first African American male elected diocesan bishop was John Burgess in 1970. In 2015, Michael Curry was consecrated as the first African American presiding bishop of the Episcopal Church. Yes, there have been moments to make your heart flutter and say, perhaps, just perhaps, things have changed, but then there is the soul crushing, *but*.

In November 2019, at the Indianapolis diocesan convention, one of the contributors, the Very Rev. Kelly Brown Douglas, dean of the Episcopal Divinity School, delivered the keynote address in which she stated, "It is only in speaking the truth about the White supremacist legacy that is ours that we will be truly able to repent of it and turn around and do something different. . . . [We need to be honest about] who we are, who we have been, and who we want to be as the Church. The Church cannot be White and Church; a decision has to be made." [15]

Yes, we have made great strides in this country in race relations; however, eleven o'clock on Sunday is still the most segregated hour in this country. If the Church cannot lead the way to the beloved community, who can? Who will? To what degree does the Church care? Is it willing to risk it all to make the face and mission of Jesus real in the world? Brené Brown has offered that to continue to ask those who are traumatized by bigotry and hatred to build the table and ask others to join is wrong. It is those who continue to benefit from racism who must do the hard work. [16] The Church, particularly the Episcopal Church as the Church of England, birthed racism in this country; therefore, the Episcopal Church must take the lead in its eradication. It began racism on these shores through the adoption of slavery; therefore, it must hold itself responsible for doing whatever is necessary to make God's kingdom real on earth because for all too many who deal with racism every day, heaven can wait.

I want to thank the writers who contributed to this work because dealing with race is difficult. Writing and discussing race makes one vulnerable to attack from those who believe this country and the Church are theirs. Writing and discussing race is soul- and gut-wrenching work; however, it is holy work.

---

15. The Very Rev. Kelly Brown Douglas, "The Work Our Soul Must Do," keynote address, November 15, 2019, *https://www.youtube.com/watch?v=qLTDDFSxMVA&t=2058s*.

16. Brené Brown, "The Quest for True Belonging and Courage to Stand Alone," interview on *The 1A*, September 12, 2017, *https://the1a.org/shows/2017-09-12/brene-brown-the-quest-for-true-belonging-and-the-courage-to-stand-alone*.

Dealing with race also requires that we admit our own complicity in upholding a system that is contrary to the life and mission of Jesus; that at times, we have permitted our religiosity to become the opiate that dulls our senses to the reality that all too many of God's sun-kissed children experience every day of their lives. While the majority of the writers are Episcopalian, other voices have contributed their take on race and the Church. Jesus transgressed boundaries and borders and in the eradication of race, the Church, the body of Christ, must get beyond its own borders and lines of demarcation to be what the Church is called to be. I also want to thank Church Publishing and Milton Brasher-Cunningham, the editor of this book; they took a chance on a very wild journey.

We begin this journey with sermons that challenge us to think about race: sermons that require a risk to be preached from the pulpit. Preaching is holy work; however, it is also fraught with danger. There are many in our pews who view preaching about race as being too political and will challenge the pastor, leave the church, or withdraw their funding. But preach we must. Then we move on to reflections and essays on advocating for Black lives in the Church and society. These essays stretch us to see Church in ways that are truly inclusive, that encourage us to ensure that our churches are sanctuaries for all God's people. Finally, we hear the call to rethink or expand Christian formation, from our seminaries to our sanctuaries. As we take this journey, there are reflections from pilgrims who traveled the Civil Rights Trail in Alabama with me in May 2019. Fifty-two people of faith—mostly Episcopalian, but also Baptist, Mennonite—and atheist, Black and White, young and not-so-young, gay and straight, clergy and lay, traveled together for five days, to learn from those involved in the struggle for Black civil and human rights. We learned from being in the company of each other and we learned from each other.

I hope these offerings begin or continue the conversations that must occur to create opportunities for people to gather and be "proximate" in the words of Equal Justice Initiative (EJI) founder Bryan Stevenson,[17] to be open to hearing voices that challenge, voices that cry out for God's justice in this time and in this place. Perhaps, just perhaps, if these conversations occur, the Church can truly be the body of Christ in a world that desperately needs God's justice today.

---

17. Bryan Stevenson, "Get Proximate to People Who are Suffering" (commencement address given at Bates College, May 27, 2018), *https://www.bates.edu/news/2018/05/27/get-proximate-to-people-who-are-suffering-bryan-stevenson-tells-bates-college-commencement-audience/*.

PART 1

Preaching Black Lives Matter

Introduction

IS THERE A WORD FROM THE LORD?

Gayle Fisher-Stewart

We really "had church today!" is a familiar expression among African Americans following a Spirit-filled worship experience. The implication of this folksy phrase is that the Spirit of God had moved with such power that all social barriers were removed and worshipers were able to "have a good time in the Lord." The passionate, celebrative style of preaching had no doubt reached the depth of worshipers' souls and had "set them on fire!" The Word of God in sermon and song had spoken to the conditions of the gathered community, who could say emphatically that they had "heard a word from the Lord."

—Melva Wilson Costen[1]

If the only thing a preacher hears from a congregation week after week is how much they enjoyed the sermon, it is very likely that the preacher is not dealing with challenging content.

—Marvin McMickle[2]

"African American spirituality is a spirituality that was born and shaped in the heat of oppression and suffering." It included a tradition of Jesus that connected the dissonant strands of grief and hope in the experience of black people who trusted in God to make a way out of no way. "Blackness is the metaphor for suffering," [Prof. J. Alfred Smith] said. "To know blackness is to be connected to the suffering, hope, and purpose of black people."

—Reggie L. Williams[3]

Bryan Stevenson, the genius behind the Equal Justice Initiative in Montgomery, Alabama, has said that racism can be eradicated when we become

---

1. Melva Wilson Costen, *African American Christian Worship* (Nashville, TN: Abingdon Press, 1993), 65.

2. Marvin A. McMickle, *The Making of a Preacher: 5 Essentials for Ministers Today* (Valley Forge, PA: Judson Press, 2018), 162.

3. Reggie L. Williams, *Bonhoeffer's Black Jesus: Harlem Renaissance Theology and an Ethic of Resistance* (Waco, TX: Baylor University Press, 2014), ix.

proximate or close to one another. Sometimes I wonder if that, in fact, is true. How much closer can you get to a person than to engage in the sexual act that creates new life? How much closer can you get to a person than to give your child over to the Black wet nurse and have that woman's milk coursing through your child, nourishing your child, providing the antibodies that will keep your child healthy? How much closer can you get to someone who works in your home every single day? Who is on duty twenty-four hours a day? Who cooks every meal you eat, who shares your living space, who shares the air you breathe? How much closer do you have to be to be *proximate*?

The German theologian Dietrich Bonhoeffer tested proximity. When he came to New York in 1931 on fellowship at Union Theological Seminary and affiliated with the Black Abyssinian Baptist Church in Harlem, under the leadership of Adam Clayton Powell Sr., he found a Black Jesus who suffered with Black Americans in a White supremacist society. For Bonhoeffer, the ministers of White churches of New York lacked content in their sermons. They preached everything except of the gospel of Jesus Christ—a gospel of resistance, of survival. He found in the worship of Abyssinian a style that had a different view of society than White churches. It was a style that acknowledged the suffering of Black people in a racist society that viewed African Americans as subhuman and legitimized brutality against them in so many ways.[4] Preaching came alive and strengthened those in Abyssinian's pews to fight against a Church and society that viewed Blacks as less than human.

In Harlem, and at Abyssinian, Bonhoeffer found the Black Jesus who understood the colonized lives of African Americans as opposed to a White Christ who was used to justify Black suffering and maltreatment. He found and worshiped a Black Jesus who disrupted White supremacy; a Black Jesus who negated the White Christ who, since colonial times, had been at the foundation of racial terrorism, served as an opiate to sedate Black people to see themselves through the eyes of Whiteness as subhuman, and to accept their unjust lot in life as a condition that had been ordained by God. The White Christ inculcated racial self-loathing for Blacks. They were taught to hate everything African: African religion, African customs, African traditions. They were taught that they descended from heathens and had no history worth the time of Whites to study. Bonhoeffer found a Jesus who was the antithesis of the Christ Whites claimed to follow, but whose actions and lives told otherwise. He found a Black Jesus who turned White supremacy on its head, who

---

4. Williams, *Bonhoeffer's Black Jesus*, 1, 21–23.

dispelled the notion of a White-centered world where "morality and racial identity are comingled and measured in proportion to the physical likeness to white bodies."[5] He came to understand that White Christianity was infected with and by White supremacy and a Black Jesus was a frightening disruption to Whites who were made comfortable when Black people accepted the structures of a White world.[6]

A Black Jesus, on the other hand, enabled oppressed African Americans to imagine him outside White societal structures and a Christianity that upheld White supremacy. A Black Jesus had a "this world" focus that pursued justice here and now, as opposed to an other-worldly orientation that encouraged Black people to accept their dehumanized lot on earth and look toward freedom in heaven. This focus in the here and now mandated activism in the politics of a racist society that denied Black people their share of what was God's. Under the tutelage of Adam Clayton Powell Sr., Bonhoeffer learned that the Black church was the center of the community and the people were involved in "applied Christianity," an active faith that changed the society in which African Americans found themselves. Powell knew that the Black church needed to reach beyond itself and to that end, he developed a worship environment that would help anyone, regardless of race, to understand the other and to engage in an active love with Jesus at the center.[7] Bonhoeffer studied W. E. B. Du Bois, who argued:

> The historical Jesus would be unwelcomed in a Christian society that is at home with white supremacy. In their general religious devotion, white-supremacist Christians are participants in Jesus' crucifixion because, in truth, their Christianity was not about Christ; white racists wedded Jesus to white supremacy, shaping Christian discipleship to govern a racial hierarchy.[8]

While Bonhoeffer's experience was in the 1930s, we find ourselves in a similar position today with White supremacy rearing its ugly head and the Church largely remaining silent. Bonhoeffer's learnings are relevant today and we must look to those who have left templates for us as we preach a word that upsets a Christianity that looks little like the Black Jesus Bonhoeffer found in Harlem who animated Black churches to be the Church, the body of Christ, in a world where suffering seemed to have the upper hand.

---

5. Williams, *Bonhoeffer's Black Jesus*, 25.

6. Williams, *Bonhoeffer's Black Jesus*, 25, 54, 58–62.

7. Williams, *Bonhoeffer's Black Jesus*, 62, 81, 90–91.

8. Williams, *Bonhoeffer's Black Jesus*, 62.

Preaching the gospel steeped in a Black Jesus of Nazareth takes courage and there are examples to guide us. Preaching requires vulnerability—especially prophetic preaching: preaching that troubles the waters of a country, a world that seems determined to live in the sin of racism. Brené Brown defines vulnerability as *risk + uncertainty + emotional exposure*.[9] Jesus risked it all to confront the unjust powers of his day. If the body of Christ is to be his representative on earth, the Church must risk it all for the gospel, a gospel that challenges this country's original sin and the role the Church played in it. The preacher must be willing to risk upsetting the congregation, at the least, to move it from its place of comfort to a place where eliminating racism becomes its call. There will be uncertainty because it is unknown how the people will initially react and later act as a result of the sermon. Finally, the preacher must risk something of themselves to let the congregation know what is in and on their heart. The Rev. Dr. Pauli Murray said there is a certain fear when a minister attempts to preach the Word of God. That fear results from the realization that we are so small and God is so great and, regardless of the level of education, the number of years preaching, or the hours of sermon preparation, our preaching will always fall short because human beings fall short and God's judgment always looms near.[10] There is no perfect sermon.

The Rev. Florence Spearing Randolph put it all on the line and opened herself to being vulnerable when she mounted the pulpit on Sunday, February 14, 1941, at Wallace Chapel AME Zion Church in Summit, New Jersey. She was about to trouble the waters with a sermon that was so controversial for its time that it was reported in both the White and Black press. A female African American, she preached a sermon titled, "If I Were White." In a sermon that would be relevant today, but was written for her particular time, Rev. Randolph lifted a mirror to the hypocrisy of America and White people in the treatment of African Americans. She preached of the need for racial justice and economic parity that could have provided the foundation for Martin Luther King Jr.'s challenge against America's three evils—racism, capitalism, and militarism—and the need for White people to take responsibility for the mess they created.

She preached during a time of war. World War II was raging, which added additional vulnerability to her words as they could be seen as challenging, not

---

9. Brené Brown, "The Quest for True Belonging and Courage to Stand Alone," interview, *The IA*, September 12, 2017, *https://the1a.org/shows/2017-09-12/brene-brown-the-quest-for-true-belonging-and-the-courage-to-stand-alone*.

10. Pauli Murray, "The Gift of the Holy Spirit," in Bettye Collier-Thomas, *Daughters of Thunder: Black Women Preachers and Their Sermons*, 1850–1979 (San Francisco: Jossey-Bass, 1998), 254.

only Christianity, but also this country's patriotism. She took a proverbial knee in the pulpit, much like Colin Kaepernick's protest against the singing of the national anthem. I can imagine this *Daughter of Thunder* skillfully opening a wound in the psyche of White Americans by declaring that if Whites "believed in Democracy as taught by Jesus [and] loved [their] country and believed . . . [the United States], because of her high type of civilization, her superior resources, her wealth and culture," then that country should be a bastion of peace and make sure all her people are cared for because "charity begins at home."[11]

From her pulpit in this supposed White church, she declared that White America needed to pull the "beam out of thine own eye" (Matt. 7:5, KJV) before finding fault with other nations. A precursor to Bryan Stevenson's call for being proximate, she called for Black and White ministers to exchange pulpits. She urged the various organizations in White churches to study Black history and realize that Black Americans had demonstrated their loyalty by dying for this country from 1776 on. But then she hit the jugular vein and said, "If I were white and believed in God, in His Son Jesus Christ and the Holy Bible," as if being White precluded believing in all three or even one, that she would challenge all who took the pulpit to speak against all that degrades God's people: racism, prejudice, hatred, oppression, and injustice. She put the responsibility for racism squarely where it belonged, telling the White race that it should show its superiority by taking responsibility for ending racial prejudice. She used scripture to make her point: if one says they love God but not a sibling in Christ, that person was a liar (1 John 4:20). She mounted her challenge to Whites to end discrimination against Blacks in housing, education, entertainment venues, and health care. She recognized and indicted systemic racism. She confronted Whites who were ignorant of Black history and called for them to put books on Black history in the libraries and to see that Black history was taught in schools. Then, with just a hint of the task that is before her, she admitted that she did not know how successful she would be if she were White, but that her conscience would be clear. She ended with a dream in which she, as a White person, was trying to avoid a Black person who was gaining on her. Finally, the Black person stood side by side with her and her wrath was kindled. The Black person was equal to her, but then she turned to act on her wrath and was "struck dumb with fear, for lo, the Black man was not there, but Christ

---

11. Florence Spearing Randolph, "If I Were White," sermon, February 14, 1941, in Collier-Thomas, *Daughters of Thunder*, 128.

stood in his place. And Oh! the pain, the pain, the pain, that looked from that dear face."[12] Would Whites act differently if Jesus were physically Black?

Randolph's sermon was daring for the time and daring for a woman because women still had a difficult time finding acceptance from men both inside and outside the Church that they had a call from God to preach. Randolph was fortunate because the African Methodist Episcopal Zion (AMEZ) Church began ordaining women in 1894. A lot was at stake for her, as a woman and as an African American to preach as she did. Race prejudice and violence were an ever-present threat. Jim Crow, segregation, and the lynchings of Blacks who did not "know their place" were never far from the minds of African Americans. It was not outside the realm of possibility that she could have been lynched. She knew she was vulnerable; she took the risk anyway.

A great preacher *brings a word* to the congregation and brings the self to the sermon. They bring scripture to life and offer a glimpse into who they are, what they believe, what they stand for, and how they have evolved. The Rev. Dr. Anna Pauline (Pauli) Murray was one such preacher. She was ordained as an Episcopal priest in 1977 at the age of sixty-seven. In 1974, she served as the crucifer at the irregular ordination of the Philadelphia Eleven, the first women *irregularly* ordained in the Episcopal Church. It was a time of change and challenge in the Episcopal Church. Women had challenged the belief that God did not call women to preach and serve at the Table in the Church. Murray was the first African American female ordained as priest in the Episcopal Church. She was used to bending the rules and norms that attempted to define the place of women and African Americans in society and the Church. Pauli Murray came to the priesthood after an illustrious career as an attorney, civil rights activist, and educator. She could have easily ignored God's call on her life, but she did not.

In five sermons preached between 1974 and 1979—"The Dilemma of the Minority Christian" (1974), "The Holy Spirit" (1977), "The Gift of the Holy Spirit (1977), "Can These Bones Live Again?" (1978), and "Salvation and Liberation" (1979)—we see an evolution of her thinking as a theologian and how she wrestled with being obedient to Jesus and being a Black Christian in a racist society and the Episcopal Church. In "Dilemma," preached three years before her ordination, she took as her text Isaiah 53:3–6, the Suffering Servant, and concluded that even in the face of racism and racial violence, the Black Christian must follow the example of Christ who went to the cross and said not "a

---

12. Florence Spearing Randolph, "If I Were White," sermon preached February 14, 1941, in Collier-Thomas, *Daughters of Thunder*, 128–29.

mumblin' word." To follow Christ as he hanged from the lynching tree was difficult for Murray and she revealed that her rebelliousness and impatience tested her ability to accept Black suffering as Jesus had accepted his. She did not want to be despised because of her race (or her gender, which was fluid).

She was torn because she wanted to be a true follower, a true disciple, but questioned whether she was able to do as the Lord did. The answer was not clear and she knew it was because she questioned the meaning of salvation as it related to life in the present, to life on earth. She said that life in the here and now should involve being safe; that people should be able to live in safety, and live without fear, knowing that God's love was available to everyone, although that was not the life for African Americans. She struggled with what many Christians have always struggled: how to love those who make it difficult to love, those who treat God's Black children as less than human, and she concluded that as long as we live as we are called to do—in community—there will always be conflict. However, if we respond with conflict, we cut ourselves off from God's love and a sense of community. If we fight back with violence, we become lost and alone. She acknowledged that African Americans fought for self-respect and pride, both which had been denied by Whites, and she knew that having self-pride was a stumbling block to salvation. She questioned whether African Americans had to make a choice between having self-pride and enduring racism and injustice without saying "a mumblin' word."

She seemed to rely on redemptive suffering because she offered that "whatever we suffer is part of God's ultimate plan; that we are in fact God's Suffering Servants in the salvation history of the world."[13] Ultimately, she offered that what African Americans endured was not a struggle between White people and Black people but a struggle between good and evil.[14] Like those in our cities who face the constant fear of meeting death at the hands of a police officer, or those who are sentenced to life in substandard housing, or those who find themselves in the snares of an unjust justice system, Murray understood that there are times when we ask about the presence of evil and the seeming inability of God to handle it.

In "Can These Bones Live Again?," a sermon using the text of Ezekiel 37:1–7, Murray said she was unable to fully grasp the Holy Spirit unless she was able to relate it to her own life. In her previous sermons, the Holy Spirit was a given; however, here she pushed back, harkening to her words in *The Dilemma*

---

13. Collier-Thomas, *Daughters of Thunder*, 257–62.

14. Collier-Thomas, *Daughters of Thunder*, 257–62.

of the Minority Christian where she confessed she was rebellious and impatient. When will her people be free? she asked. She used Psalm 137 to examine what it was to be in exile, to be exiled away from everything you know. She related exile to the experiences of African Americans, stolen from their homeland and then, during the Great Migration, experiencing exile again. Babylon of the spirit is everywhere for those who try to find their roots and as they roam rootless in a country that denies their humanity and yet is home.[15] As Nikole Hannah Jones writes in the *New York Times* "The 1619 Project," African Americans are African by heritage and American by citizenship.[16] How do we keep singing, saying everything will be all right when everything around us says otherwise?

Still, she lamented, even after all she had done in her life before and after ordination, that she might die before she was able to complete God's mission in her life. How many of us share her feeling that there is just so much to do and so many more years in the rearview mirror than lie ahead? She voiced possible doom and admitted that she was an exile who was returning to the South after a fifty-year absence. Still, she continued living into her call and "out of these dry bones, the outcasts of the earth—even women—shall arise and the House of Israel shall be reborn."[17]

Murray posed a series of questions that challenges the relevancy of the Church. These questions lead us back to Kelly Brown Douglas when she asks whether the Church is going to be White or is it going to be Church?[18] A White Church forces everyone who is not White to attempt to be something they can never be—White, which causes trauma and self-loathing. Murray wanted to know if the Church is strong enough, courageous enough to challenge the "powers and principalities," the systemic evils that destroy humanity and seem to be "virtually immune to individual morality."[19] She offered that the Church had become too ingrained in maintaining the status quo to be a force for change; the Church had been coopted and corrupted by a false world that competed with God's creation. She extolled the virtues and writings of liberation theologists, among them Gustavo Gutierrez. The civil rights activist and the theologian in her united as she argued for a life of freedom "*here* and

---

15. Pauli Murray, "Can These Bones Live Again," in Collier-Thomas, *Daughters of Thunder*, 272.

16. Nikole Hannah Jones, "The 1619 Project," *New York Times Magazine*, August 18, 2019, 26.

17. Collier-Thomas, *Daughters of Thunder*, 276.

18. Kelly Brown Douglas, "The Work Our Soul Must Do" (keynote speech, Episcopal Diocese of Indianapolis, Diocesan Convention, November 15, 2019), *https://www.youtube.com/watch?v=qLTDDFSxMVA&t=1774s*.

19. Pauli Murray, "Salvation and Liberation," in Collier-Thomas, *Daughters of Thunder*, 264.

now.[20] Sin was corporate as well as individual; the Church could not ignore corporate sin and focus solely on individual or private sin. She quoted the Rev. Dr. Martin Luther King Jr. in that for the church "to accept passively an evil system [is] as immoral as active perpetuation of it, [and] . . . a righteous person has no alternative but to refuse to cooperate with an evil system."[21] It was time to fight back and no longer accept things as they were. It was time to throw off the negative stereotypes and beliefs of African Americans that dominated White society and call out the Church that fed into that system. Finally, she said, what was needed was a "redefinition of the task of the Church in the world."[22] The Church, rather than hiding in its piety, was called to take a stand and lead the world in throwing off the powers that sought to negate God's African American children. The Church had to live into being the body of Christ, the Christ who challenged unjust powers.

Both Murray and Randolph preached dangerous sermons, although we don't know if either would have classified their sermons as such. Preaching can calm or excite; it can arouse or convict. Preaching can fill the hearer or leave the hearer empty. There is a purpose for preaching and Frank Thomas says that the purpose of preaching, particularly in the African American tradition, is to offer the hearer an assurance of God's grace in the gospel of Jesus Christ. That whatever the person may be going through, whatever is occurring in that person's life, God lifts up, strengthens, and encourages the hearer. God, in some cases, walks with that person "through the valley of the shadow of death" (Ps. 23, KJV). A good sermon can be the moral compass needed for a congregation or for society at large to repent of the evils that infect them. It can point the way to a way of life that God wants for God's people. A sermon is to always offer hope, even in the midst of despair.[23]

Regardless of the skill of the preacher, regardless of race of the preacher or congregation, there ought to be times at the end of a sermon that deals with a difficult topic that the minister is not greeted with kudos. Depending on the nature of the sermon, people might even get up and walk out because the sermon has hit a nerve or is deemed too political. Other times, the worshiper does not want to face the truth, particularly as it relates to racial oppression. Preaching against racism, lifting up #BlackLivesMatter is bound to cause some

---

20. Pauli Murray, "Salvation and Liberation," in Collier-Thomas, *Daughters of Thunder*, 266–67.

21. Pauli Murray, "Salvation and Liberation," in Collier-Thomas, *Daughters of Thunder*, 267.

22. Collier-Thomas, *Daughters of Thunder*, 269.

23. Frank Thomas, "The Nature and Purpose of Preaching," July 4, 2016, *https://www.youtube.com/watch? time_continue=11&v=Qi22PK3DA4Y&feature=emb_title.*

heartburn. According to Marvin McMickle, "preachers are made when they experience some negative reactions to what they have said but find the courage to keep saying what the Lord has laid on their heart."[24] Preaching #BlackLivesMatter can make witnesses for the Lord because the preacher has seen something in society that needs to be corrected, something that needs to be changed and has the courage to proclaim it from the pulpit. These preachers decided not to run from the truth; rather, a decision has been made to turn and face the truth head on and make a statement that can change the lives of those in their pews[25] and their community. Both Murray and Randolph faced that challenge head-on. There was the need to be vulnerable and to take a risk.

Preaching is a vital part of the worship experience. Worship is not an escape from the world; however, for many African Americans, whether in the traditional Black church or the Euro-American (White) church, it is through the worship experience that Black Christians are able to either hear about or create a world in which they are valued—one where they are able to live into God's love for all God's people. Through the worship experience, and particularly, the preached word, African Americans hear and experience the way life should be on this earth; a life that is in congruence with God's will for creation. It is through their understanding of God that they are able to live into their trust in a God who, in all too many cases, has been depicted as White and merely tolerant of those who, it was once claimed, did not descend from Adam,[26] and were unworthy of salvation—at least White salvation. As Frederick Hilborn Talbot writes, "It is through preaching that Black people are given hope as they struggle against oppression in society; as they gather to hear that God is incarnational and is present in their struggles; that God loves them, and shares in their common life and pain."[27]

Annie Woodley Brown offers that the Christian Church has been and continues to be caught between the *knowledge of good and evil* as opposed to being the countercultural voice against evil. Rather than being the face of God where all are valued and everyone is loved as one's neighbor, the Church has fallen prey to the secular world's embrace of racism.[28] Not only has it embraced the

---

24. McMickle, *Making of a Preacher*, 162.

25. McMickle, *Making of a Preacher*, 163.

26. Frederick Hilborn Talbot, *African American Worship: New Eyes for Seeing* (Eugene, OR: Wipf and Stock, 2007), 67.

27. Talbot, *African American Worship*, 67.

28. Annie Woodley Brown, "Racism and the Christian Church in America: Caught between the Knowledge of Good and Evil," *Social Work in Public Health* 34, issue 1 (March 2019), *https://www.tandfonline.com/doi/abs/10.1080/19371918.2019.1566111.*

sin of racism, the Church was at the taproot of racism in this country and that sin needs to be called out in preaching. There is a saying in the Black church that if it isn't preached from the pulpit, it isn't important.

The manure of racism fertilizes the ground in which "God's gonna trouble the waters" to experience a different way of viewing the world into which the incarnate Jesus was born; a world in which Jesus came to turn it right side up; a world in which God's people recognize that racism is the antithesis to God's creation. It is into this world that the preacher steps, who after having already prepared a sermon, sometimes has to tear it up, and begin anew. Another unarmed Black man or woman has been shot to death by a police officer. Or perhaps, the waters need to be troubled because White supremacists have burned yet another Black church. Or, another Black man has been freed from prison because of new DNA evidence that proved innocence. Or, Black children have been suspended from school because their natural hair does not conform to white standards. Or, perhaps the preacher is just tired of seeing Black bodies used as fodder for the criminal justice system or corralled in ghettos created by unjust housing and economic policies. The list can go on and on. Preaching is soul work, and preaching racial justice challenges even the best of preachers. Preaching, according to Frank Thomas, is "terrible and dangerous. It is terrible because if we do our job well, preaching troubles and shakes the foundations of the world. True preaching dares to speak truth to powerful forces that have their own 'alternative facts' and do not want to be challenged."[29]

Preaching is difficult, particularly in times when the Church and the country are polarized. The preacher can be the most polished, the most charismatic, the most dynamic, and still, preaching can cause butterflies, cause angst. Preaching about race is traumatic, teaching about race is traumatic, even with the help of the Holy Spirit. It is traumatic because it is difficult to determine how the sermon will be accepted, if the sermon will be accepted, and whether or not the sermon will move the hearers to *do something.* Crafting a prophetic sermon that speaks to both those who are in positions to change the status of the marginalized and those who are marginalized takes skill.[30] Regardless of whether or not the race of the preacher and those in the pews *match*, what for some is viewed as politics can either bring the congregation together or tear it apart. However, womanist theologian Katie Geneva Cannon reminds us that "preaching is a

---

29. Frank A. Thomas, *How to Preach a Dangerous Sermon* (Nashville: Abingdon Press, 2018), xii.

30. Phil Snider, ed., *Preaching Resistance: Voices of Hope, Justice and Solidarity* (St. Louis, MO: Chalice Press, 2018), 1.

divine activity" and when we look at race and racism, that divine activity calls for the Word of God "to be proclaimed or announced on a contemporary issue with an ultimate response to our God."[31] There is a proviso when preaching a word that disrupts, when preaching becomes dangerous: it "risks challenging those in power,"[32] and when that happens, be prepared for the preacher to be approached about preaching politics. Yet, preaching *done right* has the power to free the oppressed from the constraints of a racist society and renew hope in what could be. Preaching *done right* has the power to transform those who hear the word proclaimed if only temporarily.[33]

Preaching has the power to be a corrective, says W. Scott Haldeman:

> [Preaching] provides Christians with an opportunity to leave behind—for momentary and fragile periods—the structures of inequality and violence that pervade our lives and to imagine—and, even more, to experience—an alternative mode of being, a place and time where justice and peace are known, where a communion of love is tasted, ingested and so . . . embodied. . . . [T]o invoke poet warrior Audre Lorde, [preaching] makes us dissatisfied with anything less in our everyday lives.[34]

What is it like to preach Black Lives (Matter) if the preacher is White and the congregation is Black or the reverse? Is preaching racial justice easier if the preacher's race and the congregation's race are the same? Would there be a need to preach Black Lives Matter if, for example, the congregation and preacher are both Asian? What if the congregation and preacher look the same but are culturally different? If the preacher and congregation are White, is there a risk to the preacher when preaching about the racial issues that plague this country today? What is gained? What could be lost? Who would care?

One of the issues facing the Church today is how to attract and keep young people. While providing insight into African American millennials, Frank Thomas,[35] the creator of the first and only PhD program in African American Preaching and Sacred Rhetoric in the country, offers that the Church must

---

31. Katie Geneva Cannon, *Teaching Preaching: Isaac Rufus Clark and Black Sacred Rhetoric* (New York: Continuum, 2003), 53.

32. Thomas, *How to Preach a Dangerous Sermon*, xv.

33. Costen, *African American Christian Worship*, 67–68.

34. W. Scott Haldeman, Chicago Theological Seminary, *https://www.ctschicago.edu/people/w-scott-haldeman/*.

35. The Rev. Dr. Frank A. Thomas teaches and is the director of the PhD program in African American Preaching and Sacred Rhetoric at Christian Theological Seminary in Indianapolis, Indiana.

be relevant to this group to keep their attention. Young people are concerned with the "emergence of mass social movements. If the church does not address race . . . or is not thoughtful or skilled in addressing [this] issue, Millennials will consider church not relevant to their needs and struggles."[36] For all too many African Americans, the ability to survive a police encounter is top on their list of priorities. Black Millennials, in particular, go to church with the expectation that they will hear a word that encourages them to believe in the ideals of this country that lift up life, liberty, and the pursuit of happiness.[37] If Church does not engage the issues that affect young people's lives, we will continue to see them disconnect. Further, while people of color comprise only one-third of US millennials, the fact is that they comprise over one-half of Christians who are millennials and while they love the Jesus of the oppressed, rarely do they hear from the pulpit anything close to becoming active in the fight for justice.[38]

To preach boldly requires that one break from what is the norm of preaching in many churches: preaching sermons that are laced with a condemnation of homosexuality, that lift up heteronormative male leadership, and focus on Jesus as a "life coach who will make you healthy, wealthy, and wise."[39] Katie Cannon counsels that too much of contemporary preaching is shallow when it comes to dealing with the issues that vex American society and does little to help people deal with those issues that affect their daily lives.[40] Preaching the truth of the gospel story is difficult; however, it must be done. If the Church is not a leader, if not *the* leader, in transforming society into what it can be, then who or what organization can be called to the challenge? Preaching that challenges the status quo and provides the hearer with concrete ways of changing the world encourages resistance to the forces that negate the mission of Jesus and the *imago Dei* in God's people. Preaching boldly recognizes that preaching is not about the preacher, rather it is about God and being used by God for something greater than ourselves.[41]

---

36. Frank A. Thomas, *Introduction to the Practice of African American Preaching* (Nashville: Abington Press, 2016), 9.

37. Khalil Gibran Muhammad, "The Revolution Will Be Live-Tweeted: Why #BlackLivesMatter Is the New Model for Civil Rights," *The Guardian*, December 1, 2014, *https://www.theguardian.com/commentisfree/2014/dec/01/black-lives-matter-civil-rights-movement-ferguson*.

38. Alan Bean, "Why (White) Millennials Are Leaving the Church," Friends of Justice (blog), December 20, 2014, *https://friendsofjustice.wordpress.com/2014/12/20/why-white-millennials-are-leaving-the-church*.

39. Thomas, *Practice of African American Preaching*, 146.

40. Cannon, *Teaching Preaching*, 57.

41. Thomas, *How to Preach a Dangerous Sermon*, xv.

Preaching resistance helps to free those who wittingly and unwittingly collude with the dominant powers and helps them to repent—to change their hearts and minds and go in another direction toward freedom. Resistance preaching provides a way toward liberation from oppressive powers and enables the hearer to walk in the shoes of the oppressed.[42] Still, one of the issues that must be considered when preaching dangerous sermons is fear. People in our pews fear change. They fear the unknown. They fear conflict. They fear loss of control, power, and/or privilege. Church is where many come to escape the problems of the world and it is not unusual to hear, "I don't want to hear that stuff. I come to be comforted." The preacher cannot be swayed by those fears. There is a need to be pastoral, but ignoring what is going on in the world will not make racial injustice go away.

There is also fear on the part of the preacher. Fear of causing conflict or dividing the congregation. There is also fear that if enough people are upset, the preacher could lose the position and be without the means to care for self and family. There is also the fear that the preacher, who has spent time building up good will in the congregation, might be faced with being disliked. There is also the fear that the preacher, even after giving one's best, will not make a difference.[43] But, preach we must.

On the pages that follow are sermons that are borne out of what Walter Bruggemann calls the theology of anger that "cries out in God's name that things cannot continue as they are."[44] Preaching liberty and freedom is not for the faint of heart; however, those who do are being faithful to the gospel of Jesus, with all its risks, with all its headaches, with all its vulnerability. Preaching resistance shows that Christ's love is stronger than any force and all the princes and principalities that seem to have a toehold in today's society. Empowered by the Holy Spirit, preaching the gospel of Jesus has the power to change lives and the world as we know it. The preachers on the following pages, both lay and ordained, call us to a prophetic imagination that goes beyond the status quo and enables us to see new and yet undiscovered options for God's people.[45] Prophetic preaching borne of moral imagination propels the preacher to reveal to those with ears to hear to "public expressions of those very hopes and yearnings

---

42. Snider, *Preaching Resistance*, 5.

43. Leonora Tubbs Tisdale, *Prophetic Preaching: A Pastoral Approach* (Louisville: John Knox Press, 2010), 11–20.

44. Walter Bruggemann, *The Prophetic Imagination*, 2nd ed. (Minneapolis: Fortress Press, 2001), 65.

45. Thomas, *How to Preach a Dangerous Sermon*, xv.

that have been denied so long and suppressed so deeply."[46] The moral imagination that explodes on these pages has "the capacity to imagine something rooted in the challenges of the real world yet capable of giving birth to that which does not yet exist."[47]

Racial justice will not occur on its own. We cannot close our eyes and wish racism away. We cannot even pray it away. We can pray for strength to eradicate it. We can pray that White people have a change of heart and we can pray that Black people will love themselves as God has created them to be. Prayer must be coupled with action. Human beings have created this system of dehumanization and injustice and it will take human beings to dismantle it and create a world that reflects what God wants for all of God's people. Let us continue the work of others who came before us, and preach a word that disturbs, disrupts the status quo, yet heals. These words have been preached; these words are to be preached and the hope is that the words are heard and that action has been or will be taken on the words that have been spoken; that *shema* will rule the day, a kind of hearing that results in action. Will preachers preach a prophetic and troubling word and will preaching stir the hearts of those who hear?

---

46. Bruggemann, *Prophetic Imagination*, 65.

47. John Paul Lederach, *The Moral Imagination: The Art and Soul of Building Peace* (New York: Oxford University Press, 2005), 29.

2

Just a Few Thoughts (Questions, Really) on Race[1]

Paul Roberts Abernathy

What is race? A thing to run? If so, then, how?

A thing to which we run *to* as a shelter for safety, literally a roof under which our identity may dwell secure, a ground on which our integrity, the maintenance of that identity, may stand?

Or do we run *to* race simply, but no less significantly, as a source of pride in our presence and progress, our survival and success, as in those still heard phrases in many places, *Black* or *White* or (choose a color) *power*?

Or do we run *to* race so to run *through* race, to get to the other side, to stand with the other, so to see one another through the lens of the commonality of our humanity, as in that generation ago liberal-minded goal of a color-blind society? (A laudable ideal in theory, the pursuit of which, however, is beset by an insoluble real-world problem: even when color-blind, we all still see Black and White. It seems that we can't run *through* race to some mythological place of total color *un*consciousness.)

· · ● ● ● · ·

What is race? A thing to run? If so, then, how?

A thing if—or, if *not*, depending on one's point of view—to run *to*, then also to run *from* in fear? Fear of rejection and isolation by prejudice, which negatively prejudges us without benefit or burden of knowledge of us. Hence, a thing to run from, as in "I refuse to be identified by my race" or "I seek to pass," pretending by appearance or affect or other accouterment or action to be a member of another, preferably the politically, economically dominant race

---

1. In conjunction with the viewing and discussion of the video, *The Color of Fear*, Lee Mun Wah, April 30, 1994, *https://www.imdb.com/title/tt0484384/*.

Or do we run from race, indeed, from the other in fear of what we've been taught, of what we've learned and so believe as true about the other, about *them*, about *those people*?

Or do we run from race in fear of facing our own deep and abiding prejudice; how so quickly we judge the other based on evidence other than that which we attain by personal, individual encounter?

Race. A thing to run? No. Rather a thing *to be* as an expression of diversity. A diversity, as seen both from a theological perspective of divine intention and from an anthropological point of view of the created order itself, and, paradoxically, best shown and seen as *one*. For there is but one race, whose name is holy. And that race is wholly human.

Much the same point of Jesus's parabolic reply to that lawyer's testy question about eternal life.[2] An essential element of abundant, authentic life is our knowing and honoring our neighbor—who is anyone—and our *being* a neighbor to everyone.

Then why, O why, do we still divide ourselves, one from another, color by color? The color of fear. The fear of color, whether other than our own or our own. Despite our highest ideals and our best intentions, our history and sociology continually trump our theology and anthropology.

Let us pray and struggle still that we may find a more excellent way.

---

2. Luke 10:25–37.

3

Christmas: A Season of Peace?

A CHRISTMAS MESSAGE TO THE UNION
OF BLACK EPISCOPALIANS

Nathan D. Baxter

I don't know about you, but my heart is very troubled this Christmas. Recently an article that included photos of my participation in a march for Black lives in 2012 came to my attention. Looking at the picture, I realized that I am still troubled as a Black man—a husband, father, uncle, and grandfather. I am also troubled as a Black man who claims the Christian faith. I look around me and I see Black-on-Black gun violence, and blatant police violence on young men and women of my community. I see Black domestic violence yoked with entrenched poverty.

I see a political-economic system of school to prison tracking of our Black youth. And even with (if not because of) a Black man in the White House, I see a growing constitutional movement to reverse many hard-won civil rights and protections. I think many of us feel as insecure as did our ancestors during the days of the Fugitive Slave Act. We are not safe from racist violence on our streets and highways, nor even in our houses of worship. In my heart I feel deeply the protest chant, "NO JUSTICE! NO PEACE!"

Yet, I am a person of Christian faith—a faith that calls me to a heart of peace even in the midst of injustice.

Our Lord Jesus said, "But what comes out of the mouth proceeds from the heart, and this is what defiles. For out of the heart come evil intentions, murder, adultery, fornication, theft, false witness, slander. These are what defile a person" (Matt. 15:18–20).

Yes, I know in my heart that Christians must seek inner peace, lest, in the struggle for justice, we become the evil against which we struggle.

I am a Christian. But even more, I am an inheritor of the Black Christian tradition—a theological tradition that transcends denominations. One cannot listen to the words and melodies of the spirituals and not recognize that our slave ancestors' struggle for freedom was anchored in an inner spiritual peace.

One cannot think of the civil rights movement, its songs and sermons, and not recognize that the strength to face and overcome Jim Crow's evil was drawn from an ancestral understanding of the King of Peace: "Ride on, King Jesus." We call this "Soul Theology," which means we shall overcome only by keeping our souls anchored in the peace of Christ, even before justice comes. In this sense, the protest motto, "No Justice! No Peace!" is inverted to "NO PEACE! NO JUSTICE!" "Soul Theology" understands the essential divine truth that peace must be a matter of the individual heart before it is a social, cultural, and political reality. Keeping one's soul anchored is for us both a divine truth and ancestral witness.

The greatest contemporary witness of this aspect of "Soul Theology" was seen in the aftermath of murders at Mother Emanuel A.M.E. Church in Charleston, South Carolina. The entire nation and world were stunned when family members repeatedly stressed forgiveness of the perpetrator. Their sentiments were summed up by Wanda Simmons, granddaughter of victim the Rev. Daniel Simmons:

> Although my grandfather and the other victims died at the hands of hate, this is proof, everyone's plea for your soul, is proof that they lived in love and their legacies will live in love. So hate won't win. And I just want to thank the court for making sure that hate doesn't win.[1]

As Black Christians, they also understood the importance of inverting the great protest motto to say, "NO PEACE! NO JUSTICE!"

Perhaps this Christmas we should recapture the important message of Langston Hughes's play *Black Nativity* and remember that God made an ethnic specific statement, sending Jesus, a Jew, in a particular social location. It was God's way of saying "Jewish Lives Matter." From that specious reality came the universal witness that all lives matter. So, too, we must seek in our own realities "A Black Nativity." As critic Peter Simek wrote, "Langston Hughes' *Black Nativity* takes the biblical Christmas story and filters the scripture though the cultures of Diasporas Africa. . . . He picked up an ancient Christian tradition of adaptation and appropriation, removing the Germanic tree or the Italian crèche and replacing it with an African drum and a Harlem voice."[2]

---

1. Elahe Izadi, "The Powerful Words of Forgiveness Delivered to Dylann Roof by Victims' Relatives," *The Washington Post*, June 19, 2015, *https://www.washingtonpost.com/news/post-nation/wp/2015/06/19/hate-wont-win-the-powerful-words-delivered-to-dylann-roof-by-victims-relatives/*.

2. Peter Simek, "Does the New *Black Nativity* Retain the Heart of Langston Hughes' Classic Story?" dmagazine, November 27, 2013, *https://www.dmagazine.com/arts-entertainment/2013/11/does-the-new-black-nativity-retain-the-heart-of-langston-hughes-classic-story/*.

We will see many crèche scenes this year, signs of God's peace in a violent and desperate world. Can we see our particular Blackness in the scene, our particular source of peace in the struggle? Can we filter the sacred story through our own culture, our own experience, our own social location—give it the sounds of ancestral rhythms, a community's voice of protest, and a Soul's Theology of peace?

I began this message by sharing the photographic discovery of my angry self in a "Black Lives Matter" march for justice and peace. But later in the article I saw another sobering image of myself in a softer scene. I am still walking the protest march but now with some children who had gathered around "the priest in a dress." As we made eye contact, smiled, and chanted slogans, I noticed in them something I had not when I was walking with other ministers and adult activists. It was a peaceful determination, a sense of empowerment from being in the midst, a kindred community. So many had not known how diverse and united our local community could be. It was, in a sense, a Black Nativity. They were surrounded by mothers and fathers, pastoral shepherds, political wise men and women, and prophetic activists. Like the Christ Child, our Black, vulnerable children were courageously radiating among us—peace in the chaos—and an affirming hope in the struggle. I remember knowing in those moments that God was present. Incarnate.

This year let us share with one another the Nativity gift of peace, even as the struggle for justice continues. And let us remember the promise of our Prince of Peace: "Peace I leave with you; my peace I give to you. I do not give to you as the world gives. Do not let your hearts be troubled, and do not let them be afraid" (John 14:27).

Merry Christmas.

4

Demons

LUKE 8:26–39; JOHN 13:35

Tempie D. Beaman

In Luke's Gospel, Jesus encounters a man possessed by demons called Legion. A military legion is six thousand men. We can assume that he was possessed by not just one, but many demons. His demons caused him to be violent and self-destructive. He was so strong that he overpowered everyone and even broke his chains. He was an outcast living outside of the community where the dead were buried. To the people of the community, it was as if he was dead. He was no longer a part of the community. Who are the demon possessed in our community? Who are the outcasts, those we treat as if they were dead?

To answer these questions, I reflected on my recent trip to the historic civil rights sites in Birmingham, Montgomery, and Selma, Alabama. Reliving that journey through pictures, historical accounts, and the stories of those who actually experienced Bloody Sunday on the Edmund Pettus Bridge, the bombing of the 16th Street Baptist Church, the attacks of the dogs, the tear gas and the beatings, I am reminded that we live in a country full of demons. These demons have names, not just an all-inclusive name like Legion. But individual names like hatred and self-hatred, injustice, cruelty, intolerance, arrogance, greed, self-ishness, addiction, mental illness, and I'm sure you can name more.

But the man doesn't come to Jesus looking to be healed as others have done. He comes confronting Jesus asking, "What business do you have messing with me? You're Jesus, Son of the High God, but don't give me a hard time!" (Luke 8:26–29, MSG). The demons are behind this outburst because when Jesus saw the man, Jesus commanded the demons to come out of him. Who are the demons who confront Jesus today basically saying leave us alone? Which demons is Jesus messing with, giving a hard time today? Who is Jesus disturbing?

Our country and the world are like the demon-possessed man. We are naked before each other: seen for our hypocrisy. We claim to be a Christian nation yet our actions say, "Jesus we know who you are but leave us alone and stop giving us a hard time." We are disturbed by what we know is right, but do what we want any way. We live in graveyards that are filled with the victims of our past and present demonic behavior. People kidnapped from their homelands and sold into slavery. African families torn apart because they were seen as property, not humans, or Native American families separated because they were considered savages and their children needed to be civilized—made White. Systems and institutions were built upon the premise that white is superior and everything else is inferior. We are still tearing apart families of those who fear for their lives in their own country and have bought into the contradiction of this country as a place of safety and freedom for all. We foment violence around the world because of religious differences, ethnic differences, cultural differences. We are self-destructive, destroying our planet for profit. We are demon possessed.

Jesus doesn't send the demons back where they came from, the abyss, but gives them permission to enter the herd of pigs. The pigs are driven crazy by the demons and end up drowning. This so frightens those who saw all of this taking place that they run into the town to tell everyone what happened. When the people return, they find the man seated at Jesus's feet, fully clothed and in his right mind. Yet, what was the people's initial response? Fear. They were afraid. They were so afraid that they asked Jesus to leave their home. Why were the people afraid? Who is fearful of Jesus's actions today?

Like the demon-possessed man, we are bound with chains of division and chaos crafted out of hatred for the other, greed for profit over people's welfare, selfishness over the common good, and arrogance in the belief that our way is the only way. But our country isn't the only country that is demon possessed. The world is demon possessed. Just spend one hour watching the news and you will see these same things happening in Europe, Asia, the Middle East, Africa, all over the world. And yet, there is hope. There is a saving grace.

Just like Christ crossed the sea to step on the land where the demon-possessed man lived, there are Christians all over the world who believe in and live out the command of Christ to love your neighbor as yourself, to love your enemies and those who persecute you. There are Christians, like Christ, who confront the demons of the world and command them to leave. But there are many of us who like the townspeople are afraid. We are afraid of what goes for right; what goes for being Christ-like. We don't want our lives disturbed by Jesus. We don't want to live the way Jesus calls us to live. It is difficult to put the love of Jesus first over our own self-interests.

Recently I saw the documentary *Emanuel*, about the killing of nine members of Mother Emanuel African Methodist Episcopal Church in Charleston, South Carolina. Many of the family members of those killed forgave Dylan Roof because of their faith. The public and some of their family members and friends were amazed at their ability to forgive. But that is what Jesus calls us to do. In the face of evil, the demons of the world, we are still called to forgive, while also confronting that evil, those demons.

This is uncomfortable. Yet Jesus calls us out of our comfortable lives. By comfort, I'm not talking about material comfort, but physical and spiritual comfort. We are called to do more than send our thoughts and prayers when the demons confront us; we are called to do something as opposed to continue living our daily lives. Jesus isn't calling us to just pray. He is calling us to action. I struggle with this daily. Sometimes we are so overwhelmed by the legions of demons that we do nothing or we are paralyzed with fear. Jesus isn't calling us to confront all of the demons. But we can pick one issue—a couple of demons—that we are passionate about or can become passionate about. We can learn about it, see who's currently working on it, identify what gifts we can bring, and join others to confront it. We can do this as individuals and as church, the beloved community.

The victims of demon possession are outcasts. They are estranged from the community. They cannot rid themselves of the demons alone. They need community. As the Beloved Community, we bring the love of Christ that confronts the demons and casts them out. We are there to support, uplift, and surround the demon possessed and bring them back into community as healthy and whole persons. Whether the demons are addiction, self-hatred, mental illness, materialism, intolerance, there are so many, we have the love of Christ that overcomes all.

5

Anniversary of the Arrival of the First Africans in British North America

ISAIAH 58:9B–14, LUKE 13:10–17

Walter Brownridge

If you remove the yoke from among you, the pointing of the finger, the speaking of evil; if you offer your food to the hungry and satisfy the needs of the afflicted, then your light shall rise in the darkness and your gloom will be like the noonday. . . . Your ancient ruins shall be rebuilt. You shall raise up the foundations of many generations. You shall be called the repairer of the breach, the restorer of the street to live there. (Isaiah 58: 9b, 10, 12)

Let me begin with the context of this word from Isaiah 58. There are sixty-six chapters in the book of Isaiah, and scholars affirm that the first fifty-four chapters are the oracles of the prophet. Prophets are not astrologers nor soothsayers who "predict" the future. A prophet is one who looks at the present and, with the lens of the past, points to God's promises. One could look at the present and say, "This is the trajectory that you will head into if you don't follow God." That's not a prediction; it's more of an estimation. Through their poetry and the lyricism of even their prose, prophets offer seeds of hope. Even if doom may come from human frailty and ego and sin, we can always turn around. We can still repent and find healing and hope of a new day.

Scholars also point out that the last eleven chapters (55–66) were not written by the Prophet Isaiah, but by another prophet who extensively studied Isaiah. These chapters are deeply steeped in the message and words of Isaiah but were written approximately seventy years later. Around 608 BCE—during the Babylonian captivity—Isaiah himself was writing and saying, "Israel, Judea, Jerusalem, if you don't turn back from where you're heading, doom will come." The Babylonian kingdom had conquered Judea. Jerusalem and other nearby towns had been destroyed. Some, but not all, Jews had been taken into captivity. Out of that experience, which Jeremiah says lasted seventy years, comes some of the most beautiful poetry in the Psalms. The writer of Psalm 137 says, "By the waters of Babylon—there we sat down and there we wept when we remembered Zion. . . . For there our captors asked us for songs, and our tormentors asked for mirth, saying 'Sing us one of the songs of Zion!' How could we sing the Lord's song in a foreign land?"

These are the words of lament: the lament of the formerly enslaved grieving over their history as they recalled the pain of captivity. The experience of remembering their slavery was the result of their emancipation from Babylon. The Hebrew return to their homeland was the result of a new Babylonian emperor who permitted them to go home. Some went back home, but not all returned; some stayed in Babylon, much like a hundred years earlier at the end of the Assyrian captivity. That is how word *disapora* gets into the lexicon: *diaspora*: the dispersion of the Jews. Other dispersions of captured and enslaved peoples have happened over history and continue to this day. History may not repeat itself, but it can rhyme.

When the Jews returned to Judea in approximately 538 BCE, they found their towns destroyed and the temple reduced to rubble. Furthermore, social relations were fraught. Some Jews had remained in Judea during the captivity, and some non-Jews had taken up residence. Tensions between those two groups already existed. The returning exiles added a third group to the picture and they become scapegoats. The top 2 percent of the social structure were living off the rest. And the elite probably said, "The only good these new folks can have for us is if we oppress them as well."

This is the reality Isaiah predicted of captivity, but in third Isaiah (chapters 55–66), there is the hope of a new day of return, alongside the acknowledgment that the present still held pain, oppression, and wretchedness: "If you remove the yoke from among you, the pointing of the finger, the speaking of evil, if you offer food to the hungry and satisfy the needs of the afflicted, then your light shall rise in the darkness and your gloom be like the noonday" (Is. 58:9–10).

If we look to the stories that come after Isaiah, we hear stories of Nehemiah and Ezra and others who helped rebuild Judea and the temple. A ray of hope did come into the community. Something similar has happened five hundred years after Babylon.

Jesus of Nazareth was walking the earth and, as we heard in the Gospel lesson today, he saw a woman bent over for eighteen years. Take close note:

there is no plea heard. The woman did not ask for help and healing. She did not even sneak up and try to touch the hem of Jesus's garment. She was just stooped over. Bent over. The popular theology of the time saw her affliction as an attack of Satan. She could not lift her head toward the horizon. She could not look up at the sky. At best, she could look slightly forward, or a little to her left or to her right. She was in some ways like a small child, who, in a crowd of adults, could only see trouser legs and dresses as they frantically looked for mother and father.

The woman said nothing. She did nothing. But what did Jesus do? He saw her. He said, "Daughter, stand up straight. You are healed."

In the context of the history of sin and disobedience, of the opportunity to repent, of healing and hope and restoration, Jesus lived out third Isaiah's call to be a repairer of the breach, a restorer of streets to live on, and a giver of hope to the afflicted. And of course, there was a problem.

The religious authorities of the time said, "No, no, no, no. This is the Sabbath. This day is for something particular, and it is not for labor, and that includes healing." In attacking Jesus, they also attacked the woman. And Jesus responded by essentially breaking down the meaning of Deuteronomy. Jesus said you have to untie your donkey and feed it so it will live. The critical take-away from his words and actions is that certain things must be done out of necessity, even on the Sabbath. Wasn't the necessity of healing this woman one of those realities? Why should a woman who had suffered for eighteen years have to wait one more day? The "proper" day for healing was one day too long. The time for hope and healing was now. As the prophet Isaiah said, "You shall be called the repairer of the breach, the restorer of streets to live in" (58:12).

Fast-forward sixteen centuries and August 1619 marks the arrival of the first Africans to British North America. These first Africans were taken from Angola in West Central Africa. They were captured in a series of wars that were part of much broader Portuguese hostilities against the Kongo and Ndongo kingdoms and other states. They were put on board the *San Juan Bautista*, which carried three hundred and fifty captives bound for Vera Cruz, on the coast of Mexico. Nearing her destination, the slave ship was attacked in the Gulf of Mexico by two English privateers, the *White Lion* and the *Treasurer*, and robbed of fifty to sixty Africans.

The two privateers then sailed to Virginia, where the *White Lion* arrived at Point Comfort (ironically named), or present-day Hampton, Virginia, around the end of August. John Rolfe, a prominent planter and merchant (and formerly the husband of Pocahontas), reported that "twenty and odd Negroes" were "*bought* for victuals" (italics added). The majority of the Angolans were acquired by wealthy and well-connected English planters, including Governor Sir George Yeardley and the cape, or head, merchant, Abraham Piersey. The Africans were sold into bondage despite Virginia having no clear-cut laws sanctioning slavery.[1]

Chattel slavery already existed in New Spain, including Florida, and the Spaniards had also brought over Africans.[2] But these English-speaking colonists brought over these twenty Africans; some were chattel slaves, some were indentured servants. A few, over time, may have eventually been freed. It was the beginning of one of the great foundations of the American economy: chattel slavery.

I don't need to get into all the history here, though many people need to read it. I would advise you to go online to the *New York Times*. They have an incredible project called "The 1619 Project." You will find essays and historical accounts. The point of it is what the great historian John Hope Franklin said, "We must tell the unvarnished truth about slavery."[3] I can tell you in my education, which was from the Jesuits, this unvarnished truth was never mentioned.

My intent is not to shame, or blame, the descendants of slaveholders nor those who are the descendants of the enslaved. I am telling this story because it is a biblical story. As I said, history does not exactly repeat itself, but it damn sure rhymes. Those first Africans in America, my ancestors, were a people who were born on the water: the experience of being on ships for century upon century of the Atlantic slave trade. After one week or two weeks or three weeks of seeing nothing but a horizon of water, they began to forget who they were.

When they landed on these new shores, they began the process of seasoning, as it was said, of creating a new person. One who would be, in fact, docile and obedient as a slave. Like those Jews in Babylonian captivity, they sang songs that recalled their homeland, the old continent. But they also began to incorporate new elements of those songs because even though some had been Muslim and others held traditional African beliefs, they were introduced to Christianity. When these Africans heard the psalms, they heard the stories of Isaiah and Jeremiah, the stories resonated. Many incorporated Jesus's liberating message of hope into their reality.

---

1. This information is noted in numerous history sources. See: *https://historicjamestowne.org/history/ the-first-africans/* and *https://www.monticello.org/slavery-at-monticello/african-slavery-british-north-america/ africans-british-north-america*.

2. This information is available at *http://ldhi.library.cofc.edu/exhibits/show/african_laborers_for_a_ new_emp/the_spanish_and_new_world_slav*.

3. John Hope Franklin, "The 1619 Project," *New York Times Magazine*, August 18, 2018, 1.

My people were born on the water and came into full being on these shores. They were not Americans in their founding fathers; reality. And they were not quite Africans either to a degree. They were a "new people." Thus, we created the name African American, which developed over the centuries. They became a people not only by recognizing their existence, but also through the challenge and struggle of Native Americans, and they recognized the struggle of other people who had come to these shores or came across the borders. In the eighteenth and nineteenth and twentieth centuries, they became the real beacons of the true democracy that we try to bring to America.

History does not repeat itself exactly, but it does rhyme.

When Martin King said, "The arc of the moral universe is long, but it bends towards justice,"[4] he was diving deep into the words of Isaiah and the desire for a new day. It was the hope for one who could repair the breach. We are called to live into this calling. In her poem delivered at the inauguration of William Jefferson Clinton, Maya Angelou said that we cannot go back and undue the lessons of history, however, if we learn from history, we do not have to re-live the mistakes that were made.[5] If we face our history honestly, openly, and lovingly, a new day can be born. Restoring relations, recognizing that all who have come to these shores and who have lived here for generations and who had lived here before anyone from Europe or Africa even arrived are called to live into a beloved community. That was the dream that Isaiah lived out. That was the dream that Isaiah called the people of Israel and Judea to live into. That was the dream of God that Jesus embodied in healing a woman who had been bent over for eighteen years.

Today, Episcopal Churches in Jamestown, other parts of Virginia, and across the United States will ring bells at 3 p.m. Eastern time to commemorate that landing at Point Comfort in Jamestown four hundred years ago. To ring the bells, as the prophet Isaiah would have rung, calling us to be something better. We are invited to be restorers of the streets we live on, to be repairers of the breach, to give hope to the afflicted, to satisfy the hungry.

This bell-ringing can be seen as a metaphor for the truth that in America, we are all aliens in a strange land, and yet we are called to sing the Lord's song—even in a foreign land—that we might be the new people that God has called us all to be. May we live into that reality as followers of Jesus Christ.

---

4. Mychal Denzel Smith, "The Truth about 'The Arch of the Moral Universe,'" HuffPost, January 18, 2018, *https://www.huffpost.com/entry/opinion-smith-obama-king_n_5a5903e0e4b04f3c55a252a4.*

5. Maya Angelou, "On the Pulse of Morning," a poem written on the occasion of the inauguration of William Jefferson Clinton as the 42nd President of the United States, *https://www.nytimes.com/1993/01/21/us/the-inauguration-maya-angelou-on-the-pulse-of-morning.html.*

6

Disturb Us, O Lord

JOHN 5:1–9

Marlene Eudora Forrest

In the spring of 2018, I was called to my first parish, a predominantly White parish. As I accepted the call, I wondered how I, as an African American priest, would be able to share my truth with my congregation. I wondered how I was going to authentically be who I was and preach the gospel that God had called me to preach. I realized that I could not be afraid of my own truth; to omit pieces of who I was to make others feel comfortable was not what God was calling me to do. I was being called to take all the pieces of me and gather them up so God could do a new thing. Out of that truth I found God calling me to preach the gospel with the stories of my own brokenness weaved into it. God works through scripture, people, and circumstances, and the stories that I have been called to weave into the gospel are filled with the broken pieces of racism, hate, sexism, and more. The ugly truths are countered with the stories that set the Gospels squarely into our laps and calls us to peace in our souls and to the grace that saves our lives. My sermons were birthed out of their ugly truth of hate and racism in this country, but reflected how God moves us all and calls us to be on mission while we "court holy disruption," while we are disturbed, and as we are called to follow Jesus.

> Astonishing God, you give us a vision of the heavenly city, the new Jerusalem, your home among mortals on earth. All people and nations will stream to your city where they will find nourishment, healing, and peace. Even now your blessing shines upon all the earth to help us see a larger vision of your loving care for all creation. And so you call us to move beyond our comfortable circles, and into unfamiliar places, as we seek to share your dream of a world made new in Christ. Amen.

The lectionary provided a choice of Gospel readings. I initially chose John 14; however, as many of you know, this past week I have been on pilgrimage in Alabama as an Ambassador of Healing and Peace in Birmingham, Selma, and Montgomery. Places where many of the events of the civil rights movement occurred. Places that not only carry the history of this nation, but also carry with that history the scars of injustice and pain. And while there is pain, in these sacred places there is a deep sense of faith and hope that this world can actually be the dream God has for it.

I've been pulled by the Holy Spirit to preach not just on the selected Gospel but also on the alternate Gospel as well, and it reads like this:

> After [Jesus healed the son of the official in Capernaum] there was a festival of the Jews and Jesus went up to Jerusalem. Now in Jerusalem by the Sheep Gate there is a pool, called in Hebrew Beth-Zatha, which has five porticoes. In these lay many invalids—blind, lame, and paralyzed. One man was there who had been ill for thirty-eight years. When Jesus saw him lying there and knew that he had been there a long time, he said to him, "Do you want to be made well?" The sick man answered him, "Sir, I have no one to put me into the pool when the water is stirred up; and while I am making my way, someone else steps ahead of me." Jesus said to him, "Stand up, take your mat and walk." At once the man was made well, and he took up his mat and began to walk. Now that day was the Sabbath. (John 5:1–9)

While on pilgrimage in Alabama, I took these Gospels with me each day as my devotional. I also began to really think about what it means to be a pilgrim and prayed about what Christine Valters Painter says in *The Soul of a Pilgrim: Eight Practices for the Journey Within*, "Pilgrim means being willing to court holy disruption, to become profoundly aware of our inner movements, to claim responsibility for our choices about how we respond to this place we find ourselves in and welcome discomfort and strangeness as carrying the possibility of new revelation."[1] I pondered what message God was opening up to me.

As our pilgrimage went on, I continued to pray over these passages as we walked in the footsteps of the Rev. Dr. Martin Luther King Jr., Johnathan Daniels, John Lewis, Viola Luzzio, and many others and sat in the pews where foot soldiers sang freedom songs and prayed for change.

I prayed over these passages as we stood on soil where many were sold, lynched, and beaten because they were seen as less than human by their oppressor. I kept asking myself, "God, what are you saying to me and what word am

---

1. Christine Valters Painter, "An Interview with Christine Valters Painter," July 7, 2015, *Always We Begin Again*, https://myawba.blogspot.com/2015/07/guest-post-christine-valters-paintner.html.

I to bring back to the good people of St. Peters? How can I an African American relate this deep experience with these people who have a skin that automatically gives them 'privilege' and sometimes says to me that they represent the oppressor?" Then I recalled a prayer that is attributed to Archbishop Desmond Tutu and said to have been adapted from an original prayer by Sir Francis Drake; this prayer, along with the scriptures, seemed to sum up all that I was praying and feeling.

> Disturb us, O Lord
>
> when we are too well-pleased with ourselves
>
> when our dreams have come true because we dreamed too little,
>
> because we sailed too close to the shore.
>
> Disturb us, O Lord
>
> when with the abundance of things we possess,
>
> we have lost our thirst for the water of life
>
> when, having fallen in love with time,
>
> we have ceased to dream of eternity
>
> and in our efforts to build a new earth,
>
> we have allowed our vision of Heaven to grow dim.
>
> Stir us, O Lord
>
> to dare more boldly, to venture into wider seas
>
> where storms show Thy mastery,
>
> where losing sight of land, we shall find the stars.
>
> In the name of Him who pushed back the horizons of our hopes
>
> and invited the brave to follow.
>
> Amen.[2]

I realized from all these prayers and passages I had been given that God was calling me to urge you to be open to the Holy Spirit, the one who teaches us, the advocate sent in the name of God and who calls us to be like Jesus and to bring peace—a peace that will require us to stir things up and be willing to court holy disruption and to not only be disturbed by the things that we see in the world, but also to disturb. To stand in the gap for those who have no

---

2. The prayer can be found at various sources on the internet: Desmond Tutu, "Disturb Us O Lord," *Godspace*, March 2, 2012, *https://godspacelight.com/2012/03/02/disturb-us-o-lord-a-prayer-by-desmond-tutu-4/*. Also: *https://unfinishedsymphony.org/2013/02/24/disturb-us-a-prayer-by-archbishop-desmond-tutu/*.

voice. For those who feel that God has forgotten them. For those who after decades of fighting for justice continue to be the subject of bigotry, prejudice, discrimination, and hate. God is calling us to disturb what is the status quo. To disturb those systems that oppress. To disturb those processes that allow us to continue to be separate and unequal. To claim responsibility for our choices about how we respond to this place we find ourselves in and welcome discomfort and strangeness as carrying the possibility of a new revelation. God wants us to be disturbed and shaken by these things so that we can press forward and stir the waters.

We must not continue to be like those who stepped in front of the man who was ill for thirty-eight years and sat by the pool. We must be disturbed by those who step in front of others and proclaim a healing that is not for them. We must not be the people who step in front of others out of our own sense of privilege, not allowing those who are in greater need than we are to reach the healing that they require and that our mighty God has declared for them.

God is asking us to see fully the injustices, hurts, and pains in the world and be so disturbed by them that we want to stir things up for change and court holy disruption as we seek a just society. God is asking us to shake things up. Bishop Jake Owensby says, "The Kingdom is wherever God's Love is shaking things up and bringing things to new life."[3] God wants us to live a cross-shaped life and that takes us loving so deeply and passionately that we are shaking things up, stirring the waters and disturbing the things that are not in line with the example that Jesus set for us.

God was disturbed by the state of things and sent God's only begotten Son to stir things up, to disturb things, to court holy disruption, and to shake up the world. Jesus condemned injustice and called out those who were treating others unjustly. And even with this he continued to value every creature. Jesus is calling us to stand up for the marginalized, the oppressed, the forgotten, those whose dignity and value have been stripped from them.

My siblings in Christ, we are the hands, feet, and heart of God in this world and we are all his ambassadors for healing and peace. We are the foot soldiers of the present day. We are the ones who God is calling to disturb things until they are made right. We are the ones who God is calling to stir the waters and to go up the river and make a change. We are the ones who God is calling to come to the table and make room for all. We are the ones who God is calling to court holy disruption to level the playing field for all.

---

3. Jake Owensby, "Show Up and Look Alert," MinistryMatters, November 13, 2018, *https://www.ministrymatters.com/all/entry/8527/show-up-and-look-alert.*

Oh God, give us a vision of the heavenly city, the new Jerusalem, your home among mortals on earth. Let us stir things up so that all people and nations will stream to your city where they will find nourishment, healing, and peace. Let your blessing shine upon all the earth to help us disturb, to shake things up and be willing to court holy disruption as Jesus did so we can see a larger vision of your loving care for all creation. And call us to move beyond our comfortable circles, and into unfamiliar places, as we seek to share your dream of a world made new in Christ as we, like the man by the pool, stand up, take up our mats, and walk the pilgrim's way. Amen.

7

Strategies of Resistance

DANIEL 3:14–20, 24–29

Wilda C. Gafney

There is more than one way to tell a story, especially a story as important as the Christian story; this also applies to the stories that make up our sacred stories. Today we explore that plurality in a lectionary of my devising, rather revising—because I think there is danger in only retelling the same stories, no matter how beloved.

Among our sacred trove of stories are two versions of the Daniel story; even more exist outside of the Christian canons. One of those canonical stories was preserved in Hebrew and Aramaic by the descendants of the Judeans who survived the Babylonian exile and created the mother text for the Hebrew Bible and the Protestant version of the story. That is the source of our Second Lesson and Canticle. The other canonical story was preserved in Greek by the descendants of the Judeans who fled to Egypt instead. That is the source of our First Lesson. Together those lessons and canticle are in narrative order telling a more complete story.

The book of Daniel is a text of resistance. It is a cagey, strategic piece of resistance. It is an anti-imperial text disguised as an anti-imperial text. Empires don't mind their subjects mocking failed and fallen empires. In their egocentrism, they read that calumny as their own praise because they are top dog now. So the cagey authors of Daniel disguised a critique of the lingering and declining Greek Empire in a retroactive critique of the centuries-past Babylonian Empire. And they put that critique on the lips and at the pen of Daniel, a beloved figure whose origins were even older than the Babylonian Empire, or its predecessor Assyrian Empire, or the great dynasties of Egypt, or even the founding of the people of Israel. Daniel was a figure of legend whose stories were told in each generation with new stories added to his canon from time to time.

I invite you to hear the story as subversive as it really is. In the First Lesson, three young people have been taken captive by the empire and forced to assimilate to its culture, made to wear its clothing, eat its food, speak its language, and answer to the names they give them—names which stuck to them even in the stories of their own people. The tentacles of empire reach deep, even into the hearts of people who are working faithfully to decolonialize themselves. It matters that these are young people. In the larger story of Daniel, they are taken as children to be assimilated so that they will love the empire that colonized their people more than they love their own selves. Empires have always underestimated young people, whether it was civil rights protestors, dreamers, or high school gun reform activists.

When our lesson begins, these young people are being enculturated in the worship of the empire and required to pray to the gods of the empire at the cost of their subjugated, colonized lives. One of the lessons of this text is that empire is rapacious and insatiable. They were already speaking the language of empire. They had already had their names changed from Hananiah, Mishael, and Azariah to Shadrach, Meshach, and Abednego. But it wasn't enough. The empire wanted more—more of them, more of their souls.

As long as there is a corner of your soul that is free, uncolonized, unconquered, unbought, and unbossed, empire will by any means necessary seek to uproot that liberty and colonize the last vestige of your right mind, heart, and soul. African and Native Americans know this story all too well as do the indigenous peoples of every nation conquered by an empire. In the face of the empire's ravenous desire for their abject and total submission, Hananiah, Mishael, and Azariah clung fast to God of their foremothers and fathers and rejected the empire's religion.

I'm calling this sermon "Strategies of Resistance"—ours, not theirs, because they didn't really strategize. They just said no. No to the god of empire. No to its worship and veneration. They didn't negotiate; they didn't equivocate. Sometimes we just need to say no to the manifestations of empire in our world. No to the slaughter of school children. No to military-grade weaponry in the streets. No to families ripped apart by militarized immigration assault troops. No to bad preaching. No to death-dealing theology. No to violence against women. No to bullying gay and trans teens to death. No to incompetent and corrupt government. No to everything that stands against the life-giving love of God and the liberty it grants. No and hell no.

The empire responded to their rejection of its attempt to colonize their minds, their spirits, their souls, and their ancestral religion with lethal rage. The empire covets good religion. It knows if it gets a toehold in pulpits and pews, seminaries and sanctuaries, books and blogs, texts and tweets, it can sanctify its hierarchies and disparities as the word and will of God. The empire prepared to kill Hananiah, Mishael, and Azariah. It was to be a spectacle lynching. A spectacle lynching was when good White folk would make an event out of a lynching, bring their sweethearts, wives, children, and a basket of goodies to nibble while they watched the show. They'd often set their victims on fire (as Nebuchadnezzar planned to do), pose with their burning corpses, and later cut off pieces of them to take home as souvenirs.

Activist-archivist James Allen collected one hundred and forty-five photos of spectacle lynchings in the US. They are featured in the volume *Without Sanctuary*[1] which I commend to you. The strategies of resistance required to outlaw lynching lasted well into the twentieth century. Sometimes resistance is an intergenerational struggle.

The most significant strategy of resistance employed by the three young people was the willingness to let the empire spill their blood. Sometimes resistance means being willing to die. Sometimes it means preparing to die. Sometimes it means dying. Sometimes it means rising from the dead—but I'm getting ahead of next week's story. We are not far from the fiftieth anniversary of the assassination and martyrdom of the Rev. Dr. Martin Luther King Jr. He and many others in the civil rights movement resisted not just segregation but White supremacy with their very lives. White supremacy is a colonizing force that transcends national borders and is every bit as much a manifestation of empire as any nation with imperial imagination and aspirations. The three young people prepared to die in resistance to the empire.

The Hebrew text moves quickly to a story of miraculous deliverance, but not so fast—there is more to the story. The Greek story picks up where the Hebrew one leaves off and fills in the gap. The young people responded to their impending extrajudicial killing with the songs of their ancestors. They sang to the God no empire could strip from them. They told the story of God's faithfulness to their people. As the empire's rage burned against them in literal fire, they used the breaths they thought would be their last to deny the empire power over them, over their story, and over their song, because our stories and our songs are tools of resistance. The empire set out to destroy this last act of resistance. But something happened when they refused to surrender their heart and minds, songs and prayers, poetry and theology, even if they had to lay their bodies down. God appeared in the midst of the resistance.

---

1. James Allen, Hilton Als, John Lewis, and Leon F. Litwack, *Without Sanctuary: Lynching Photography in America* (Twin Palms: Twin Palms Publishers, 2000).

The resistance writers used the book of Daniel to tell their people that the empire would not be defeated with the master's tools. They couldn't defeat it with military might. They couldn't defeat it with economic might. But if they kept their minds right and stayed on the God who delivered their ancestors, no empire would ever be able to destroy them, no matter what their political reality. In the words of the Gospel, "you will know the truth, and the truth will make you free" (John 8:32).

Our words have power. That is why fascists burn books, ban films, silence scholars, censure artists, and assassinate prophets. They bully and sue, intimidate and obfuscate, and they use their words to rewrite our stories, revise our histories, and stamp their image on our art and culture. And they lie. They lie about us. They lie about our culture. They lie about our history. They lie about God. With their lies they construct a god who is not God and expect us to bow down and worship it.

But these young activists on the page and the older activists behind the pen have shown us how to resist: Don't let the empire tell you who you are. Don't let the empire assimilate you into its culture. Don't let the empire tell you your cultural and culinary practices are inferior. Don't let the empire clothe you—body or mind. Don't let the empire tell you who God is. Don't let the empire use your life to advertise its glory. Resistance is not futile. But resistance is costly. We follow one who resisted empire to the cost of his life and we are called to do the same. How much more ought we be willing to put our lives on the line knowing the promise of resurrection than those young people, literal or literary, who were willing to go to a death from which they had no sure promise of escape? Amen.

8

Listening for Black Lives

A SERMON TO MYSELF
AND MY WHITE COLLEAGUES

MARK 5:34

Peter Jarrett-Schell

He said to her, "Daughter, your faith has made you well; go in peace, and be healed of your disease."

Sometimes the Spirit leads us to apparent contradictions. That being the case, I'd like to talk about listening; specifically, listening for Black lives. For a White preacher like myself, the challenge of this book, *Preaching Black Lives (Matter)* is an inherently thorny one. My people are the producers and beneficiaries of White Supremacist structures that demean both Black lives and the importance of those lives. This is not solely a historical matter. Consciously or otherwise, we participate in and reaffirm these structures every day. Therefore, we have a special moral responsibility to bring them down.

But all too often when we raise our voices to denounce White supremacy (if we raise them at all), we do so in ways that re-inscribe patterns of White supremacy. All too often, the very act of raising our voices draws attention away from Black witnesses, who are more capable than we to testify about the importance of their own lives. Speaking from a position of power, like a pulpit, only amplifies this effect of re-centering Whiteness. So we work at cross purposes, undercutting the very people for whom we aspire to advocate.

If we are silent, we tacitly support the forces of White supremacy, and the unjust profit they deliver to us. If we speak, we repeat patterns of White supremacy that perpetually privilege White voices. We are in a devil's bind. What is to be done?

There is no easy answer, but we might begin by taking a cue from one of our own, a White man, indeed a very White man, who was nonetheless a foster child of the Black church,[1] one murdered for his witness on behalf of those whom Whiteness demeaned:

> It is God's love for us that He not only gives us His Word but also lends us His ear. So it is His work that we do for our brother when we learn to listen to him. Christians, especially ministers, so often think they must always contribute something when they are in the company of others, that this is the one service they have to render. They forget that listening can be a greater service than speaking.[2]

If we do not listen, we will not understand what is required, for Black lives alone can tell what justice they require. If we do not listen, we will never know our own blind spots. If we do not listen, and indeed, allow ourselves to be transformed by the voices we hear, there is no hope for us.

We who are called White must preach for Black lives. The sin that threatens them is ours, and our Savior will not excuse us if we fail to raise our voices. But if we are to preach for Black lives, we must first learn to listen for Black lives. Reading the witnesses of this book might be a good place to start. But for us, listening, rather than merely hearing, is no easy feat.

In her book *White Fragility*, the secular educator Robin DiAngelo describes and critiques the defensive responses we (that is White people) deploy when encountering, and especially when challenged on, the issues of race and racism.[3] She makes the point that while these defenses are often unconscious and reflexive, they are not innocent, but rather, weaponized. They work to derail honest conversations on racism, and thereby obliterate even the possibility of confronting and dismantling the structure of White supremacy.

DiAngelo is an atheist, but if we were to translate her ideas into a theological framework, we might say that White fragility represents sin's effort to remain unexamined. In the face of such dissembling fragility, DiAngelo's prescription is simple: "toughen up." Her central argument is:

---

1. By his own acknowledgment, Bonhoeffer's radical understanding of discipleship was profoundly shaped by his time as a member of Harlem's Abyssinian Baptist Church, and the teaching of its then pastor, the Rev. Adam Clayton Powell. Sr. Dr. Reggie Williams documents and explores this connection in his book *Bonhoeffer's Black Jesus: Harlem Renaissance Theology and an Ethic of Resistance* (Waco, TX: Baylor University Press, 2014).

2. Dietrich Bonhoeffer, *Life Together: A Discussion of Christian Fellowship* (San Francisco: HarperSanFrancisco, 1978), 97.

3. Robin J. DiAngelo, *White Fragility: Why It's So Hard for White People to Talk about Racism* (Boston: Beacon Press, 2018).

Stopping our racist patterns must be more important than working to convince others that we don't have them. We do have them, and people of color already know we have them; our efforts to prove otherwise are not convincing. An honest accounting of these patterns is no small task given the power of white fragility and white solidarity, but it is necessary.[4]

And it is necessary. White fragility shouts like hell to drown out Black voices. We must learn to muzzle it, if we ever hope to listen for Black lives.

When Christians encounter a new moral claim, it's almost reflexive to ask ourselves: "What would Jesus say about this?" Often, this question leaves us sorting through complicated and conflicting testimony. But there are those blessed, startling moments when Christ's witness is so clear as to silence all debate.

As we consider DiAngelo's claims regarding White fragility, the story of Jesus's encounter with the Syrophoenecian woman offers just such a testimony.

> [Jesus] set out and went away to the region of Tyre. He entered a house and did not want anyone to know he was there. Yet he could not escape notice, but a woman whose little daughter had an unclean spirit immediately heard about him, and she came and bowed down at his feet. Now the woman was a Gentile, of Syrophoenician origin. She begged him to cast the demon out of her daughter. He said to her, "Let the children be fed first, for it is not fair to take the children's food and throw it to the dogs." But she answered him, "[Lord], even the dogs under the table eat the children's crumbs." Then he said to her, "For saying that, you may go—the demon has left your daughter." So she went home, found the child lying on the bed, and the demon gone. (Mark 7:24–30)

For many Christians, myself included, this is one of the most cringeworthy passages of the Bible. There are multitudes of verses of scripture that we weaponized to support discrimination, disenfranchisement, even genocide. But this may be the only time we hear such words come explicitly from the mouth of Christ. Hearing what sounds like racism from a man we proclaim as Messiah should give us pause.

Before proceeding, let me offer two disclaimers. First, historically, it's not quite accurate to label Jesus's rebuke as "racist." Both racism and race are recent inventions, scarcely more than five hundred years old. As Du Bois famously noted:

---

4. DiAngelo, *White Fragility*, 129.

The discovery of personal whiteness among the world's peoples is a very modern thing—a nineteenth and twentieth century matter, indeed. The ancient world would have laughed at such a distinction.[5]

Racism—that is, the project of sorting humanity into a small number of groups based on an arbitrarily chosen set of physical attributes, with the purpose of establishing and enforcing a universal hierarchy among them—is a decidedly new idea. But ethnocism—that is, the project of arguing for and enforcing various hierarchies of human ancestry—is certainly ancient. And it can fairly be described as a kind of antecedent to racism.

This distinction is more than simply academic. One of racism's fundamental lies is that race is both eternal and natural. In fact, it is neither. When we uncritically and anachronistically read racism and race back into scripture, we contribute to the lie of race's inevitability and immortality. And if we attribute divine characteristics to human constructions, we are rightly called idolaters.

That said, while Jesus's comment to the Syrophoenician woman is not racist, it is decidedly enthnocist. Mark is content to imply this fact (though it takes very little inference to catch his meaning). Matthew's account of the story is more explicit. Before rebuking her, Jesus declares "I was sent only to the lost sheep of the house of Israel" (Matt. 15:26). Jesus asserts a clear hierarchy: Israelites are privileged over Gentiles; and on this basis, the woman's daughter should be left to suffer. Though the statement is not racist, per se, its effects are similar.

His words also fit the popular short-hand definition of racism: prejudice + power. Jesus is prejudiced against the Syrophoenecian woman; and he holds in his hand the power to free her daughter, or not, as he chooses. So if Jesus's rebuke is not technically racist, in the historical sense, we can still reasonably understand it as a fore-type of racism. Having delivered this disclaimer, for the sake of convenience, and to communicate the urgency of this passage, I hope you will forgive me if I call Jesus's behavior "racist" going forward.

The second disclaimer is this: given that my stated purpose is to consider the story of the Syrophoenecian woman in light of DiAngelo's "White fragility," and given that I've identified Jesus's rebuke as a fore-type of racism, a reader might infer that I am attributing something like Whiteness to Jesus.

To be clear, Jesus is neither historically nor theologically White. Ethnically, he did not belong to any of the diverse groups that have been assimilated into

---

5. W. E. B. Du Bois, "The Souls of White Folk," in *Darkwater: Voices Within the Veil* (New York: Harcourt, Brace & Co, 1920), 29–52.

Whiteness. Sociologically, he was a working-class Israelite living under Roman occupation, from a town of ill-repute: he did not have the social capital of Whiteness. Theologically, Jesus's clear orientation is toward the margins, thus Whiteness cannot be his subject. As James Cone famously noted: "He *is* Black, because he *was* a Jew."[6] Whiteness has no part in him.

That said, we must also acknowledge that at various points in his ministry, Jesus wields significantly greater social power than those who surround him: as an able-bodied man, as an Israelite within Israelite lands, as a respected and educated teacher, as a renowned healer, and as an adult. Though he is not White, the way he conducts himself in these moments can be instructive for those of us who participate constantly in the social power of Whiteness.

Disclaimers aside, what can DiAngelo teach us about Jesus and the Syrophoenician woman? And how will it help us listen for Black lives? DiAngelo identifies a number of defenses that White people deploy when confronting the issue of racism. Among them is White solidarity, which is the unspoken agreement among Whites to protect White advantage and not cause another White person to feel racial discomfort by confronting them when they say or do something racist.[7]

At the first sign of racial trouble, we circle the wagons to defend other White people from charges of racist conduct, or even from confrontations with simple facts regarding the racist institutions of our society. As regards Jesus and the Syrophoenician woman, it seems that we transfer this same impulse onto Christ.

If you make a search of sermons and biblical commentaries on the story of the Syrophoenician woman, you will notice very quickly how White scholars and pastors seem intent on circling their wagons around Jesus. Though he is not White, perhaps we recognize in his power and in his prejudice the same racist dynamics that surround us. Or, perhaps, we imagine him to be White. Either way, we feel compelled to defend him from the charge of racism before it is even stated. What does this look like in practice?

DiAngelo notes that one of the most prevalent defensive responses of White fragility is to prioritize intent over results.[8] We assert that so long as our conscious intentions were not racist, then we are absolved from the racist effects of our actions.

---

6. James H. Cone, *God of the Oppressed* (Maryknoll, NY: Orbis, 1997), 123.

7. DiAngelo, *White Fragility*, 57.

8. DiAngelo, *White Fragility*, 69.

This seems to be the preferred defense of biblical commentators. One way or another, they will declare that Jesus does not intend the racism that we hear. In my review of these commentaries, I find three versions of this argument.

The first notes that in the Greek, when Jesus uses the word "dog," he is using the diminutive form (κυνάριον), in contrast to the standard (κύων) that Jesus uses to describe the dogs who lick at the poor man Lazarus's sores (Luke 16:21). Thus, according to this argument, when he calls the Syrophoenician woman a dog, he is describing her not with contempt, but rather affection.[9]

The absurdity of this argument comes clear if we simply read his words again, replacing "dogs" with the diminutive, and more affectionate, "puppies": *It is not fair to take the children's food and throw it to the [puppies.]*

This is, of course, no less offensive, only more patronizing. And regardless, this reasoning still leaves the woman's daughter to suffer and die.

The second line of argument emphasizes Jesus's declaration, "Let the children be fed first." From here, the commentators assert that Jesus's intention is not to deny the Syrophoenicians needs; but rather, to defer them. Essentially, these commentators argue, he is simply telling the woman to wait her turn.[10]

There are two problems with this line of argument. The first is that the statement "Let the children be fed first," appears only in Mark's version of the story, not Matthew's. For Matthew, at least, this detail is irrelevant. More fundamentally, this line of interpretation is uncomfortably reminiscent of the court's decision in *Plessy v. Ferguson*. It would be akin to telling those who had to go to the back of bus that they were not being denied, only deferred. After all, in the end, the bus is still going to the same destination. And once again, his reasoning leaves the woman's daughter to suffer.

The final version of this argument is a favorite of White interpreters with liberationist aspirations. I regret to say, I have preached it myself on one occasion. This argument states that by denying the woman in a racist fashion, Jesus provides her the opportunity to speak for, and claim, her own justice. Thus, he empowers her.[11]

This argument requires such contorted mental gymnastics that it is remarkable it does not cause aneurysms. Imagine a potential employer who tells

---

9. John Macarthur, *Macarthur Study Bible New King James Version* (Nashville: Thomas Nelson, 1998), 1475.

10. John Gill, "Commentary on Mark 7:4." *The New John Gill Exposition of the Entire Bible*, 1999, accessed September 07, 2018, *https://www.studylight.org/commentaries/geb/mark-7.html*.

11. Holly J. Carey, "Jesus and the Syrophoenician Woman: A Case Study in Inclusiveness," *Leaven* 19, no. 1 (2011): article 8.

an applicant, "We're not hiring you because you're Black." When the applicant protests, the employer says, "You're hired. I just wanted to give you the chance to speak up for yourself." One can only hope that a civil rights lawsuit would follow.

Another defensive mechanism DiAngelo identifies is focusing on the messenger, rather than the message.[12] That is, we invalidate criticism based on the method of its delivery rather than its content, colloquially: tone-policing. A particular favorite is the assertion that criticism must be delivered privately, or it is invalid.[13] DiAngelo notes the absurdity of this rule, in that the racist behavior being critiqued is frequently public. Thus, the public space is preserved for racism, and antiracism is regulated to private spaces (where it is generally ignored anyway).

In reading the story of the Syrophoenician woman, I was surprised to notice how I engaged in that kind of tone-policing within my own mind. Through decades of reading this exchange, I had always imagined it as a private encounter. The witness of Mark's account is unclear, though his statement "yet [Jesus] could not escape notice" at least suggests there might have been others present. Matthew, on the other hand, is very clear about the fact that the Syrophoenician woman had an audience.

By imagining the scene as a private one, I effectively moved the woman's criticism to a venue I deemed more appropriate, and thus, allowed Jesus to save face (at least in my sight), which is to be expected: the defenses of White fragility operate even in the absence of external criticism, sabotaging the healthy parts of our own minds, so we cannot see for ourselves the structures of White supremacy that shape our lives.

Here, in all these various interpretations of the passage, we see the defensive reactions of DiAngelo's *White Fragility* deployed to protect Jesus against the charge of racism. This is not particularly surprising. As DiAngelo notes, White fragility is endemic in our society.

What is surprising is to watch how Jesus reacts. Let us consider the scene again, from the beginning. Jesus delivers a racist rebuke: "It is not fair to take the children's food and throw it to the dogs" (Matt. 15:26). The woman responds with a bit of rhetorical brilliance—a pointed quip, a comic reversal of his words: "Yes, Lord, yet even the dogs eat the crumbs that fall from their masters' table" (Matt. 15:27). Perhaps she speaks meekly, using the language of his

---

12. DiAngelo, *White Fragility*, 121.

13. DiAngelo, *White Fragility*, 123.

own racism in an effort to ingratiate herself to him, thus subverting the rules of an oppressive system for her own need. Or perhaps she tosses his words back to him in a witty and sarcastic rebuke. We can't really know. Regardless, the fundamental content of her retort is: Jesus is wrong. Specifically, his prejudice has led him to a false and unjust conclusion.

And now we encounter a startling and graceful surprise. In contrast to his later day interpreters, Jesus offers no defense; no explanation, no gas-lighting, no appeal to intent, no evasion or disengagement, no tone policing. He does not recenter himself. Instead, he simply states: "For saying that, you may go—the demon has left your daughter" (Mark 7:29).

A short phrase, but there is so much in that statement.

"For saying that . . ." that is, he amplifies her voice. He acknowledges, for anyone who is listening, that the woman's critique was valid and her witness has proved it. This healing he will perform is not a matter of mercy, but one of justice. She was right and he was wrong. By contrast, White fragility moves to recenter our own voices. And if we do happen to engage in antiracist action, we frame it as a kind of largess of character, rather than simply a matter of paying what is owed.

". . . [Y]ou may go . . ." that is, he asks nothing further of her: neither thanks, nor recognition, nor absolution, nor even reconciliation. Whereas, White fragility demands that should we do right, we must be thanked, and acknowledged, and forgiven, and told we are friends again and that all is well.

"The demon has left your daughter." Finally, he amends his behavior, and delivers her justice. (Mark's account is kind enough to confirm for us that the girl was, in fact, healed.) He makes amends and focuses on what must be done. White fragility, by contrast, will focus on intention, sentiment, and statement, rather than change, action, and restitution.

At one point in her work, DiAngelo recounts posing a question to people of color:

> "What would it be like if you could simply give [White people] feedback, have us graciously receive it, reflect, and work to change the behavior?"[14] "It would be revolutionary,"[15] a man of color replied with a sigh. Mark 7:29 shows us what that revolution could look like in practice.

We might ask ourselves—and I do—why the Evangelists would include this very unflattering story of the Messiah whom they loved, and his racism. We

---

14. DiAngelo, *White Fragility*, 112.

15. DiAngelo, *White Fragility*, 112.

might wonder why they reported this singular and unique story of Jesus losing an argument. That is a good question.

In one anecdote, DiAngelo recalls a moment when her own thoughtless racist behavior is brought to her attention. She approaches the woman she wounded to work for repair. She listens, she acknowledges, she commits to change, she makes restitution, as far as was possible, and says "thank you." And then she recalls, "I ask Angela if there is anything else that needs to be said or heard so that we may move forward. She replies that yes, there is. 'The next time you do something like this, would you like feedback publicly or privately?' she asks. I answer that given my role as an educator, I would appreciate receiving the feedback publicly, as it is important for White people to see that I am also engaged in a lifelong process of learning and growth."[16]

Like DiAngelo, Jesus is an educator: "Teacher" is the title to which he most frequently answers. As an educator, the inclusion of this story is important, because in it he shows us how to receive criticism, even rebuke, when we have engaged in racist behavior. When reading this story from Mark, Jacob Slichter noted admiringly, "He had the courage to do his learning publicly."[17] Unfortunately, such courage is rare; but if we hope to learn how to listen for Black lives, we must claim it.

When we contrast, on the one hand, how simply, directly, and readily Jesus receives criticism for his racist behavior, and, on the other, the convoluted contortions interpreters use to explain his racism away; when we consider our own reluctance to acknowledge and name his behavior as a kind of racism, and how this reluctance blinds us to the actual Good News of the story (that is, that the woman receives justice, that Jesus repents and changes, and that it is possible for us to do the same), then we must consider this conclusion: White fragility not only keeps us from talking meaningfully about racism; it also keeps us from hearing the gospel. We court a double danger when we allow White fragility to deafen us; when we let it stop us from listening for Black lives.

For Black people, this danger is measured in harassment, lost jobs, broken bones, and worse. For us, the danger comes in the possibility of spiritual death. As Bonhoeffer notes:

> He who can no longer listen to his brother will soon be no longer listening to God either; he will be doing nothing but prattle in the presence of God.

---

16. DiAngelo, *White Fragility*, 139–40.

17. Jacob Slichter, personal communication, April 18, 2019.

This is the beginning of the death of the spiritual life, and in the end there is nothing left but spiritual chatter and clerical condescension arrayed in pious words.[18]

Thus, it can be rightly said, if we are to preach for Black lives, indeed, if are to preach at all, we must first learn to listen for Black lives. And this involves following Christ's example, putting aside our defensiveness, and receiving the witness of Black voices, whatever tone they take, as the manifest grace of God in our lives.

---

18. Dietrich Bonhoeffer, *Life Together* (New York: HarperCollins, 2009), 97–98.

9

The Pilgrimage

ACTS 16:25–26; ISAIAH 60:20–23

Rebecca S. Myers

About midnight Paul and Silas were praying and singing hymns to God, and the prisoners were listening to them. Suddenly there was an earthquake, so violent that the foundations of the prison were shaken; and immediately all the doors were opened and everyone's chains were unfastened.

Sometimes opportunities just show up and I had the privilege of being part of a pilgrimage organized by the Washington, DC, chapter of the Union of Black Episcopalians to civil rights sites in Birmingham, Montgomery, and Selma, Alabama. Those who participated were called "Ambassadors of Healing."

While I had been to some of these sites over the years, there were new museums and memorials that I wanted to visit. Also, going with UBE presented a wonderful opportunity to be among Episcopalians and our friends; it suggested a spiritually centered trip.

One of the new museums we visited was the Legacy Museum in downtown Montgomery, Alabama. The museum was founded by the Equal Justice Initiative or EJI. It is designed to show how the legacy of slavery led to lynching, which led to Jim Crow, which led to today's mass incarceration of people of color.

At the entrance of the museum, we saw videos and maps teaching about the domestic slave trade. In 1808, the "importation of slaves" was outlawed. Yet slavery still existed in the United States. As had been happening for many years, children born of mothers who were enslaved were also enslaved. Virginia became the place that provided the most enslaved people from their Commonwealth to the "deep or lower south." Virginia had the largest domestic slave trade.

The domestic slave trade is often known as the Second Middle Passage, the first one being the trip from the African continent to the United States.

This Second Middle Passage was just as brutal. People brought to Montgomery sometimes marched on foot for hundreds of miles and were kept in pens, sometimes with the animals, as they awaited being sold at auction. The Legacy Museum recreates these pens and, using holographic imagery, brings the experience of those enslaved to life.

In one pen, a young boy and girl appear, continually asking for their mother from whom they had been separated. In another pen, people appear and continually sing. Even as we looked and listened to the stories in the other cells, you continually heard the singing from the first one. Those songs and the singing, not only during that time but throughout the civil rights movement and even into today, were important and powerful.

Our group was fortunate to have tour guides at many of the sites who had participated in the various movements—some as young as eleven years old and others in their early or late teens. Now in their seventies and eighties, they provided a firsthand account of marching so their parents could vote, or not using buses for over a year so they could ride anywhere on the bus, or demanding equal access to all public facilities. They provided a firsthand account to the violence such seemingly simple requests elicited, including the deaths of their friends and loved ones. We were told this movement was a spiritual movement with political and economic consequences. It was led from the churches, not from the political parties or businesses. The movement was grounded in God's justice and in God's love.

In our reading from Acts, we hear a story of a young girl who was enslaved to two men; they made a lot of money because of her ability to see into the future. The two men did not see her as a human being. Like slave holders and oppressors throughout the ages, they only saw the money they could make by exploiting her talent.

Paul and Silas had been staying with Lydia in the city of Philippi. This young, enslaved woman followed them around, proclaiming that Paul and Silas were bound to God and indeed offered salvation. After a number of days, Paul was able to get the foretelling to stop. We are told that the woman was no longer able to tell of future events. The two men who had enslaved her were not concerned about her at all and were furious with Paul and Silas. They had Paul and Silas horribly beaten and thrown into jail.

And what did Paul and Silas do? They did what freedom fighters and Christians have done across time: they sang. On our pilgrimage we, too, sang—"O Freedom," "We Shall Overcome," and "Ain't Gonna Let Nobody Turn Me Around."

Paul and Silas sang. They prayed and they sang. Yes, they were caught in a political system, accused of violating the laws of the community. They were jailed by the political authorities of the city. They had challenged the economic system of the time that said it was right for two men to make money from the talent of another person, that it was perfectly right to enslave someone for personal economic gain.

Yet, Paul and Silas knew that all of this aberrant political and economic behavior, laws, and societal norms were a corruption of the spirit, a corruption of the soul. That's what Jesus Christ had taught them. Jesus Christ had taught them a way to live that fed their souls, that created communities where all could be soul-fed. They knew going against the corruption of the world could get them killed, yet the liberation they felt from living in the way Jesus taught was so powerful, death did not scare them; death had lost its sting.

And that's why the pilgrimage to these sites in Alabama was so powerful, especially being able to meet people who lived the movement. The civil rights movement was and is a spiritual movement, with political and economic consequences.

We are required by our love for Jesus Christ, who shed his blood for us, to work for and live in a world where all are free and souls are fed. The prophet Isaiah says it this way in chapter 65:20–23:

No more shall there be in it
 an infant that lives but a few days,
 or an old person who does not live out a lifetime;
for one who dies at a hundred years will be considered a youth,
 and one who falls short of a hundred will be considered accursed.
They shall build houses and inhabit them;
 they shall plant vineyards and eat their fruit.
They shall not build and another inhabit;
 they shall not plant and another eat;
for like the days of a tree shall the days of my people be,
 and my chosen shall long enjoy the work of their hands.
They shall not labor in vain,
 or bear children for calamity;
for they shall be offspring blessed by the Lord—
 and their descendants as well.

At the one end of the Edmund Pettis bridge in Selma, close to where the march from Selma to Montgomery for voting rights began, there is a park commemorating the march. One of the monuments is to Representative John Lewis. As a college student, Lewis was with the Student Nonviolent Coordinating Committee or SNCC, and suggested the march as a way to press the politicians in Montgomery to ensure voting rights for all. The quote from Rep. Lewis that is on this monument says, "When we pray, our feet move."

May our praying move our feet to continue the work for God's justice right here and right now, so that everyone's chains will be broken and the doors to the prison will be opened.

Amen.

10

Which Is It?

THE TOWER OF BABEL
OR THE NEW COMMANDMENT?

GENESIS 11:1–9, JOHN 13:34–35, JOHN 19:30, NAB

Kevin C. Pinckney

Question: Where will you stay when it is finished?

Answer: In one of the many rooms Jesus prepared.

Let us begin our journey to the city of heaven. From what I understand, a room has been prepared for us. How much will it cost? What do we owe? Those questions you may ask, but you should know that the price has been paid. We do not have a mortgage on this house, or rent for the room.

You ask: How is this possible? Who owns such a house? What do I owe?

Answer: It is in the Father's house. It has been purchased for you. And, the cost? The house had to be purchased before you could even enter the city called "The Kingdom of Heaven."

You cannot enter the city until the paperwork on the house has been finished. What was written in the Old Testament had to be fulfilled. The foundation had to be laid.

The kingdom of heaven could not be entered until Jesus said his last word and died. Because he did, you may go into the room prepared for you.

> When Jesus had taken the wine, he said, "It is finished." And bowing his head, he handed over the spirit. (John 19:30, NAB)

It is finished. Jesus went to the closing for us so we could enter the city, house, and room prepared for us. The mortgage has been paid. The papers have been signed. It is finished. Welcome. Enter your city. Your house. Enter the room that Jesus prepared for you.

[Jesus said] There are many rooms in my Father's house. If there weren't, I wouldn't have told you that I am going away to prepare a place for you, would I? (John 14:2, ISV)

Jesus has prepared an inclusive house. The "many rooms" do not necessarily mean he is quantifying the spaciousness of God's house. Jesus has prepared a place for the authentic you, the you God created, the you he has come to learn about over the course of your life.

Jesus is not color-blind. He applauds the individuality when he recognizes you and is designing the room he prepares for you. After all, there are many rooms, and those many rooms are contained within God's house—a house that is meant to be filled.

> **Question:** If Jesus is not color-blind, does that mean heaven is segregated?
>
> **Answer:** Jesus is reassuring the people that there will be a place for them. Each of them. There is no segregation according to race or color.
>
> **Question:** I want to be certain. May I request a walk through? May I preview the room?
>
> **Answer:** All your life you have been given a preview. You only had to listen and live the words you have been told.

Jesus took the foundation from the Hebrew Bible. Jesus built the structure, designed the room. You only had to see what he said in the Gospels. You had to let your spirit hear the words deep down in your soul. You would feel the room come to life through those deeds and those actions to know what your room will be like.

No, heaven is not segregated. Believing that it is puts us in a dangerous place. A place that is not filled with his love. Earthly segregation is evil: people viewing the "not me" through a myopic lens of fear filled with incomprehensible suspicions.

> The whole world spoke the same language, using the same words. While men were migrating in the east, they came upon a valley in the land of Shinar and settled there. They said to one another, "Come, let us mold bricks and harden them with fire." They used bricks for stone and bitumen (tar) for mortar. Then they said, "Come, let us build ourselves a city and a tower with its top in the sky, and make a name for ourselves; otherwise we shall be scattered all over the earth."

The LORD came down to see the city and the tower that the men had built. Then the LORD said: "If now, while they are one people, all speaking the same language, they have started to do this, nothing will stop them from doing whatever they presume to do. Let us go down and there confuse their language, so that no one will not understand what another says."

Thus the LORD scattered them from there all over the earth, and they stopped building the city. That is why it was called Babel, because the LORD confused the speech of all the world. It was from that place that He scattered them all over the earth. (Gen. 11:1–9, NAB)

How soon do they forget the "New Commandment"?

[Jesus said,] "I give you a new commandment: love one another. As I have loved you, so you also should love one another." (John 13:34, NAB)

You may be in one room together or separated among the many rooms. What you will share is the love. It is the love that will bring together the tenants within His house.

[Jesus said,] "This is how all will know that you are my disciples, if you have love for one another." (John 13:35, NAB)

I repeat. How soon do they forget the "New Commandment"?

It is possible to appear to be segregated. A Black church. A White church. A Latinx church. An Asian church. A dichotomy of churches, as may appear to be the end result of the Tower of Babel. But Jesus left one Church.

I saw a meme that said (I'm paraphrasing) to be a person in the United States of America means that your ancestral origins are:

1. Native American
2. Immigrant
3. Enslaved victim
4. Refugee

It seems that these categories are just another way for human beings to separate ourselves; they don't even seem to be complete or accurate. And yet, they exist, more often than not, to highlight differences as opposed to showing how we are alike.

The movie *Black Panther* introduced me to "colonizers." It was an epiphany. I was aware of colonization, but had never really matched the word to people. Colonizers: those who colonize. History was taught to me through the perspective of the United States of America colonizers. I was told the grand tales of the explorers who colonized the world, without using the word "colonizers."

That fear from Babel seemed to disappear. They cared not but to explore the exotic and live amongst those who were *different*.

But to hear the story from the perspective of a Wakandan? To hear the story from the perspective of woke, indigenous people?

What was the way of colonizers?

Someone, some group of someones, who came from Babel is upon their shores. Upon their land. At first, very much uninvited. Colonizers. Strange languages. Strange customs. Babel. Why were they here? What was their way?

The indigenous are seen as weak. They lived through the spirit of the New Commandment. Out of love, they shared. That was their way. Their custom. Their spirituality. Now we are still transfixed by the parameters of the "us" and the "not us," where the colonizers are "not us."

When the Tower of Babel fell, humanity was young. It was too soon for uniformity among the people. God had made and remade the earth for God's children to inhabit. The land was baptized from the Great Flood and refreshed to nourish the surviving children. The children were of the same house, but it was time for them to inherit the Earth and to learn the beauty of God's gift to them. Babel happened to ensure the children populated the world. It was not time to reach the heavens and lord over all that was. But it seems as though superiority over others and other things never left some.

In the United States of America, it came to pass that one "race" subjugated all others in order to gain the "riches" of the land. It was never a matter of not knowing what one ethnicity had within its grasp. It was a matter of the spirituality of the people who allowed the "not us" to be welcomed.

How soon did they forget the "New Commandment"?

The objective now may be racial reconciliation. The "not us" have to remember Babel, but more importantly, the "not us" need to remember before Babel. What if Babel took place so humanity could learn about a colorful world, a world that defined beauty in all of its manifestations?

The resulting beauty would fill and decorate God's house with many rooms of colorful design where Jesus prepared your room, and his room, and her room, even their rooms. But it was never said that the room Jesus prepared was a closed-off space. What if the room allowed others to see in and to visit and to share the love? The "not us" need to remember the love that existed after the Great Flood and before the confusion at the Tower of Babel. Once recalled, perhaps racial reconciliation may commence.

[Jesus said,] "This is how all will know that you are my disciples, if you have love for one another." (John 13:35, NAB)

11

Samaritan Sunday

LUKE 16:19–31

Gene Robinson

If you were coming to church to hear some good news this morning, this might not have been a great morning to come. We've got Amos, one of the great prophets, reading the riot act to the Jews because of their unfaithfulness to God. And then the first letter to Timothy, which is probably not written by Paul but by one of his protégés or associates, is also talking about being comfortable and wealthy and still being a person of God. And then if that wasn't enough, we have the story of the rich man and Lazarus. Where is the good news in all that? We aren't given a whole lot of details about either the rich man or Lazarus, but the writer, Luke, tells us, gives us a little hint about where he's going because the rich man never has a name in this story, but the beggar at the gate with sores on himself and looking for scraps from the rich man's table, he's named. And Abraham calls him by his name. This rich man, whose name was probably known far and wide because he was rich and, therefore, probably powerful, doesn't even rate a name in the afterlife. But Lazarus, who got the short end of the stick in real life, has been taken to the bosom of Abraham.

The sin of the rich man was not that he was rich or not even his attitude toward Lazarus; it was the disconnectedness he chose from Lazarus. I wonder out loud, did he really even want to see Lazarus at his gate? Occasionally he might have thrown some change his way or some scraps of food, but honestly, he just didn't care all that much. Now, it's entirely possible this rich man was really a nice guy. Maybe he worked hard; maybe he had an entrepreneurial spirit. Maybe he gave generously to his synagogue. Maybe he was really on ok guy; maybe he just didn't connect to this man sitting at his gate.

On the other hand, he might have been awful. We're told that he was neither awful nor good, just that he was rich. Now, Lazarus, maybe he was a good guy. Maybe he was a poor man's hero; maybe he was poor and generous in spite of the misery he lived in. He might have been a drunk or an addict or both or worse. We are not told. We are just told he was poor. I'm going to do a side bar, so I'm going to the side. So, this story is about privilege—all kinds of privilege—though it seems to be about the privilege of wealth. As we go through the story, I want you to think about all those kinds of privilege. It's about White people who have privilege and, as a result, benefit from a culture set up to favor them at the expense of people of color. Or it's the privilege of being male, which comes at the expense of women. Or it's about being able bodied, or being documented, or being—you fill in the blank. Whatever the privilege is, it's about what the privileged person does. If we as White people are not working to undo the systemic racism that is America, then we are a part of it; we are racists unless we are working day and night to dismantle it.

If you are a man and you are talking to and about women in a way that doesn't respect them as a human being and a child of God, if you're not trying to dismantle the system that benefits men at the expense of women, then you are a misogynist. And so on and so on.

It's not that this rich man had wealth, it's that the wealth seduced him into thinking he wasn't connected to those on the losing side of privilege.

With any kind of privilege, we don't have to hate anybody or treat anybody poorly to participate. If we are not working to undo that system and we are benefiting from it, then we are a part of it. This story is about much more than wealth. It makes me wonder if the rich man wanted to see Lazarus at his gate; was he intentionally blind to the beggar?

Fast forward: they are both dead. The rich man is in Hades and Lazarus is at Abraham's side. And the rich man hasn't learned much. He's still ordering around people he considers beneath him.

"Send him to me with a fingerful of water to quench my thirst."

"Would you go back to tell my brothers so they will know how bad this is?"

Abraham says, "Look, you had the Bible; it's full of the law and the prophets; it told you what to do. You wouldn't even listen to somebody coming back from the dead." We know that's true, right? We know somebody who came back from the dead and how often do we not listen to him?

This story is not just about fabulously wealthy people; it's not Bill Gates or Jeff Bezos. It's about us because, compared to the people of the rest of the world, we are unbelievably rich. You might not have as much money as someone else you've heard about, but there's hardly a person sitting here who is not rich in a meaningful way. If you're squirming a little, good. That's precisely what we're supposed to be doing because we are inextricably linked and connected to the most vulnerable among us—regardless of the reason for their vulnerability.

We are linked to them and God means for us to be connected to them. To treat them like human beings. God wants us to pay attention and to reach out in some meaningful way that keeps us connected.

Samaritan Ministries is here today offering us a quite specific way to stay connected to people who are in dire straits. And what I love about Samaritan Ministries is that they do that work with infinite respect for the people who are the recipients of that work. This is not Madame Gotrocks giving money to the poor and pitying them all the time. It's about empowering unemployed people and homeless people and they do it in a way that builds up their integrity and not tears it down. It makes them feel better about themselves. You are going to hear more about them.

The rich man needed Samaritan Ministries. He needed first of all, to see the man at his gate, and then he needed to look for ways to stay connected to him. The funny thing about staying connected is that we can't treat someone like dirt if we are connected to them. We can't treat them as less than a child of God if we are connected to them. If we are really ready to get our hands dirty to help them out. If we are willing to give up some of our wealth to help them out, it will be fulfilling.

The great chasm between the rich man and Lazarus isn't just in heaven or hell. It is right here on earth. It's about connecting now and not when it's too late. How do we that? This might sound odd. Pay attention when you are watching TV. When a program comes on about a 100,000 people being killed in Yemen and there are attacks from Saudi Arabia that you and I are funding, don't change the channel. Listen to it and weep; get mad; get active. It's important that we not turn away from these folks at our door. I don't care what you think about immigration law, I am telling you that circumstances are so bad in El Salvador and Guatemala and Honduras, that people in those places would be crazy not to come here, or at least send their children here. When I was working in El Salvador, I sat with a woman whose fifteen-year-old son had been recruited by a gang. When he wouldn't join, they killed him and raped his sister in front of her. She said to me, "I wish I had sent them north to the border."

Don't turn away from stories like that. They are the truth; they are the stories we learn when we stay connected, when we remind ourselves day after day that they are children of God, just like you and me. So, when we hear about voter suppression in Georgia, we must care about it, even though we are in DC. We can't maintain this privilege whether it be from wealth, or from race, or gender, or able bodies, we can't use that privilege to feather our nests anymore at the expense of someone else.

I get it that we can't be connected to everybody, but we can be connected to somebody. There is some person who is facing some grievance going on in the world that we can be a part of solving. We don't have to do it all, but when we meet Jesus he's going to want to hear what we did for at least somebody. Otherwise, we are going to be looking up from Hades and seeing these people gathered around Abraham and wish we had listened.

Now, this story isn't really about heaven and hell and all that kind of stuff; it's about what we do with what we have. I don't know how it will happen, but I think that at some point in our lives, or in our deaths, we will be made to see what we did and who we really were—and that just may be hell.

About two chapters after this story in Luke's gospel there is another story. Jesus is in Jericho and a blind man sitting by the road cries out, "Jesus, Son of David, have mercy on me." Son of David was the messianic term, not just a nice term. The blind man was saying, "Here is the one we have been waiting for."

And Jesus says, "Bring him here." The crowd had been trying to shush him up because, after all, he was just a blind man sitting on the side of the road trying to beg for enough to subsist, but then they say, "He's calling for you," and the man jumps up and goes to Jesus and Jesus asks him the most interesting question.

"What do you want me to do for you?"

The man says, "I want to see again."

My question today is, "What do we want Jesus to do for us?" Could it be that we want to see all the people we have intentionally decided not to see? The world and God are waiting for us to treat them with infinite respect. It is not a big ask. Amen.

12

What Does the Lord Require?

JOHN 4:1–27

Glenice Robinson-Como

From the beginning of time, one of the most difficult tasks for us has been to live among one another, knowing who we are and whose we are. Throughout the scriptures, God continuously beckons us into reconciliation with the earth and with one another. Yet, as much as we say we are working for reconciliation with one another, we find another Charlottesville event, a political ploy, or another injustice where the poor and disenfranchised continually suffer and the rich and privileged prevail.

If we are truly living through the lens of the gospel, if the "Good News" is truly for all people in all places, then why is it that still today we cannot embrace and fully live out the ministry of Christ where all are precious and of value to God? Perhaps we sometimes forget that we need one another to see the face of God in ourselves, our lives, and in each other. The richness of the gospel invites us into knowing that we each bear something in which the other needs in order to fully continue the work of building up the body of Christ. This knowledge makes our work for a just society a cooperative effort; an effort in which we bring together all of our God-given gifts and use them as an offering to God. Lest we forget that justice in any form has always been a gospel issue and to negate justice is in opposition to everything in which Jesus came into the world to accomplish. From the beginning of time God has shown us who we are to be in the world and the book of Micah could not be clearer: "And what does the Lord require of you but to do justice, and to love kindness, and to walk humbly with your God?" (Micah 6:8).

Many who live within the realm of power and privilege have shared their journeys of inclusivity with me. They say they are not color-blind, which is quite bothersome because if you do not see color, you are truly not seeing God. You do not see me. God created us to be a kaleidoscope of color, culture, and creativity. Yet many still find their journey as reconcilers to be uncomfortable, painful, or even awkward toward those who are different from us in their thoughts, words, or deeds. The unknown territories of oppression can be difficult, they can be scary, and yes, they can be costly. As Jesus said, "For what will it profit them to gain the whole world and forfeit their life?" (Mark 8:36). Jesus calls each of us to be inclusive of all persons, to ensure there is a seat at the table for everyone, even if they differ from us. It is within our differences in which Christ expects us to grow, to accept, and to render respect for one another. The gift of caring relationships within the realm of our differences and uncertainties is truly where the power of transformation occurs. The work of racial reconciliation is difficult work; when we feel the pain of racial conversations and encounters, it is then that we are positioned within the heart of the struggle. For within the midst of the struggle, within the midst of the fire, is where the spirit opens a pathway toward healing and change.

If we think about the story of the Samaritan woman at the well (John 4), we will recall that she risked everything, knowing she was despised by Jews and bore the mark of an outcast. Many first-century men rarely spoke to women; women were considered property and held no social status. The very fact that women daily retrieved water for the community and family self-defined their status and their worth. It confirmed they were regarded more as a servant than as a member of the family. Yet it is here at the most unlikely place and with the most unlikely person that Jesus ministers to one deemed "the least of these." Of all who lived in Samaria, Jesus chose the most unlikely person to proclaim the gospel and in turn, she rushed to tell all that she heard within her community.

We are not told the woman's name, but still her story stands as a living witness of the love of Christ who knows everything about us yet still loves us and constantly invites us to drink deeply from the well of life. Jesus's ministry to those considered as the outcasts of society reveals his great worth and love for all humanity and the woman at the well stands as a symbol and an offering of hope to us today. The Samaritan woman reminds us of how Jesus interacted with those the world has labeled as not good enough, not worthy enough, or those who were marginalized and placed outside of our social circles. As gospel bearers. may we also be reminded that we are also commissioned to go into the Samaritan communities of today and offer advocacy, support, and love.

At the heart of John's Gospel, may we also remember that the work of racial reconciliation will cost us something as a gospel bearer. Actually, we should expect our work together to bear some type of cost, for it is through the giving and emptying of ourselves that we become more Christ-like. Our mission and purpose must always be like a second skin to us, for this is the very ministry in which Christ modeled during his earthly pilgrimage.

Recently my family and I visited an exhibit at the Bible Museum in Washington, DC, entitled, "The Tapestry of Light." The exhibit is an interpretation of John's apocalypse presented in tapestry form. It is the first known to be created by a woman, Dr. Irene Barberis. The artist utilizes light to demonstrate medieval ideas of "illuminating the soul."[1] She uses light in an incredible way. Each time you view a scene, various colors of light change the tapestry and reveal a different message and image. This is what I feel the light of Christ does to each of us. The light of Christ touches us, transforms us, heals us, and sends us out into the world to share in ministry together. In all of our experiences in life, it is the light of Christ that reveals our deepest pains and begins the work of healing and restoration. We are truly God's tapestry of light and love. I pray through our spiritual healing we each will seek to be continuously transformed by the power of God's light, in order that we might work to change the world.

---

1. "The Tapestry of Light Project," The Bible Museum, *https://www.tapestryoflightproject.com/about.*

13

The Wall of Whiteness

Cara Rockhill

I am pale. Really pale. Even by white standards, I'm pale. Growing up, as far as I was concerned, my skin was a liability. I was constantly late to summer activities because I was applying sunblock. Since I was a kid, I was terrible about reapplying sunblock, meaning I basically stayed sunburnt from May until September. Adult Cara is admittedly a little annoyed at child Cara. But that's for me to work out in therapy.

When I preach, I talk a fair amount about my skin. I try to put myself in the story, show what work I've done and why, and lead people through the process by showing I went first. My process starts with a long look at myself from the outside in: my pale skin, my blue eyes, my freckles.

I am White. And not just White; pale. According to one of those ancestry tests, I am 82 percent British, 16 percent Scandinavian, and 2 percent unidentifiable. My ancestors followed a migratory pattern that led to my pale skin. I stand before you as a result of ancestors who lived in the mountains of Britain (specifically Scotland); Rockhill even means the people who lived on the mountain—the rock hill.

White skin—a liability that constantly hurt—stayed red all summer, and flushed when I talked, walked outside, walked inside, or cried. And then I grew up. I became a lawyer. Then a priest. I began to understand. My skin wasn't a liability. My skin was a head start. It was not a head start I asked for, but it was one I got. It was not something I intentionally sought, but the color of my skin was, without a doubt, a factor in my educational and professional success.

The color of my skin allowed my grandparents to buy land in a certain area, which made it easier for my mother to buy the house that I grew up in. She bought it from my grandparents. Because of where I grew up, which remains a majority white area, I went to excellent schools. I got into college. My mother understood credit, and set me up so that I would have good credit as an adult. Having good credit allowed me to rack up a lot of student debt in order to get advanced degrees.

Those advanced degrees made me the Rev. Dr. Cara Rockhill. I didn't ask for any of those advantages, but I got them. I benefitted from redlining (when my grandparents could buy land, but the descendants of slaves could not); I benefited from a well-funded school system because generations of higher income earners meant higher taxes collected for schools. I benefitted from my mother's education and understanding of credit.

I can't speak of the experiences of those with darker skin, but I can hold my experience and understanding in contrast to that of others. For example, in *The Bluest Eye*, Toni Morrison writes about a little girl named Pecola who considers herself ugly because of her dark skin. She believes she would be beautiful and able to escape her oppressed life if only she had blue eyes. The underlying issue is much deeper than how Pecola looks. There is internalized racism, inherited self-hate, self-loathing, and a diminished sense of self, which led to how Pecola views herself.[1]

The opposite is true for me, and for the majority of Episcopalians. We were raised in a society that lifts up the color of our skin. My skin, my pale skin, is often complimented by strangers, and has been most of my life. The development of American culture, in which the Episcopal Church played a huge role, created the form of racism that runs rampant in America today. Toni Morrison gave voice to the internalized racism of little girls of color (and, in other works, of adults of color). And she made me, with my bright blue eyes, think differently about the world I thought I saw.

I've spent a lot of time unpacking racism: internalized racism, privilege, Whiteness, my Whiteness, the witness of the church, systemic racism, and White supremacy. As a faith leader and preacher, this is a huge part of what I am called to do—to look to myself and then help lead others. It is an ongoing evolution for me. One that I thought I was making good progress. And then one day, I realized that I hadn't spent any time considering that my skin, my White skin, is a barrier between God and me. There isn't a question mark at the end of that sentence. It's a fact. That thought stopped me in my tracks.

My call shifted in that moment when I realized that I was called to tear down these barriers—within myself first, and then to help others. These walls are human constructions. God isn't a big fan of walls (I'm thinking Jericho and Babel; we know what God does to big walls). Have you ever stopped and considered a picture of Jesus? Jesus was many things, but a blond-haired, blue-eyed

---

1. Toni Morrison, *The Bluest Eye* (New York: Alfred A. Knopf, 2000).

man was never one of them. Jesus as a White man is a White construction; God made him dark-skinned and dark-eyed.

Just last week I spoke at a Bible study and asked if anyone else struggled with the idea of Jesus acknowledging slavery as an acceptable part of life. I got a lot of answers about slavery as just a fact of life back then—and how far we've come as a society. I got crickets when I asked how Jesus accepting slavery made people feel; they hadn't thought about it. They hadn't let those words sink in. They hadn't dealt with racism.

I can't blame them; it wasn't until I started intentionally to do this work that I stopped to think about how the Bible has been used to subdue and subject other humans. I didn't enjoy thinking about how I bought into the idea of "things were different back then," nor about what parts of me are still influenced by internal racism and systemic racism.

I try to gently ask questions to lead people into this process. I share that simply being raised to understand that Jesus looks like me left me struggling with the idea that my skin raised me to think of God as a colleague, an equal, a friend I can just chat with whenever, instead of, well, God. I ask how often we attribute something to God opening a door (or window), when it was White privilege that opened that opportunity?

None of these questions is easy. It's a lot more fun to think about race and privilege in theoretical terms. It's much easier to just be academic. The actual work can't just be academic though. We must take an honest and vulnerable look at ourselves and our history as Christians. We can't merely accept that things were different back then. We must actively strive to be different ourselves, to recognize where that history impacts our present, and to do the difficult work of tearing down the walls humans built, even if we didn't build them.

If we are truly to love our neighbors as ourselves, we must first love ourselves. Our history is part of who we are. If we don't do the work, and instead just ignore or sweep the unpleasant parts away, we're not fully loving ourselves. We still have walls.

God enters through our wounds and scars, not over our walls.

This work doesn't lead to being ashamed of our skin. This work leads to a fuller understanding of who God created us to be.

As a preacher, helping us to be the people that God created us to be is at the top of my to-do list.

I must first walk the path, then invite others to join me.

I will continue to circle the wall of my Whiteness until it crumbles.

14

The Absent God

LUKE 12:32–40; HEBREWS 10:39–11:16

Rob Stephens

Our text includes one of Jesus's several parables about a master leaving his servants and slaves with the keys to the house. Today we are told to keep the lamps lit and to stay "dressed for action," which the direct translation would be more like "gird your loins." Which, if you it look up, isn't as racy as it sounds.

These stories never sat well with me as a kid growing up in church. They seemed to be saying, "Watch out! You never know when God is coming for you!" "Keep your head on a swivel, Jesus could show up at any moment and catch you stealing that last oatmeal cream pie from the closet." And yes, I would actually eat that last oatmeal cream pie, and pray for forgiveness before the last bite was down just to make sure I didn't get caught in sin. It was a stressful life.

Now that I've grown up and get to enjoy the luxuries of adulthood like eating ice cream every night and sometimes in the morning, where the only real regret is physical and not existential, I find myself in a different quarrel with these texts.

I don't like that we're talking about masters and slaves or servants as if it is a legitimate metaphor in the first place. I imagine I would be more interested in how the servants could squat on the land and create a model of cooperative ownership, as they do in Acts, so that when the master returned he would no longer be able to rule over the others. Of course, the master would be welcome to join the co-op.

When my kindhearted and thoughtful spouse, Hershey, read that introduction, she told me it was one of the *Whitest* things I had ever written. "You can't even handle a *parable* about not being in charge. You have to theorize your way out of it, and then call it moral!"

Well, what can you do? I still didn't like the stories. And as I read this portion of scripture, I found myself even more put-off by Jesus's anxiety-inducing warnings. Just ten verses earlier, Jesus tells the disciples, "Therefore I tell you, do not worry about your life, what you will eat, or about your body, what you will wear. . . . Can any of you by worrying add a single hour to your span of life?" (Luke 12:22, 25).

Come on, Jesus, which one is it: perpetual neurotic vigilance or Hakuna Matata, no worries, be happy?

As I said, this parable is not an isolated incident. Jesus tells several of these parables about a master of the house going on a journey and coming back unexpectedly to judge the servants. There is the parable of the talents, where servants receive the talents and the master comes back to see what they did with them. There is the parable of the bridegroom and the ten bridesmaids, half of whom were disowned because they didn't bring enough oil for their lamps. Each one caused me to feel like God acted more like a hidden camera or a big brother waiting around the corner to jump and catch me in the act, than like the all-loving God I knew.

So I wasn't at first keen on this scripture, but, as many of you know, it's the scriptures that make us the most uncomfortable that are often the ones we need to hear the most.

These stories of Jesus are called by some scholars the "parables of stewardship." They tell stories of people, often described as servants or slaves, left in charge of a place that does not belong to them, and who are judged by their behavior in the absence of the rightful owner. They are stewards of the property, lands, and people left to them. But on another level, as Justo González argues, they are also stories about the *absence* of God. In fact, he argues that the theme of God's absence is central to Jesus's ministry and message while he walked this world.[1] If the idea of a "Gotcha God" who was waiting to catch us in sin wasn't off-putting enough, now we have a God who comes up missing.

Jesus knew that the disciples—and all of us—would find ourselves at times feeling the absence of God. There are other parables where *we* are the ones who leave God and wander away from God's love, like the lost sheep, the lost coin, or the prodigal son. And in fact, as a good repentant Protestant, I like those parables more. In them, I am in control. I am the sheep who wanders, the son who took my inheritance and ran away. I can find comfort in my human depravity. I know what to do when I'm lost.

But what about when it feels like God is lost? What about when a twenty-one-year-old drives ten hours to kill twenty-two strangers in a Walmart in El Paso, twenty-two children of the Most High God. They weren't lost sheep or

---

1. Justo L. González, *Luke* (Louisville: Westminster John Knox Press, 2010).

prodigal sons and daughters. The oldest was ninety years old and the youngest was fifteen. What about when another white man kills nine human beings in less than a minute in Dayton, Ohio?

What can we say about God when the most explicitly White supremacist president since Woodrow Wilson makes a statement condemning White supremacy and the next day—while he is in El Paso supposedly comforting victims who were targeted because of anti-immigrant xenophobia he has fueled—has his administration carry out what ICE (Immigration and Customs Enforcement) would proudly call the largest raid in US history? Nearly seven hundred workers were handcuffed in Mississippi factories in a campaign of terror, many leaving children unattended and traumatized. Where is God when these mass shootings and terror campaigns against immigrants are most horrifying not in their uniqueness, but in that they have become a mundane reality of American life.

Yes, I don't think I've liked these "stewardship parables" because they are asking us to be responsible for a broken world. But we are reaping the horror of what happens when stewards get confused by the freedom and responsibility given them, that is, given to us—those of us who have come to think we are the master just because we have the keys to the kingdom; those who, like the unfaithful slave in the following part of chapter 12, begin to use that freedom to control the world around them and, drunk on power, beat others into submission.

What does God want from us in God's absence? Henry Nouwen says, "As we become aware of God's absence we discover God's presence, and as we realize that God left us, we also come to know that God did not leave us *alone*."[2]

It may be instructive to take a look at where we find ourselves in the Gospel story. Midway through Luke we are no longer dealing with the "let the little children come to me" Jesus (Matt. 19:14). This is not the Jesus of sweet lullabies and Christian love songs. This Jesus has turned the corner toward Golgotha and his own crucifixion. He is looking at the world with brutal clarity.

Jesus in the middle of Luke is not comforting in the traditional sense. Later in chapter 12, verses 49 and 51 he will say, "I came to bring fire to the earth, and how I wish it were already kindled! . . . Do you think that I have come to bring peace to the earth? No, I tell you, but rather division!"

It is as Sonia Sanchez described the immortal brilliance of Toni Morrison this week on *Democracy Now!* podcast, saying Toni Morrison looked at the

---

2. Quoted in Justo González, *The Living Reminder: Service and Prayer in Memory of Jesus* (New York: Seabury Press, 1977), 46.

world with a cold and warm eye. She helped us look at the world with great clarity and to speak truth about it with "unmolested language."[3]

Yes, the prophetic love and ministry and unmolested language of our brother Jesus prepares us for times like now. When, to use Toni Morrison's words, "the parasitical nature of white freedom" comes to hound our souls. It is a parasitical White freedom because it is a freedom that garners its strength from oppression.[4] This corrupted American freedom is what allowed our founders to have no problem holding "liberty and justice for all" in one hand and people in chains in the other, to paraphrase Karen and Barbara Fields.[5] It is a form of "freedom" that requires slavery to affirm its freedom. It is a warped version of freedom that is most threatened by the real thing.

It is in times like these when God feels so painfully absent that it also becomes so clear what God's justice does NOT look like—how untenable a world without God and without God's mercy and justice would be. In God's absence, the beauty of humanity and creation becomes all the more urgently important because we see how precious it is.

This is what the story of the good steward means to me. We must keep our loins girded and lamps lit, because the paradox of Christ is that it is through the Crucifixion, in and through death, that death is destroyed. The paradox of Christ. That is how Dr. King says, "Somehow I know, only when it is dark enough can I see the stars."[6] Somehow! We must learn to look at the world as our ancestor Toni Morrison did, with cold and sober eyes at the brutal reality in which we find ourselves; with the cold, hard unmolested truths that the soul-killing myths of White freedom, White supremacy, and, yes, White Christianity are parasitic and grotesquely warped idols that leave no one unscathed. We must look at the world and one another with the warm eyes of the Resurrection, with the warm eyes that see each other as human beings, each with a divine spark, with a warmth that can only be described as hope.

Two weeks ago I joined hundreds of other people of faith and moral witnesses in El Paso and marched on a detention center where hundreds of

3. "'Toni Morrison Will Always Be with Us': Angela Davis, Nikki Giovanni & Sonia Sanchez Pay Tribute." *Democracy Now!*, August 7, 2019, *https://www.democracynow.org/2019/8/7/remembering_toni_morrison*.

4. Toni Morrison, *Playing in the Dark: Whiteness and the Literary Imagination* (New York: Vintage, 1993).

5. Karen E. Fields and Barbara J. Fields, *Racecraft: The Soul of Inequality in American Life*. (London: Verso Book, 2016).

6. Martin Luther King Jr., "I've Been to the Mountaintop," April 3, 1968, *https://speakola.com/ideas/martin-luther-king-jr-ive-been-to-the-mountaintop-1968*.

refugees were being caged. We were there for a Moral Monday at the Borderlands. We were two miles from the Walmart where the tragedy would occur less than a week later. The organizers from Repairers of the Breach who had gotten in earlier used that Walmart for last-minute supplies throughout the week.

On Monday night after the action, our friend and comrade Ilka Vega from the Hope Border Institute took me to the top of a parking deck to look out over the city of El Paso. That night from the parking deck, when you look out over the city lights, you could not tell where the United States of America ends and Mexico begins. Yes, only when it is dark enough can we see past the borders, beyond the walls created by human beings.

This thing called faith is a paradox because it is not logical. We don't need faith for something we are sure is going to happen. It doesn't make sense. It defies our desire to control and be in charge. The brutality of El Paso, Dayton, Orlando, Charleston, Pittsburgh, and too many other tragedies are not God's plan. And we are called in those moments to even more desperately cling to a vision of a better world, to trust that this world is not final, that there is something beyond us all, a city called heaven, that is calling to something deeply within us all, to be responsible right now for all of creation.

That's why we call it faith and not a fact. Our faith tells us God is here, even when everything around us seems to suggest God is absent. In that faith, we must more boldly consider what it means that God left us the keys to the kingdom. We can't pray our way out of it. We can't logic our way out of it. We've been given the keys. And we are not in charge. We have been given something so big and scary. While the master is away, we care for one another. The truth is we cannot bring the master back when it feels like God is missing. But everything we do can bring the kingdom here to earth.

Beloved, let us strive to be like those saints described in Hebrews:

All of these died in faith without having received the promises, but from a distance they saw and greeted them. . . . But as it is, they desire a better country, that is, a heavenly one. Therefore God is not ashamed to be called their God; indeed, he has prepared a city for them." (Heb. 11:13–16)

Let us be able to say boldly, "But we are not among those who shrink back and so are lost, but among those who have faith and so are saved" (Heb. 10:39). God, give us the faith that is "the assurance of things hoped for, the conviction of things not seen" (Heb. 11:1). Amen.

Reflection Questions

1. Do you find it difficult to preach about race in your context? What is your context? Is your race and the race of your congregation the same or do you find yourself in the minority?

2. If you and your congregation are non-Black, do you believe it is important to preach about race, to lift up #BlackLivesMatter?

3. If you have preached about race, what has been the reaction of your congregation?

4. If you preach about race, is it primarily during Black History Month or other *ethnic* events? Why is that?

5. If you have preached about race, have you been confronted by a member or members of your congregation, advising you not to be *political*?

6. What books have you read to assist you in preaching about racial issues? How many were written by people of color?

7. Have you taken any courses in, for example, Black liberation, in seminary or undergrad or graduate school?

8. Which of your sermons could you add to this collection?

PART II

Advocating
for Black Lives

15

From the Trenches

ADVOCATING FOR BLACK LIVES (MATTER)

Gayle Fisher-Stewart

I had the privilege of growing up in a tradition that didn't believe in the myths and the legends because we had to bear the brunt of them.

—*Dr. Eddie Glaude Jr.*

The gap between what Church is and what it claims to be, what it could still be, is so wide, it's heartbreaking.

—*The Rev. Peter Jarrett-Schell*

The trip began innocently enough. It was one of those church bus trips for lunch, shopping, and a boat ride. During our free time, I wandered the streets of a quaint little town on the Maryland Eastern shore. There were all varieties and races of people—residents, tourists, shoppers. They were Black and brown and other colors. As I walked, I noticed an Episcopal church, pre–Civil War, surrounded by a cemetery. As I read the names on the tombstones—some faded, some clear—I decided that one Sunday I would drive back and visit the congregation.

We were early. Only one usher was on duty when we arrived. I introduced my parents and myself and indicated the church we attended. We were offered a slight smile and told to "sit anywhere." It just happened to be a Sunday celebrating their patron saint. As people filed in, only the members who sat next to us spoke. Again, I introduced us. The service began, with bagpipes and kilts galore and nary another Black face in the place. That was not all that unusual; I've been in plenty of Episcopal churches where the Black faces were none, or few and far in between. There was a certain coldness that I attributed to Episcopalians being the *frozen chosen*. Most Episcopal church members will tell you that they are warm and welcoming, but the truth tends to be the opposite. We tend to be warm and loving to our own. The chill was perceptible.

At the announcements in the middle of the service, the minister asked if there were any visitors. We stood and introduced ourselves, again saying that I was Episcopalian and naming the churches we attended. What struck me was that there was no "If you are ever in the area, you're always welcome." There are many Sundays when we have had visitors at our parishes, and most visitors already have a church. Still, we offer the invitation to come again, to visit again, to join us again, to say you are always welcome if you are in the area. But not this church. Perhaps, I thought, it was an oversight that would be corrected at the end of the service as we greeted the minister. That was not to happen. As we filed out, we were told, "Have a nice day." There was no "Thank you for coming" or "Come again." I am Episcopalian and I did not feel welcome in an Episcopal church. Perhaps, it was just a congregation that seemed "cold" to visitors, even visitors who are Episcopalians; however, I had to ask myself, "Was it because we were Black?" The church was fairly full; if there were Black members, I'm sure they didn't all take off the same Sunday. Could it be that the members of this church could not or refused to see the *imago Dei* in us? Could it be they were not willing to see that we were also children of God? Perhaps they were welcoming and loving, just not to outsiders—Black outsiders.

The Episcopal Church is overwhelmingly White. It has always been overwhelmingly White. Our history tells us it was the Church of the slave master; the plantocracy. As the Very Rev. Kelly Brown Douglas has challenged, the Episcopal Church has "a decision to make. Are we going to be White or are we going to be Church? One cannot be at once White and Church."[1] Perhaps, just perhaps, the majority of the Episcopal Church likes being White or is blind to its Whiteness; after all, Whiteness is perceived as normal in America.

Truth be told, it is difficult navigating Blackness in a country that uplifts Whiteness, although Blacks have managed. Being White has always been viewed as being better, prettier, more intelligent, more capable, more industrious and while integration was necessary, it hurt the Black community because we bought into the *White is better* lie. We left the communities that nurtured us—if we were successful navigating redlining—because we believed White neighborhoods were better. We sent our children to White schools because we believed them to be better than our Black schools. While the resources might have been deficient, our teachers nurtured our children. Our businesses suffered because we wanted to *shop White*. We left our churches because we

---

1. The Very Rev. Kelly Brown Douglas, "The Work Our Soul Must Do" (keynote speech, Diocese of Indianapolis Diocesan Convention, November 15, 2019), *https://www.youtube.com/watch?v=qLTDDFSxMVA&t=1768s.*

believed White churches were also better. Some Blacks preferred services where the Holy Spirit was more subdued and controlled. We gathered to worship along color lines. Some churches were home to the lighter-hued and professional African Americans, while others were home to the darker-skinned folk and the working class. We learned well. We segregated ourselves. We learned the lessons of the White world. Whites discriminated against us and we turned around and discriminated against us. We thought we had assimilated, that we had become *White*, at least in a societal way, only to realize we were still Black and would never be fully accepted in a country that prized Whiteness.

If the Church replicates or, in some ways, originates racism, we must ask the question, why bother? Why bother being a part of an institution that is the antithesis of Jesus? James Cone claimed that the White church was the anti-Christ.[2] Would it not be better to be part of Thurman's religion of Jesus without the creeds, beliefs, and liturgies of a church that continues to devalue Black life?

Another question that must be asked is what is the cumulative effect of witnessing the Church that negates the commandment to love one's neighbor as one's self? While not written as an apologetic for the Church, Joy Degruy's *Post Traumatic Slave Syndrome: America's Legacy of Enduring Injury & Healing*[3] provides some insight into why historically Black and predominantly Black churches continue to exist.[4] While it is difficult to empirically prove a direct connection between the trauma experienced by once-enslaved Africans and how African Americans view themselves today, science does tell us that the effects of trauma can be cumulative.[5] Values, beliefs, and perceptions can be passed down through generations and they can be negative or positive. For example, there is still a White standard of beauty in this country and the world. While many African Americans wear their hair natural, without chemical straighteners and heat, many still want the "good hair" look. Long hair, straight hair, good hair, light skin obtained either through genetics or skin lighteners are still values in the Black community. Recent cases in which Black children have been sent home from predominantly White schools (PWS) or

---

2. James H. Cone, *Said I Wasn't Gonna Tell Nobody* (New York: Orbis Books, 2018), 51.

3. Joy Degruy, *Post Traumatic Slave Syndrome: America's Legacy of Enduring Injury & Healing* (Baltimore: Uptone Press, 2017).

4. All too many historically Black, to include historically Black denominations, and predominantly Black (having once been White) churches find themselves in gentrifying areas with Whites not choosing to become members of churches where they will be in the minority.

5. Degruy, *Post Traumatic Slave Syndrome*, 104.

Black employees have been sent home from work because their hair was in violation of professional (meaning White) grooming standards, continues the belief that there is something wrong with Black hair and affects the self-esteem of African Americans. For Whites and Blacks, Black hair is not professional: it is not neat, it is not White. The legal battles fought in the 1970s to have Black hair accepted in the work place are being fought again. In February 2019, New York City banned discrimination against Black hair.[6] In July 2019, California became the first state to ban discrimination against Black hair[7] and in September 2019, Montgomery County, Maryland, also passed a bill banning discrimination against Black hair.[8] These laws act as passes Blacks had to carry when Black codes prescribed every aspect of Black life. African Americans need permission to wear our hair as God has created it.

Living while Black is traumatizing; it is trauma. While slavery and lynchings are a part of the past, the nicks and scratches of everyday living in a racist society continue to accumulate. Psychologist Monica Williams calls this accumulation of daily nicks and scratches *race-based traumatic stress injury.*[9] These microaggressions, which may be subtle (such as visiting an all-White church and wondering if one is welcome and then not being welcomed), result in the self-question, "Is it because I'm Black?" The nicks build up and wear at one's self esteem. Joy Degruy writes that as a result of daily microaggressions, esteem becomes "vacant" or absent and African Americans come to believe that they have little self-worth,[10] even in the eyes of God—who has been, most likely, pictured as White. These microaggressions can also transfer to the church when Black preaching, Black worship style, and Black music are considered not to be *proper or in due order*; that they are inferior to White or European-style worship, preaching, and music.

A few of years ago, a friend of mine posted on Facebook about her daughter's first day at a predominantly White school. When her daughter came

---

6. Charisse Jones and Zalati Meyer, "What's in a Hairstyle? A Lot. New York City Bans Bias against Black Hair," *USA Today*, February 18, 2019, *https://www.usatoday.com/story/money/2019/02/18/Black-hair-protected-same-laws-ban-discrimination-nyc-says/2906013002/.*

7. Dustin Gardiner, "California Bans Bias against Black People Based on Natural Hairstyles," *San Francisco Chronicle*, July 3, 2019, *https://www.sfchronicle.com/politics/article/California-bans-discrimination-against-Blacks-14069995.php.*

8. Kolbie Satterfield, "New Montgomery County Bill Makes It Illegal to Discriminate Based on Your Hair," September 24, 2018, *https://www.wusa9.com/article/news/local/maryland/natural-hair-bill-makes-discrimination-illegal/65-500e6476-87a5-4eb3-bb04-8b7377195ce8.*

9. Jenna Wortham, "Racism's Psychological Toll," *New York Times*, June 24, 2019, *https://mobile.nytimes.com/2015/06/24/magazine/racisms-psychological-toll.html.*

10. Degruy, *Post Traumatic Slave Syndrome*, 108.

home, she could see something was wrong. At first, my friend attributed it to the first day at a new school. She assumed that soon the daughter would make friends and fit in, but the look was too downcast, so she asked her daughter what was wrong.

"They won't play with me because I am too dark. Do you think if I painted myself White, they would play with me?"

In her book *Breathe*, Imani Perry writes of her fear for her Black sons in a White society that fails to see their humanity. At a book talk in Washington, DC, she spoke of her inability to breathe knowing the danger society holds for her sons; she asked when it might be possible for her to take a breath. I told of my experience, that I feared for the life of my son, particularly as it relates to policing in America; although I am a retired police officer, and my son is forty-three years old, I still do not breathe. I hold my breath until I know he is safely home, knowing that even home is not a safe place for African Americans. Perry writes, "Do I cover my home in the blood of the proverbial sacrificial goat, praying that we have been passed over? That the blood-thirsty fear lands at someone else's door? I am tempted, but I know that prayers don't prevent tragedy; they hold you up as you pass through it. Sometimes."[11] Shortly after the birth of her Black son, a friend of *New York Times* columnist Claudia Rankin told her that "the condition of Black life is one of mourning."[12] This mourning is lived daily, lived constantly; it forms a veil over each Black baby born.

> Though the White liberal imagination likes to feel temporarily bad about Black suffering, there really is no mode of empathy that can replicate the daily strain of knowing that as a Black person you can be killed for simply being Black: no hands in your pockets, no playing music, no sudden movements, no driving your car, no walking at night, no walking in the day, no turning onto this street, no entering this building, no standing your ground, no standing here, no standing there, no talking back, no playing with toy guns, no living while Black.[13]

We live in the *sometimes*; the sometimes of trauma that tells us every single day that we are different, we are not welcome, we are not wanted—even in church.

---

11. Imani Perry, *Breathe: A Letter to My Sons* (Boston: Beacon Press, 2019), 2.

12. Claudia Rankin, "The Condition of Black Life Is One of Mourning," *New York Times Magazine*, June 22, 2015, *https://www.nytimes.com/2015/06/22/magazine/the-condition-of-black-life-is-one-of-mourning.html*.

13. Rankin, "Condition of Black Life."

Our collective trauma has been ignored—we should "get over it," "move on," "there is a level playing field"—however, we strive for racial reconciliation knowing that the cry for reconciliation is bankrupt. How can there be reconciliation when the races have never been one? Something that was never one cannot be put back together; it cannot be made whole. It cannot be reconciled. The Rev. Kelly Brown Douglas's question about whether the Episcopal Church wants to be the Church or be White is not rhetorical; we must ask the question anticipating a response. We must ask why the Church—any church or denomination—would want to engage in the work of eradicating and eliminating the trauma racism has rained upon its ebony-hued children, when it has benefited from America's original sin? When Jesus was incarnate, he showed God to the world; the Church, as the body of Christ, has been left to continue that work, but the Church has too often abdicated its responsibility. Rather than show the Jesus of the Gospels, the Church has shown Jesus as racist. The Church must repent, confess its sin in an active way, and turn toward God, and act in a way that is different than that which sees some of God's people as less than human.

There is an invisible Church in plain sight—not the invisible church of Albert Raboteau and the hush arbors of slavery, although it is not much different. Rather, it is a church where Blacks, African Americans, come together in podcasts, webcasts, conferences, to have courageous conversations, and push back on the orthodoxy, orthopraxy, and orthopathy of those—primarily Whites—who profess to follow a Nazarean Jew named Jesus as savior.

Millennials Lisa Fields (founder of the Jude 3 Project and an African American evangelical) and Michelle Higgins have opined that there is a lack of repentance on the part of White Christians for the sin of racism against God's saved and unsaved children of ebony grace. The White church's walk must match its talk concerning America's original sin, a sin the White church benefited from both materially and financially and which the Church justified with a flawed theology.[14] To keep Black millennials, the Church must act in a manner that shows them that their lives matter.

Is it possible to be Episcopalian and Black without assimilating to the dominant White Anglo-Saxon Protestant culture or to be seen as other than Episcopalian? We ought to be able to bring our Blackness to the Church in whatever form it may render itself. We should be able to call on the ancestors,

---

14. Michelle Higgins, "The Idea of Racial Reconciliation Is Bankrupt: White Supremacy, the Church and How to Move Forward," *Current Magazine*, August 29, 2017, *https://relevantmagazine.com/current/michelle-higgins-the-idea-of-racial-reconciliation-is-bankrupt/*. Lisa Fields, "Change the Story," The Jude 3 Project, August 30, 2019, *https://jude3project.org/podcast/change*.

raise holy hands, and have emotive and spirit-filled preaching without getting the side-eye from those who are offended that what is occurring is not Anglican or proper.

In 1992, political scientist Andrew Hacker published *Two Nations: Black & White, Separate, Hostile, and Unequal* in which he opened the sore of racism by means of a parable in which a White person is notified by the government that a mistake had been made at his birth; rather than being White, he should have been born Black. The letter said that at midnight the "mistake" would be corrected and he would become Black. He would not only have darker skin, he would have the bodily and facial features associated with being an African American and having African ancestry. However, his knowledge of his former self and his former life would remain intact, even though he would not be recognizable to anyone he knew.[15] He would be "White" in Black skin. I can only imagine that anyone White reading the book would give a sigh of relief and secretly think, "I'm glad that could never happen." Or perhaps, the thought would be "Thank God, this is only someone's imagination." When White students were presented with this story and asked how much they should be compensated for the *mistake*, they answered $1 million for each year they would be expected to live as a Black person. There is value in Whiteness that penalizes Blackness. Eddie Glaude Jr. calls it the "value gap," where White lives are valued more than Black lives.[16] The students in the scenario believed they should be given punitive damages for having to live as a Black person.

While we talk about how to rid the country and Church of racism at various levels, how many Whites know about the Jude 3 Project, founded by Lisa Fields, where predominately Black lay and ordained theologians discuss the issues that vex Black people in this country? We also need to recover the art of Black preaching. How many Whites know about or would attend the first doctoral program in African American Preaching and Sacred Rhetoric at Christian Theological Seminary in Indianapolis?[17] While Blacks who attend PWS (predominantly White seminaries) and take homiletics, which may have a Eurocentric bent, would Whites consider taking a Black preaching course? If not, why not?

---

15. Andrew Hacker, *Two Nations: Black and White, Separate, Hostile, and Unequal* (New York: Ballentine Books, 1992), 42.

16. Eddie S. Glaude Jr., *Democracy in Black: How Race Still Enslaves the American Soul* (New York: Crown Publishers, 2016).

17. For more information, see *https://www.cts.edu/academics/degree-programs/phd-in-african-american-preaching-and-sacred-rhetoric/*.

In *Souls of Black Folk*, W. E. B. Du Bois wrote that "the problem of the 20th century is the problem of the color line."[18] That problem is still with us; in response, the Episcopal Church has taken up the challenge of racial reconciliation with its missional document, "Becoming Beloved Community." However, before the Church can challenge society, it must first deal with the elephant that sits in front of the communion table—that racism is alive and well in the Church. Historically Black churches, while facing a similar decline in membership as White churches, face an additional issue. Whites may join multiracial churches (as opposed to multicultural), but are hesitant to join predominantly Black churches. Whites are uncomfortable with being in the minority, something Blacks face every day as they live in a racialized country. Jemar Tisby offers a critique of integrated churches, saying there is a downside, even as we look at the limited racial progress in our society. Most integrated churches will still be predominantly White unless Whites integrate into historically or predominantly Black churches. Black spaces permit African Americans to find community and relationships that are important for mental and cultural health. Tisby writes, "We want spaces to lament when the next unarmed Black person is killed by law enforcement."[19] In other words, African Americans crave space where it is okay to be Black and not have to wear the clothing of assimilation, the clothing of Whiteness, where Blacks do not have to wear Paul Lawrence Dunbar's "mask that grins and lies."[20] They don't want to leave who they are at the church's doorstep.

The gospel message is about reconciling ourselves to God and to each other; however, that dream has been elusive. Korie Edwards offers that true integration in and of our churches is fraught with twists and turns that may never be straightened. Interracial churches work when Whites are comfortable, when their worship style is dominant, and others assimilate to their dominant culture.[21] In her research, Edwards has found even when churches were interracial, Whiteness was still the primary culture in all aspects of church life. Non-White members assimilated; they left who they were at the entrance to fit in and be accepted. Too often, that desire to fit in leads to internalized racial

---

18. W. E. Burghardt Du Bois, *The Souls of Black Folk: Essays and Sketches* (Chicago: A.C. McClurg & Co., 1920), 13.

19. Jemar Tisby, "The Downside of Integration for Black Christians," The Witness, August 21, 2017, *https://thewitnessbcc.com/downside-integration-Black-christians*.

20. Paul Lawrence Dunbar, "We Wear the Mask," accessed November 1, 2019, *https://www.poetry foundation.org/poems/44203/we-wear-the-mask*.

21. Korie L. Edwards, *The Elusive Dream: The Power of Race in Interracial Churches* (New York: Oxford University, 2008), 6.

oppression, which means that the style of worship, the music, liturgy, mission-
ary, and theological interests were consistent with White values.[22] Interracial
churches, which most likely began as White congregations with African Americans joining, generally do not adopt African American worship styles and practices.[23] Interracial churches morph toward White desires and norms because of
two additional factors: the fear that Whites will leave (and they have the ability
to do so) and that African Americans care that they leave.[24]

Chanequa Walker-Barnes laments the reason why she gave up church. A
clinical psychologist and associate professor of practical theology at Mercer
College McAfee School of Theology, Walker-Barnes was tired of attending
churches that failed to deal with the issues that affect Black life in America. She
gave up on church because she could not worship "with her whole body."[25] She
knows other African Americans who feel the same way and they are committed
followers of Jesus. They are lay and ordained, professors at seminaries; these are
"biblically-literate [people] who deeply love Jesus." As the Episcopal Church
is attempting to reclaim Jesus, it is interesting that Walker-Barnes says that she
and other followers of Jesus cannot find Jesus in church, so they are looking in
places outside of church where the issues that affect Black life are lifted up and
given serious consideration. She asks a profound question, as she paraphrases
Howard Thurman, "What word does Christianity have to offer for those of
us who live with our backs constantly against the walls of White supremacist
heterosexist patriarchal ableist capitalism?"[26] For her, there is no word forth-
coming. "We were willing to give up our preferred worship style for the chance
to really try to live this vision of beloved community with a diverse group of
people. That didn't work."[27]

In these churches pastored by Whites, African Americans are finding a failure to address, for example, the police shootings of Black people. There have
been prayers offered for shootings that have occurred in this country (for example, school shootings), overseas (the shootings in Paris and Brussels), and there

---

22. Edwards, *Elusive Dream*, 8.

23. Edwards, *Elusive Dream*, 23.

24. Edwards, *Elusive Dream*, 128.

25. Chanequa Walker-Barnes, "Why I Gave Up Church," Bearings Online, October 12, 2017, *https://
collegevilleinstitute.org/bearings/why-i-gave-up-church*.

26. Walker-Barnes, "Why I Gave Up Church."

27. Campbell Robertson, "A Quiet Exodus: Why Black Worshipers Are Leaving White Evangelical Churches," *New York Times*, March 9, 2018, *https://nytimes.com/2018/03/09/us/blacks-evangelical-
churches.html*.

have been prayers for law enforcement officers who have been killed, but nary a word said for unarmed Black people who have been killed by the police. Some say that preaching on race is divisive and "not a matter of the gospel."[28] Too many Whites, including White pastors, believe that we are in a post-racial era: The civil rights era has come and gone. It did what it was supposed to do, laws have been passed, and it is time to move on. Nothing could be further from the truth. White normativity is the foundation of interracial churches and that normativity sees as normal Whiteness along with White culture and values.[29] As this country has experienced, when the percentage of African Americans reaches a tipping point, Whites begin leaving, as White children experienced difficulty adjusting to being around a majority of Black children.[30]

I am reminded of Mother Teresa who said she once believed that prayer changed things, but then she realized that prayer changed us and we change things. Prayer works if we get off our knees and do something. Black millennials have outgrown the Church that is only about tradition and are not swayed by large praise bands, sermons that appeal to the emotions and scapegoat the ills of society as sin without indicating that people choose to sin. They are tired of churches that have stained glass windows and other icons that perpetuate Whiteness and White supremacy. They are tired of churches that do everything except make disciples. They are tired of and disappointed with churches, particularly Black churches, that have failed to be in the forefront of the Black Lives Matter movement.[31]

What follows in this section are stories of confession, catharsis, and hope. However, as Ibram X. Kendi has written, while there is hope that this country can become antiracist, there is also the possibility for hopelessness because it wants to hold onto its Whiteness.[32] Do Black lives matter in the Episcopal Church? Kendi writes that Black death matters to the life of this country; however, some Americans would rather see Black people die than face their death-dealing perceptions of what American truly is and "seem to love."[33] Of course, we could accept the false narrative of a postracial church, with the

---

28. Robertson, "Quiet Exodus."

29. Edwards, *Elusive Dream*, 10.

30. Brad Christerson, Korie L. Edwards, and Michael O. Emerson, *Against All Odds: The Struggle for Racial Integration in Religious Organizations* (New York: New York University, 2005), 73.

31. Thomas, "Exodus."

32. Kendi, "Hopefulness and Hopelessness of 1619."

33. Ibram X. Kendi, "Sacrificing Black Lives for the American Lie," *New York Times*, June 24, 2017, *https://www.nytimes.com/2017/06/24/opinion/sunday/philando-castile-police-shootings.html*.

election of Presiding Bishop Michael Curry in 2015, just as some believed in a postracial America with the election of President Obama in 2008. However, the backlash to Obama's election gives insight into the impotency of the Church. The term "postracial" is as old as this country. Americans have viewed this country in all of its configuration as postracial since Thomas Jefferson penned the words, "all men are created equal."[34] Just as Kelly Brown Douglas has offered that the Episcopal Church cannot be both White and Christian, "Black people and the post-racial myth cannot both live in the United States."[35] We can keep our heads stuck in the sand, we can continue to breathe in the opiate of religion that dulls the senses to the tragedy that is life for all too many of God's children, or we can follow Jesus to the wall and love all God's children as God loves us. We can wait until Jesus comes, as the Negro spiritual goes, to "fix it Jesus, like you said you would," or we can speak the truth and let it fall where it may.

As you read these stories, these reflections, that follow what is your story? Are you willing to share it?

---

34. Kendi, "Sacrificing Black Lives."
35. Kendi, "Sacrificing Black Lives."

16

Activists and Churches

Jennifer Amuzie

I don't consider myself particularly radical or particularly churchy, but it happens enough that I've come to terms with the fact that I'm probably both: a friend adds me to a Facebook group for evangelists, or DMs (direct message) me some clobber verses, or says outright, "I don't know how you can be a [fill in the blank] and in church." And I usually don't try to explain. The Church has done terrible things and is full of people who have done terrible things. I am a regularly disappointed woman of faith.

Activists love churches. If a "faith leader" can come to your protest and the press arrives, the chances that your protest will be covered by the media goes up—even higher if you have someone in a clerical collar, and higher still if they gets arrested. Churches are exciting for organizers too: they are communities with prebuilt ladders of engagement and absorption, ready for mobilization. And, of course, in the pantheon of social movements, the civil rights movement stands like a shining star: dramatic societal change in a little over a decade run by a network of churches and pastors who were ready to boycott, break the law, be arrested, and be photographed doing it. I know that this is simplistic and romantic. It is also one-sided: activists love churches, but churches don't love them back.

In his letter from a Birmingham jail, the Rev. Dr. Martin Luther King Jr. describes the conflict for the churches and faith leaders that see themselves as moral beacons—they are still institutions. At best, a church's pleading that oppressed people have patience is a reference to their own unwieldiness: bylaws need to be drafted, steering committees need to approve changes. At worst, it's a reference to the benefits of oppression that they are unwilling to recognize. At best, a faith leader is enamored with the role as the mediator; at worst, the privilege of an educated cisgendered heterosexual man and all the authority that God and the people gave him to wield, makes him unwilling to pass the mic. Even the story we tell ourselves about the civil rights movement is one of privilege, as if queer people and women and people who weren't college educated were not at the center of this wild, radical story of their own liberation.

I grew up on a small island off the coast of South Georgia. St. Simons Island is the birthplace of Anna Alexander, a woman as holy and good as Stephen the deacon and the first martyr. If she weren't Black and a woman, she would have been a deacon, but her saintliness in the face of the twin demons of patriarchy and White supremacy was only enough to give her the diminutive: deaconess. St. Simons Island is also known for a rebellion of seventy-five Igbo people who survived the Middle Passage and then ran the slavers' ship aground in Dunbar Creek and walked into the sea. These are my people, continually asserting their humanity. Church folks. Activists.

Activists aren't innocent. My friends who can't watch without tasting tear gas in their throats, who go to get booked and have their fingerprints damn them to exile, won't tell you that there are fair-weather folks in their midst, but I see the way the people who have the most to lose are the first to sacrifice their bodies. The Church carries the same sort of cowardice. I see the way organizers don't recognize risk or labor, and I hear all the times I was urged to be less of a Martha and more of a Mary. I bristle under the instruction to be patient, to wait and realize that White moderates are everywhere—in the pews, in the power mapping sessions—value looking good over being good. I am a woman of faith, however, and I choose to identify as such: a little bit naive and dumb, flinging my body completely into the good and holy work of standing together, facing the devil and facing the sea, loving and not quite being loved back.

17

Our Duty to Preach #BlackLivesMatter

Claudia Marion Allen

"I know that that which I now speak will bring me into conflict. This I do not covet, for the conflict has seemed to be continuous of late years; but I do not mean to live a coward, or die a coward, leaving my work undone. I must follow my Master's footsteps."

—*Ellen G. White, "Our Duty to the Colored People"*[1]

He just laid there. Uncovered. Unbothered. Apparently unvalued. On August 9, 2014, Michael Brown was shot and killed by police officer Darren Wilson in Ferguson, Missouri. Officer Wilson initially stopped Brown for jaywalking[2] and the exchange allegedly escalated resulting in Wilson shooting Brown "at least six times, including twice in the head,"[3] according to the autopsy report published in the *New York Times*. What was most devastating was that Brown's dead body was left unattended in the middle of the street for four hours.[4] Pictures of his motionless body spread across the internet like wildfire. In each and every shot, he just laid there as though his blood was supposed to seep into concrete rather than course through his veins.

---

1. Ellen G. White, "Our Duty to the Colored People," Manuscript 6, 1891, Ellen G. White Writings, November 4, 1889, *https://text.egwwritings.org/publication.php?pubtype=EGWManuscript&bookCode=Ms61891&lang=en&collection=2&section=all&pagenumber=1&QUERY=our+duty+to+colored+people&resultId=16*.

2. Max Ehrenfreund, "The Risks of Walking While Black in Ferguson," May 4, 2015, *The Washington Post*, *https://www.washingtonpost.com/news/wonk/2015/03/04/95-percent-of-people-arrested-for-jaywalking-in-ferguson-were-Black/?utm_term=.e16cf4622f09*.

3. France Robles and Julie Bosman, "Autopsy Shows Michael Brown Was Struck at Least 6 Times," *New York Times*, August 18, 2014, *https://www.nytimes.com/2014/08/18/us/michael-brown-autopsy-shows-he-was-shot-at-least-6-times.html*.

4. Julie Bosman and Joseph Goldstein, "Timeline for a Body: 4 Hours in the Middle of a Ferguson Street," *New York Times*, August 24, 2014, *https://www.nytimes.com/2014/08/24/us/michael-brown-a-bodys-timeline-4-hours-on-a-ferguson-street.html*.

Julie Bosman wrote that "neighbors were horrified by the gruesome scene."[5] A local resident named Keisha provided the best description of how his corpse was treated. Interviewing her a week after the shooting, Marc Lamont Hill quoted her: "They just left him there . . . like he ain't belong to nobody."[6] That was what enraged me. That was the language I needed to help me express my frustration and disbelief at his body lying in the street like roadkill. As the photos filled my timeline, I kept asking myself, how could they leave him there for so long? How could the authorities justify his decaying body left uncovered for children to run past? Why was it okay for death to be displayed like that? Does the gospel have anything to say about it?

Hill describes the state leaving Brown's body unattended for four hours as more than an injustice in his book *Nobody: Casualties of America's War on the Vulnerable, from Ferguson to Flint and Beyond*. He suggests such disdain and lack of care was inhumane. The posthumous treatment of Michael Brown communicated that he was

> Nobody. [He had] No parents who loved him. No community that cared for him. No medical establishment morally compelled to save him. No State duty-bound to invest in him, before or after his death. Michael Brown was treated as if he was not entitled to the most basic elements of democratic citizenship, not to mention human decency. He was treated as if he was not a person, much less an American. He was disposable.[7]

In other words, the death and posthumous treatment of Michael Brown evidenced that his life did not matter to the state.

The neglect of the state communicated that Michael Brown's life did not matter; the silence of the Church made Christians across the nation complicit in that message. As state officials left his body in the street, most preachers and pastors closed their eyes, trying to ignore the travesty instead of providing any rebuke or hope. Across denominational lines, Christians sang, "Blessed assurance, Jesus is mine." We shouted in the aisles because Jesus is a "way maker, miracle worker, and light in the darkness." Many of us cried hallelujahs because God's a "good, good Father." But when the singing subsided, we listened to sermons that made no mention of this precious life lost. Sitting in the midst of Du Bois'

---

5. Bosman and Goldstein, "Timeline for a Body: 4 Hours in the Middle of a Ferguson Street."

6. Marc Lamont Hill, *Nobody: Casualties of America's War on the Vulnerable, from Ferguson to Flint and Beyond* (New York: Atria Books, 2016), 10.

7. Hill, *Nobody*, 10.

"frenzy,"[8] many of us took what James Baldwin alluded to as the opiate drug of church[9] and tried to escape the harsh realities of living in a racist America.

We ignored Brown's dead body no differently than the state did. Many preachers sermonized on the Beatitudes, taught on faith, challenged us with the sanctuary, inspired us to become our best selves, and comforted us with grace. We stood behind pulpits and warned against being prodigal sons and daughters and tried to entice with the hope of the second coming, all while disregarding the pain of grieving parents, the confusion of predominantly Black communities, and the outrage of a nation. We preached a socially disengaged Christ because, for many of us, speaking about spirituality is separate and more important than speaking to social unrest.

This religiosity that is so heavenly minded that it is of no earthly good causes us to preach sermons filled with dogma but devoid of love; sermons that speak to spirituality but neglect to mention the relevant ills and issues of society. It is our mishandling of the hearts and minds of people during times of social crisis that has caused Christian churches to lose influence, integrity, and interest with those we long to serve. In order to regain our influence, integrity, and the interest of those we long to serve, preachers and pastors must begin preaching sermons that present Christ as a God who cares about the effects of sin on society. Every preacher has a spiritual and social responsibility—yes, a duty—to preach against injustice from the pulpit. Preaching should directly rebuke injustices like racism, family separation, and discrimination against women.

In 1891, Ellen G. White, founding member and esteemed prophetess of the Seventh-day Adventist Church delivered "Our Duty to the Colored People," a speech written to show that not only do Seventh-day Adventists have a spiritual mandate to preach that Black lives matter, but that all preachers of the Gospel of Jesus Christ have a duty to preach that Black lives matter.

#BlackLivesMatter: More than a Tweet

After the death of Trayvon Martin and the exoneration of his killer, vigilante community watchman George Zimmerman, Alicia Garza wrote a series of

---

8. W. E. B. Du Bois, "Of the Faith of the Fathers," in *The Souls of Black Folk* (New York: Dover Publications, 1994), 116: "Finally the Frenzy of 'Shouting,' when the Spirit of the Lord passed by, and, seizing the devotee, made him mad with supernatural joy, was the last essential of Negro religion and the one more devoutly believed in than all the rest. It varied in expression from the silent rapt countenance or the low murmur and moan to the mad abandon of physical fervor,—the stamping, shrieking, and shouting, the rushing to and fro and wild waving of arms, the weeping and laughing, the vision and the trance."

9. James Baldwin, *The Fire Next Time* (New York: Vintage International, 1993), 20.

social media posts entitled "A Love Letter to Black People." Garza admonished her readership, demanding that we "stop saying we are not surprised. That's a damn shame in itself. I continue to be surprised at how little Black lives matter."[10] Garza's friend Patrisse Cullors was so moved by those three words that she responded, "Declaration: Black bodies will no longer be sacrificed for the rest of the world's enlightenment. I am done. I am so done. Trayvon, you are loved infinitely. #Blacklivesmatter."[11] And the hashtag was born.

It wasn't long before the tweet began trending on social media. But while many on Twitter were using it, a Pew Research study cited that the tweet gained its highest peak usage "over the ten days spanning July 7–17, 2016" when "the #BlackLivesMatter hashtag was mentioned [in] an average of nearly 500,000 tweets daily."[12] This surge was due to the killings of Alton Sterling, Philando Castile, and the killing of five police officers in Dallas, Texas. All happened within two days of each other. Because of continuing instances "from July 2013 through May 1, 2018, the hashtag has been used nearly 30 million times on Twitter, an average of 17,002 times per day."[13] Such high usage suggests that many resonate with the declaration and feel that this series of social and political events have demonstrated the need to declare the value of Black life.

But this popular hashtag has grown to become more than a trendy tweet. In an article for *The Feminist Wire*, Garza writes that "Black Lives Matter is an ideological and political intervention in a world where Black lives are systematically and intentionally targeted for demise. It is an affirmation of Black folks' contributions to this society, our humanity, and our resilience in the face of deadly oppression."[14] She continues:

> Black Lives Matter is a unique contribution that goes beyond extrajudicial killings of Black people by police and vigilantes. . . . Black Lives Matter affirms the lives of Black queer and trans folks, disabled folks, Black-undocumented folks, folks with records, women and all Black lives along the gender spectrum. It centers

---

10. Jelani Cobb, "The Matter of Black Lives," *The New Yorker*, March 14, 2016, *http://www.newyorker.com/magazine/2016/03/14/where-is-black-lives-matter-headed*.

11. Jennings Brown, "One Year After Michael Brown: How a Hashtag Changed Social Protest," August 7, 2015, *http://www.vocativ.com/218365/michael-brown-and-black-lives-matter*.

12. Monica Anderson, Skye Toor, Lee Rainie, and Aaron Smith, "An Analysis of #BlackLivesMatter and Other Twitter Hashtags Related to Political or Social Issues," Pew Research Center, July 11, 2018, *https://www.pewresearch.org/internet/2018/07/11/an-analysis-of-Blacklivesmatter-and-other-twitter-hashtags-related-to-political-or-social-issues/*.

13. Anderson et al., "An Analysis of #BlackLivesMatter."

14. Alicia Garza, "A Herstory of the #BlackLivesMatter Movement by Alicia Garza" October 7, 2014, *The Feminist Wire*, *https://thefeministwire.com/2014/10/Blacklivesmatter-2/*.

those that have been marginalized within Black liberation movements. It is a tactic to (re)build the Black liberation movement."[15]

It is this ideological framework that transitioned the twitter statement from a hashtag to a movement.

Black Lives Matter first appeared as a network beyond twitter in August 2014, after the death of Michael Brown. Organizing what they called "the Black Life Matters Ride," Darnell Moore and Patrisse Cullors "developed a plan of action to head to the occupied territory in support of our brothers and sisters. Over 600 people gathered."[16] It is because of this kind of focus and practical presence that the trending hashtag #BlackLivesMatter went from something you simply type in a tweet to becoming "a member-led global network of more than 40 chapters."[17] Their ideological framework partnered with their social and political action in Ferguson in what Garrett Chase describes as "part viral social phenomenon, part civil rights movement." He argues that "Black Lives Matter draws on common themes from previous civil rights movements, but it is a marked departure from previous chapters of the centuries-long struggle for Black freedom and equality in America."[18] This "marked departure" is seen in the network's origination and growth through social media. Never before has any African American social movement been able to reach so many African Americans across the nation so quickly. It possesses and articulates the age-old, fundamental belief of every African American throughout our laborious time here in these "yet to be United States"—that we are human and deserving of humane treatment regardless of our race, gender, class, education, sexual orientation, or even criminal record.

This is why the silence of Christian preachers was so loud. In a time where Black people were crying out, demanding they be treated as human beings and not criminalized based on the color of their skin, preachers refused to rebuke their systematic demise and validate the spiritual and biblical sanctity of their lament. Instead, our silence suggested that the marginalization and criminalization of our people is what is sanctioned by God. While we are not accomplices in the destruction and degradation of Black people, our silence has made us complicit in their oppression.

---

15. Garza, "A Herstory of the #BlackLivesMatter Movement."

16. Black Lives Matter, "Herstory," *https://blacklivesmatter.com/herstory/*.

17. Black Lives Matter, "Herstory."

18. Garrett Chase, "The Early History of the Black Lives Matter Movement, and the Implications Thereof," *Nevada Law Journal* 18 (May 30, 2018), *https://law.unlv.edu/nevada-law-journal/vol18/early-history-Black-lives-matter-movement-and-implications-thereof-1757.*

Silence and Seventh-Day Adventists

The Seventh-day Adventist Church is an example of a Christian denomination that, as an institutional whole, is predominately silent concerning issues of racism and the systematic oppression of Black people. Although several individual Seventh-day Adventists, both Black and White, are extremely vocal within their own local congregations and spheres of influence, it is critical that we understand the importance of institutional church culture. For while the church is not restricted to its four walls or its denominational by-laws, its institutional ministerial culture and expression of God is intimately attached to its practice of justice for the oppressed. This, unfortunately, is where the Seventh-day Adventist denomination has historically fallen short. Samuel G. London in his book *Seventh-Day Adventists and the Civil Rights Movement* explicates this truth in great detail. Marking the significant contributions individual seventh-day Adventists made, London shows how the denomination's theology influenced how and why most Seventh-day Adventists, particularly the world church at large, chose not to participate or give voice to the movement. He writes, "During the 1950s and 1960s, some white Adventist leaders used certain theological and philosophical concepts within Adventism to discourage political activism among church members. The roots of these ideas show how Adventist leaders used them to oppose the denomination's entry into the civil rights movement."[19] This thinking is rooted in Adventism's firm belief in the separation of church and state. It is their strong belief in this separation that has many White Adventists, and even some Black Adventists, believing that mission and evangelism do not include the rebuke and resistance of oppressive sociopolitical powers within any government or regime.

What is ironic is that while White American Adventists refused to speak up or lend their voices during the civil rights movement, urging members to refrain from political engagement, Harold Alomia documents the German chapter of the denomination's support and political engagement with Hitler and Nazi Germany. Alomia writes,

> Following in the footsteps of the Christian majority, the Seventh-day Adventist Church cannot be commended for its actions during the Nazi regime. Echoing the praises for the rise of Hitler to power, Adolf Minck, President of the Adventist German Church, penned his satisfaction with the election of Adolf Hitler in the August Edition of *Advenbote* (the official periodical

---

19. Samuel G. London, "Theology, Politics, and the Retreat from Social Activism," in *Seventh-day Adventists and the Civil Rights Movement* (Jackson: UP of Mississippi, 2009), 66.

of the Seventh-day Adventist Church in Germany at the time): "A fresh enlivening, and renewing reformation spirit is blowing through our German lands. . . . [T]his is a time of decision, a time, . . . The word of God and Christianity shall be restored to a place of honor."[20]

Alomia further cites that "not only did the Seventh-day Adventist leadership sing praises to the Nazi government, it even went so far as 'strongly recommending' how its members were to vote in every plebiscite of the Nazi regime."[21] Much of what attracted Adventists to the Nazi regime was Hitler's elevation of the superiority of Christianity and his promotion of a vegan/vegetarian diet, or what many Adventists identify as "the Health message."

But the Seventh-day Adventist Church's engagement or lack thereof with certain racially charged sociopolitical movements is not a controversy restricted to the past. The denomination has a long history of racism and segregation that includes the refusal of medical care to a Black woman[22] simply because of her race, along with segregation in the General Conference cafeteria, and the denial of African American students to enroll in some of their universities.[23] With such a history, one would think the denomination would jump at the opportunity to right its wrongs and champion the work of anti-racism and racial reconciliation, but the Seventh-day Adventist Church did not make an official statement on racism until June 27, 1985. In it then General Conference President Neal C. Wilson declared:

> The Seventh-day Adventist Church deplores all forms of racism, including the political policy of apartheid with its enforced segregation and legalized discrimination. Seventh-day Adventists want to be faithful to the reconciling ministry assigned to the Christian church. As a worldwide community of faith, the Seventh-day Adventist Church wishes to witness to and exhibit in her own ranks the unity of love that transcends racial differences and overcomes past alienation between races.[24]

---

20. Harold Alomia, "Fatal Flirting: The Nazi State and the Seventh-day Adventist Church," *Journal of Adventist Mission Studies, Digital Commons at Andrews University* 6, no 1 (2010), *https://digitalcommons. andrews.edu/cgi/viewcontent.cgi?article=1042&context=jams*.

21. Harold Alomia, "Fatal Flirting."

22. Benjamin Baker, "The Lucy Byard Story," *Columbia Union Conference*, March 2019, *http://www. columbiaunion.org/content/march-2019-feature-lucy-byard-story*.

23. Cleran Hollancid, "More about the Legacy of Race in Seventh-day Adventist Culture," *Adventist Today*, March 26, 2017, *https://atoday.org/more-about-the-legacy-of-race-in-seventh-day-adventist-culture/*.

24. "Racism," *Official Statements of the Seventh-day Adventist Church*, *https://www.adventist.org/en/ information/official-statements/statements/article/go/-/racism/*.

The statement is encouraging. It denotes a movement in the right direction. But there has not been one official statement on racism and its effect on African American Seventh-day Adventists from the denomination's leadership since then. Presently, the General Conference President Ted Wilson has not issued one statement rebuking or speaking to the plethora of police shootings, the mass incarceration of African Americans, or any other systematic injustice targeted at Blacks in America.

Many Seventh-day Adventists who are afflicted by these concerns and are passionate about providing aid and justice to those affected find encouragement in the support and statements of division leaders like Dan Jackson, president of the North American Division; regional conference presidents; and local pastors. These are all Adventist leaders who have published statements responding to the pain systematic racism has caused. For example, President Jackson published a statement from the North American Division on the death of Michael Brown stating:

> As a part of the larger family of America, Seventh-day Adventists grieve with Michael Brown's family and extend our heartfelt condolences for their tragic loss. . . . We pray that justice will replace injustice, that truth will replace deceit, that inequality will be replaced by equitable brotherhood and that God's peace will prevail.[25]

But even though this statement acknowledges the incident and offers condolences and support to those affected, it still does not rebuke the systematic manifestation of racism through these fatal cases of police brutality. There is no explicit, public outcry against racism and its destructive force on African Americans in this country. The strategic and intentional silence of Christian churches like the Seventh-day Adventist Church is producing a spiritual fatigue within its membership, as well as limiting the reach and efficacy of its evangelism.

What's fascinating is that such silence during injustice, the promotion of oppression, and even the vague stances against discrimination are not an accurate representation of the historical or foundational beliefs of the denomination or its founding parents. In fact, Adventism was birthed during the abolitionist movement and was institutionalized the same year President Lincoln signed the Emancipation Proclamation. January of 1863 Lincoln freed the slaves and

---

25. Monte Sahlin, "Adventist Leaders Speak Out on Unrest in Ferguson, Missouri," *Adventist Today*, August 21, 2014, *https://atoday.org/adventist-leaders-speak-out-on-unrest-in-ferguson-missouri/*.

in May 1863 the Seventh-day Adventist Church became an official Christian denomination. Founding member and prophetess of the Seventh-day Adventist Church, Ellen G. White, was an open and well-known abolitionist.

She was born Ellen Gould Harmon on what scholars believe was November 26, 1827, to a Methodist family. Converting to Millerism[26] at fourteen years old,[27] Ellen White had her first vision at the age of seventeen and began operating as a prophetic voice for the movement. After marrying James White on August 30, 1846, Ellen White's life became quickly consumed with small group studying, preaching, receiving visions, and writing those visions in several lengthy books. Because of her ministry, a small group dedicated to understanding scripture eventually became identified as the "Seventh-day Adventists," tied to their belief in the seventh day Sabbath and the advent, or second coming, of Jesus Christ.

Ellen White wrote of visions of heaven, described explicit scenes with Christ and his disciples from the New Testament, and wrote letters to leaders and officials as the denomination continued to grow. She was, through her writing and preaching, a spiritual teacher of theology, a moral teacher on behavior and diet, and a social teacher on the duty of Whites to abolish slavery and repair the social and psychological damage done by slavery by uplifting African Americans financially, educationally, and spiritually. Her legacy as a social teacher for racial activism is most famously seen and studied in her speech to thirty-one General Conference officials in March 1891, entitled, "Our Duty to the Colored People." The speech has become for many Adventists the foremost written text on race relations in the Seventh-day Adventist Church. Her admonition provides great clarity and spiritual direction for a Christian's moral responsibility to those who are oppressed and marginalized.

Beginning with "there has been much perplexity as to how our laborers in the south shall deal with the 'color line,'"[28] White inferred that the General Conference had had multiple conversations about race relations within the Seventh-day Adventist Church. Without mincing words, White declared, "The Lord Jesus came to our world to save men and women of all nationalities. He died just as much for the colored people as for the White race."[29] What is of

---

26. A Protestant sect led by William Miller that believed that Jesus would return in 1843.

27. Ben Baker, "'I Do Not Mean to Live a Coward or Die a Coward': An Examination of Ellen G. White's Lifelong Relationship to Black People" (dissertation, Howard University Department of History, December 2011).

28. White, "Our Duty to the Colored People."

29. White, "Our Duty to the Colored People."

great significance in this speech is that White declared that she was aware that the sentiments she was soon to express will not only be potentially dismissed, but would garner her disciplinary measures. She stated:

> I know that that which I now speak will bring me into conflict. This I do not covet, for the conflict has seemed to be continuous of late years; but I do not mean to live a coward or die a coward, leaving my work undone. I must follow in my Master's footsteps.[30]

Her declaration should encourage each and every preacher of the gospel. The truth of the matter is that speaking out against injustice, demanding that African Americans receive the respect and restitution they deserve, and calling out the hypocrisy and sin of racism are all spiritual and moral responsibilities that may result in many of us being punished within our respective denominations. The founding prophetess of the Seventh-day Adventist Church was punished for her work in antiracism and racial reconciliation. But that did not stop her from speaking truth to power. We must be committed to doing the same and to say with the Psalmist, "God is our refuge and strength, an ever-present help in trouble. Therefore we will not fear, though the earth give way and the mountains fall into the heart of the sea" (Ps. 46:1–2).

Preaching Black Lives Matter will bring many of us into conflict with our denominations and our politically narcissistic governmental officials who are only concerned with accumulating and allocating wealth for the 1 percent. But this should not deter us from declaring the justice of God and our command to be peacemakers in the earth. We must never shrink. We must vow never to "live a coward or die a coward, leaving [our] work undone." The spirit of the Lord is upon us to feed the hungry, free the wrongfully imprisoned, heal those with no health insurance, liberate all who suffer under the heavy hand of State sanctioned violence and oppression.

It is for this reason that White followed up her declaration of commitment by reestablishing the nature of Christ:

> It has become fashionable to look down upon the poor, and upon the colored race in particular. But Jesus, the Master, was poor, and He sympathizes with the poor, the discarded, the oppressed, and declares that every insult shown to them is as if shown to Himself.[31]

---

30. White, "Our Duty to the Colored People."
31. White, "Our Duty to the Colored People."

Oftentimes our treatment of the poor and Black and Brown persons in this country is as though we believe that Christ was a rich Anglo-Saxon Pharisee. But in the words of theologian Vincent Harding, "Jesus, 'the poor Jew' of Nazareth, the disinherited, threatened subject of Roman power"[32] was a person of color who himself was poor and oppressed. It is for this reason that long before James Cone could articulate it, Ellen White declared that God is on the side of the oppressed.

With great power and passion, Ellen White declared not just the likeness of Christ to the oppressed, but declared the humanity of African Americans: "The Black man's name is written in the book of life beside the White man's. All are one in Christ. Birth, station, nationality, or color cannot elevate or degrade men. The character makes the man."[33] Her declaration was critical because the church was currently worshiping separately. She said:

> Men may have both hereditary and cultivated prejudices, but when the love of Jesus fills the heart, and they become one with Christ, they will have the same spirit that He had. If a colored brother sits by their side, they will not be offended or despise him. They are journeying to the same heaven, and will be seated at the same table to eat bread in the kingdom of God.[34]

After describing the practice of segregation and superiority within the Church, White challenged any notion of the sanctity of segregation declaring, "You have no license from God to exclude the colored people from your places of worship. . . . They should hold membership in the church with the white brethren. Every effort should be made to wipe out the terrible wrong which has been done them."[35] In other words, White's admonition to these church leaders went beyond declaring the oppression of Jesus Christ and the humanity of African Americans, and proceeded to rebuke the disdain and racism within the hearts and individual actions of the leadership.

But while White preached to these General Conference officials that Black lives mattered and that individual acts of racism were a sin against God birthed in the heart, she moved to rebuking the institution for its participation and complicit perpetuation of racism through their silence and inactivity. She

---

32. Vincent Harding, "Foreword," in Howard Thurman, *Jesus and the Disinherited* (Boston: Beacon Press, 1976), iii.

33. White, "Our Duty to the Colored People."

34. White, "Our Duty to the Colored People."

35. White, "Our Duty to the Colored People.

urged that not only was it their responsibility to preach and rebuke racial injustice, but also to institutionally participate in their social, financial, educational, and spiritual restitution and restoration.

> Are we not under even greater obligation to labor for the colored people than for those who have been more highly favored? Who is it that held these people in servitude? Who kept them in ignorance, and pursued a course to debase and brutalize them, forcing them to disregard the law of marriage, breaking up the family relation, tearing wife from husband, and husband from wife? If the race is degraded, if they are repulsive in habits and manners, who made them so? Is there not much due to them from the white people? After so great a wrong has been done them, should not an earnest effort be made to lift them up?[36]

Her oratorical example showed that not only should Christians preach about the humanity of African Americans, the importance of Christ's connection to oppression, and the rebuking of sin and racial superiority in the heart and individual behavior, but that our preaching and our lives should display a commitment to the holistic restitution and restoration of African American people. She believed this work is the duty of the Seventh-day Adventist Church, yea all Christians, but especially White Christians.

Many of you reading this come from Christian traditions similar to that of the Seventh-day Adventist Church. You believe in the Lord Jesus Christ and the separation of church and state. You pride yourself on being keepers of the Word, and children awaiting Christ's soon return. And all of these things are beautiful and should not be changed. My encouragement is to position these beliefs around Christ, who is the center of all we believe and do. I believe that, like the Adventist Church, which began as a spiritual and religious movement, many Christian churches and believers have moved away from the fire and passion of their foreparents. No longer do we speak with the power they had or hold our institutions and congregations to the standard of a Christianity that is both preached and lived; a Christianity that seeks to save the body and the soul of the lost. Instead, we are distracted by the contemporary consumerist nature of Church feeding the spiritual entertainment needs of our parishioners instead of preaching truth that restores brokenness and facilitates transformation. This silence and irrelevant preaching are stifling the impact and growth of

---

36. White, "Our Duty to the Colored People."

the realm of God. Until we are willing to rebuke the violence that is happening to Black and Brown bodies, African American and Latinx people will never be able to hear anything we have to say about their souls or lives in the hereafter. We must, with great consideration, explicitly and directly rebuke the injustices of institutional racism, sexism, and the separation of families at the border based on fear on the foreigner.

Through the example of Ellen White, we can learn the importance of using our platforms and privilege to speak against individual and institutional racism. We can see that no matter the consequence, it is our spiritual and social duty to rebuke racism in our speech, restore oppressed people through our love, and replace oppressive systems through our activism. That means that preaching takes place both inside and outside the pulpit. It's not just an oratorical performance that takes place on Saturday or Sunday morning. It's not just a spiritual plea to reconcile sinners back to their loving Savior. No preaching is a lifestyle of activism. It is a commitment to interceding on behalf of the oppressed, the marginalized, those whose voices have been muzzled, and whose being has garnered them violence and discrimination. We exemplify this intercession in word, and in word made flesh. Let us start standing between oppressors and the oppressed with our words and our actions, inside our pulpits and outside our pulpits. Just like the hashtag #BlackLivesMatter, we are called to move our preaching beyond our words and into our daily actions. Preaching #Black-LivesMatter is more than just a sermon that supports a hashtag. It's more than preaching a sermon acknowledging the humanity of Black people. Preaching #BlackLivesMatter is a lifestyle of intercession that includes speaking and acting that expresses the incarnate love of God in a racist society. May people look at us and truly see the words of God made flesh, again.

18

Why Are We So White?

BEING A BLACK BISHOP IN A DIOCESE THAT WANTS TO DISMANTLE RACISM

Jennifer Baskerville-Burrows

I felt called to enter the discernment and election process for bishop of the Diocese of Indianapolis for many reasons—but it took me a while. As an African American/Native American from New York City, I had more than my fair share of presumptions of what Indiana was like. Stories of the influence of the Ku Klux Klan loomed large. When I finally read the profile for what the diocese was searching for in their next bishop, one sentence caught my eye: "We wonder why when we gather at diocesan convention we are so White." I thought, any diocese that is willing and able to ask that out loud is a diocese I want to know more about. As the Holy Spirit and the people of God would have it, I was elected and consecrated bishop of the Diocese of Indianapolis, breaking a stained glass ceiling as the first Black female diocesan bishop in The Episcopal Church.

I constantly marvel that God would call me to serve in Indiana. I'm still a New Yorker at heart, and here I am serving the church in a southern Midwest state that was home to some two hundred sundown towns between 1860 and 1940.[1] Those were places where it was not illegal for Blacks to live, just nearly impossible. If Black people were in one of these towns and wanted to live, they needed to be out by sundown. Signs were usually posted at the edge of town making this fact known. It was one of the ways the North dealt with Jim Crow.

I received a quick education about sundown towns when I made my first episcopal visit to St. Stephen's Church in New Harmony, Indiana, in October 2017. New Harmony, founded as a utopian community, is the site of Paul Tillich's grave; arts and music in the Harmonist style are plentiful. As I arrived

---

1. James W. Loewen, *Sundown Towns: The Hidden Dimension of American Racism, Reprint Edition* (New York: New Press, 2018).

in town, I was immediately impressed by the hospitality. St. Stephen's had posted "Welcome Bishop Jennifer" signs at a couple of points around town. I later learned that those wonderful welcome signs had been placed where the sundown signs had once stood. The priest-in-charge and the vestry had talked intently about how to acknowledge their history and, going forward, how to change the story about race in their artistic, utopian community. It was a beautiful gesture that generated important conversations, both internal and external, about an unspoken history. The internal conversation involved the acknowledgement of a shameful narrative. The external conversation brought me and other members of the New Harmony community into a dialogue about what those welcome signs were signifying beyond mere hospitality. This kind of truth-telling engendered trust and deepened the relationship between bishop and congregation almost immediately.

Now in the fourth year of my episcopacy, I get to have many such conversations and I get to wonder alongside people of many races and backgrounds about the "color" of our diocese. Like all conversations about race and White supremacy, it is profound and challenging work. And, thanks be to God, we are having these necessary conversations with more frequency in the Episcopal Church and in other places where such topics were previously just not discussed. As a Black woman in authority helping to provide, nurture, and sustain the spaces where a majority White community can have these conversations, I find this work liberating, exhausting, and transformative.

Though the current political and social climate have brought urgency to conversations about race and diversity, I believe the work of reconciliation and deepening relationship across racial differences has always been the Church's business. These matters are central to Christian identity. The biblical and theological concept of *imago Dei*, the image of God, informs how I understand the world and the diversity of people and creation that inhabit it.

In the creation narrative in the first chapter of Genesis, God completes the work of calming the chaos and creating all living things, and then decides to create humankind. Chapter 1, verse 26 says, "Then God said, 'Let us make humankind in our image, according to our likeness . . .'" To see the diversity of humankind is to understand that the image of God is complex. There have been many interpretations of the *imago Dei* throughout Christian tradition. Some of these interpretations have found the human reflection of the divine in physical resemblance, in the capacity to reason, and in the power to exercise dominion over creation. A more modern view contends that the image of God describes life in relationship.

This construction of the image of God is not made from a set of physical or intellectual attributes, but rather by transcending the self through relationship. Put simply, to be created in God's image is to be in relationship. God in the Holy Trinity exhibits perfect relationship in community. By creating humanity not in a solitary state, but as relational from the very beginning, God establishes that to be created in God's image means to be in relationship. To discount a portion of humanity is to discount the fullness of God. We cannot be one in Christ if some are part of the image of God and others are not.

As chief pastor and teacher, I have the privilege and responsibility of encouraging our diocese to embrace this understanding of *imago Dei* by having difficult conversations about White supremacy, anti-Blackness, White privilege, and racism. The fact that the majority of the Diocese of Indianapolis is White doesn't exempt us from these conversations. Indeed, it makes them more urgent. I encourage our entirely White congregations to talk about race on their own before attempting to do so with people of color with whom they have little relationship. As is the case across much of our church, many of our congregations here in Indiana do not reflect the diversity of their neighborhoods. If there is to be a shift toward growing into true diversity and mutuality, we have deep and difficult work to do on our own first.

Alongside antibias and antiracism trainings, book discussions, and the like, we must ask some rather simple but difficult questions. In conversations around our diocese I will posit that perhaps the question is not so much, "Why is our diocesan convention so White?" but "Why does my parish look the way it does?" To break that question down: "Who is in my friendship circle? Who do I allow into my life or at my dining table? Who has access to the things I value most, like church? Do they only look like me?"

The answers to those questions can take us to convicting and heartbreaking places as we confront the realities of our divided society. It is nearly impossible to find a pressing social issue in which systemic racism doesn't play a role: gun violence, immigration, poverty, education, employment, transportation access, and on and on. While solving these seemingly intractable challenges can prove overwhelming, our church communities can provide space to do the ongoing personal work that is necessary to undo and unlearn racial superiority and internalized racial oppression.

Many people, of course, find the prospect of wrestling with these questions in community to be daunting, to require courage, vulnerability, and trust. From time to time I'll share what it is like for me to be the only person of color in the room or church as I go about the ministry of bishop in our diocese. The reality of my experience is important for understanding who I am not only as bishop, but as a fellow Christian who hopes, dreams, and works for a time when being the "lonely only" is more exception than rule. And yet, I admit to being incredibly hopeful as I witness our congregations going ever deeper to learn, reflect, and attempt change.

Dismantling systemic racism is essential to the church's witness of God's love in Jesus and is rooted in our baptismal vows to honor the dignity of every human being. We are called to undertake this work as an ongoing practice of growing in Christian maturity, which is nothing less than learning to live and love more like Jesus, seeing God in the other no matter their race, class or station in life.

I pray that this work will transform us. I am in it for the long haul and look to the day when the question about what we look like at convention will be moot because we will have grown to reflect truly the *imago Dei*—the image of God in all of its diverse beauty.

19

Real Presence and How It Makes Black Lives Matter (Black LGBTQ)

Antonio J. Baxter

If baptism begins the welcome and reconciliation into the journey of faith, the Eucharist (The Lord's Supper) is the ongoing presence, welcome, reconciliation, and the promise of new life and the unique, profound kingdom of God. The Lord's Table has been at the center of many theological disputes and the cause of various schisms and splits within the Church (the body of Christ). The study of the different models of the Lord's Supper in comparison with the scriptures moves one from the process of embedded theology to deliberative theology about the Eucharist.

Outside the Roman Catholic Church, both the models of Martin Luther and Ulrich Zwingli have been heavily influential in the concept of the Lord's Table, particularly for Christians in the United States. Examining these models helps us examine how we approach the mission of the Church in the world because the mission of the Church and how it relates to the world determines how we understand the Lord's Supper. In Luther's "real presence," the Lord's Table draws all who may come for the presence of God and God's sustaining grace. In Zwingli's memorial, the remembrance of Christ and his Passion and Resurrection draws to the table those who remember and reflect on the triumph of now and the "to come." Comparing the two models raises interesting questions. How do they relate and correspond to the idea of an open table or open feast? And how does the idea of the open feast relate to the witness of the Church to Black LGBTQ members of the Black church who have often felt marginalized and on the boundaries? The Lord's Supper has been used to exclude and say that some (Black LGBTQ) do not belong even in the Black church. However, the Lord's Supper stands open and welcoming for all.

Martin Luther's model of the Eucharist is characterized as consubstantiation because of ubiquitous presence.[1] Luther was in opposition to the Roman Catholic position on transubstantiation, which is a rationalization of the mystery of Eucharist in how bread and wine become the body and blood of Christ. Thomas Aquinas established the foundation of transubstantiation in looking at the accidents (outward appearance) and substance (inward reality) through the framework of Aristotelian philosophy (while a shirt may be red, or made of cotton or silk, these are distinct from it being a shirt—what we can see outside).[2] So while we see bread and wine, the real substance is not seen by the eye (body and blood), although the nature of what makes up the body and blood (bread and wine) are seen. Luther thought the rationalization was not needed because the concepts of the body and blood and the bread and wine could be all held together.[3]

Luther made the case borrowing imagery from Origen, who used a piece of iron that is heated until the color changes red as his metaphor. When a piece of iron is heated to that point, it demonstrates two substances.[4] Both iron and fire make up the heated iron. Luther stated it was possible for the bread and wine and the body and blood to all be held together in the Eucharist. Luther explained the presence of Christ in the Eucharist by using Christ's risen body. In the risen (glorified) body of Christ, Luther argued that the divine nature of Christ empowered him to be able to be everywhere (omnipresent).[5] Scripture backs Luther's claim. Jesus proclaimed he would be with us always (Matt. 28:19–20), which adds evidence to Luther's point that Christ's glorified body is omnipresent.

Luther referred to the bread and wine in other language as well. He said the bread and wine acted as a last will and testament of promised inheritance to those who took it once the promiser had passed away.[6] It declared a death of the one who made the promise (its full activation becomes available after the promiser has passed away). It identified the promise of eternal life and communion with all the saints of God in the new kingdom of God, which included

---

1. Daniel L. Migliore, *Faith Seeking Understanding: An Introduction to Christian Theology* (Grand Rapids, MI: William B. Eerdmans, 2014), 302.

2. Migliore, *Faith Seeking Understanding*, 301.

3. Migliore, *Faith Seeking Understanding*, 302.

4. Migliore, *Faith Seeking Understanding*, 302.

5. Migliore, *Faith Seeking Understanding*, 302.

6. Dr. Sathi Clarke, "The Holy Eucharist" (lecture, Wesley Theological Seminary, Washington, DC, April 9, 2019).

grace and forgiveness to all who confessed salvation through Christ.[7] Luther also stressed that Christ's body and spiritual presence in the Eucharist was present to all, even to those who might eat and drink unworthily of it. If the bread and wine were a witness to the promises of Christ, then all who came to meet and receive Christ opened themselves to become unified into the family of Christ (heir-member of the church).

Luther's reference to the Lord's Supper as the "last will and testament" provides an opportunity for all who come to the Table to share in Christ's remembrance and in the coming opportunity presented in the "coming" kingdom of God.[8] The Eucharist is an opportunity to affirm that Christ provides grace and forgiveness to all and the opportunity is there for all. In this presentation of the Lord's Table, Luther's model presents an opportunity to make the Lord's Supper an open table, and just maybe an open feast (to some degree).

Ulrich Zwingli's model of the Eucharist is characterized as memorialist. Zwingli was a major figure in the reformation movement in Switzerland. He thought Luther's position of consubstantiation through ubiquity was as elusive and as much a rationalization attempt as the Roman Catholic concept of transubstantiation.[9] He thought that scripture indicated that Christ was seated at the right side of God the Father. For Zwingli, this biblical reference of Christ being seated at the right hand of God meant that it was not possible for Christ's presence to be anywhere else.[10]

Zwingli treated language such as "this is my body" and "this is my blood" as language that pointed us to remember the salvation of the believer through the passion, death, and resurrection of Christ. It was a call to meditate and ponder on the event. Zwingli believed the language was allegorical. He pointed to scripture where Christ referenced himself as a vine (John 15:5) and described how Christ was speaking figuratively; he was not an actual vine. Zwingli believed that describing the bread and the wine as Christ's actual body and blood was a misuse or a misunderstanding of scripture.[11] With no scripture providing the foundation of human authority to invoke Christ's presence in the bread and wine, he believed there is no basis for Christ's presence in the bread and wine.

---

7. Clarke, "Holy Eucharist."

8. Clarke, "Holy Eucharist," 19–20.

9. Clarke, "Holy Eucharist" 21.

10. Clarke, "Holy Eucharist," 19–20.

11. Clarke, "Holy Eucharist," 19–20.

Zwingli also used the metaphor of a lover setting off for a trip and leaving flowers as a remembrance of the lover until their return to establish what memorialism was. The flowers served as a token to remember until the return of the lover.[12] Zwingli made note of there being no scripture reference to justify the bread and wine becoming the body and blood by the pronouncement of the pope or any other presbyter.[13] The memorialist perspective views the sacraments more as ordinances. These ordinances were instituted by Christ himself and the command was passed from him to the apostles. These ordinances serve as an expression of obedience and commitment.[14] The act of the Lord's Supper is how we show our commitment and loyalty to Christ. Sharing the Lord's Supper retells of the story of Christ's work in salvation history work and demonstrates our commitment to him and to the Church. The language of ordinance and Zwingli's description of the act of receiving communion as demonstration of one's loyalty and commitment recalls Christ's act, but also seems to present language that restricts access to the Lord's Table. The language provides a criterion by which one must submit to be able to take part at the Table. It hints that unless one believes or adheres to commitment the way it is prescribed by a certain doctrine, one is not allowed to be a participant at the Table.

How do Luther's consubstantiation because of ubiquitous presence and Zwingli's model of Eucharist relate to the "open table" or the "open feast"? The open table welcomes all to the table to be recipients and served at the Lord's Table. It welcomes all, those who some may call lawbreakers and those who some might think of as saints. No one is denied a seat at the Lord's Table; whatever restriction can be thought of to deny a person (race, socioeconomic status, religion, nationality, caste, marital status, sexual orientation, felon, innocent, baptized, non-baptized) cannot be a barrier. Christ broke the barrier in his salvific work! The Table is not only made open, but the feast to some degree is open. Jürgen Moltmann says the Eucharist—the commemorative sign of Christ's suffering and death, the foreshadowing sign through resurrection and eternal life, and the demonstrative sign of Christ's grace in our anticipation of his coming—is an open feast due to the forward direction in which to God's new world and the reconciliation of this new creation to God is made present.[15]

---

12. Clarke, "Holy Eucharist," 19–20.

13. Clarke, "Holy Eucharist," 19–20.

14. Migliore, *Faith Seeking Understanding*, 303–4.

15. Clarke, "Holy Eucharist," 31–33.

Luther's consubstantiation, because of ubiquitous presence, correlates with the idea of the open table and open feast as opposed to Zwingli's memorialist model. For Luther, there are real benefits to the presence of Christ in the bread and wine. He believed that recipients of Eucharist received the exchange of the forgiveness of sin through the presence of Christ in the bread and wine. The Eucharist invited a direct encounter with Christ (in the bread and wine) to be assured of the forgiveness of sin and acceptance. Zwingli rejected such notions and found it to be absurd that forgiveness came through bread and wine. For Zwingli, forgiveness was found in the cross of Christ.[16] While Luther would have concurred with that point: he would have insisted forgiveness was won at the Cross. However, he thought it was distributed in the bread and wine and given through the word.[17] The forgiveness of sin makes real the possibility of life and salvation. This was an important point for Luther because lives hung in the balance, both in the present life and in eternity. Luther said forgiveness of sin overcame the evil trio of sin, death, and the devil:

> Pure, pure, wholesome and soothing medicine that aids you and will give you life in both soul and body. . . . For here in the sacrament you are to receive from Christ's lips the forgiveness of sins, which contains and brings with it God's grace and Spirit will all his gifts, protection, defense, and power against death, the devil, and every trouble.[18]

The open table is an invitation to receive this for those who partake.

Paul in 2 Corinthians 5:15 indicates that Christ died for all. He also states that through Christ, God is reconciling the world to himself. The diverse creation is involved in God's plan. Luke 14 points to an invitation to all that are on the outer edges, not just natural friends and companions; outsiders and the marginalized are encouraged to come and enjoy the great banquet that has been prepared. Based on Luther's assertion of the power of the Eucharist to distribute forgiveness, scripture that God is reconciling, and Christ's invitation, God's Table invites persons with different theological beliefs and does not require baptism and confirmation as prerequisites (corresponding with some characteristics of Moltmann's open feast).[19]

---

16. Gordon A. Jensen, "The Sacrament of the Altar," *Lutheran Quarterly* 31, no. 1 (Spring 2017): 5.

17. Jensen, "Sacrament of the Altar," 5.

18. Quoted in Jensen, "Sacrament of the Altar," 5.

19. Clarke, "Holy Eucharist," 31–33.

Luther's consubstantiation, when held against scripture, correlates with the idea of the open table and some elements of the open feast, which is remarkable because it provides a place for Black LGBTQ believers not only to be at the table receiving openly and freely, but also administering it in the Black church. Black church denominations, such as African Methodist Episcopal (AME), African Methodist Episcopal Zion (AME Zion), National Baptist Convention USA, Church of God In Christ (COGIC), and Pentecostal Assemblies of the World (PAW), to this day either have resolutions or statements in which they condemn same-gender marriage or forbid LGBTQ people to serve openly in ordained ministry.[20] However, through the ubiquitous presence of Christ and its correlation to the open table and open feast, Black LGBTQ believers must challenge the Black church to see the Black LGBTQ believers' right to be at the Lord's Table with the ability to be in communion with others (including in communion with a partner in marriage and openly true to who they are to serve in ordained ministry).

Jesus shared a meal with tax collectors (a group of Jewish collaborators with the Roman occupiers of Israel who collected taxes for the Roman government in excess to make themselves wealthy) and offered living water to an outcast Samaritan woman.[21] The apostle Paul, in Galatians 3:28, reminds us that Jew or Greek, slave or free, male or female all disappear in Christ. Paul's words are important because they lay the foundation for all to come together and share a meal. It points us toward all being the same in Christ when we come to the Table, particularly for the Eucharist.[22] Our distinctions, though diverse, become one in the image of Christ at the Lord's Table. Having endured a history of being excluded from the Table and seen as a heathens with no hope of equal salvation with Whites, the Black church must see its hypocrisy when it uses scripture to support exclusion and justify oppression. Christ's presence in the bread and wine breaks downs barriers and demands all be eligible to receive and serve (via holy orders or ordination). Christ's body in the bread and wine at The Lord's Table transcends distinctions, and undoes biologized body in terms of gender.[23] The body escapes these constructs and points to the manifold

---

20. *Human Rights Campaign: Faith Positions*, accessed May 7, 2019, *https://www.hrc.org/resources/faith-positions*.

21. Martha Smith Tatarnic, "Whoever Comes To Me: Open Table, Missional Church, and the Body of Christ," *Anglican Theological Review* 96, no. 2 (Spring 2014): 292.

22. Jay Emerson Johnson, *Peculiar Faith: Queer Theology for Christian Witness* (New York: Seabury Books, 2014), 128.

23. Any Buechel, *That We Might Become God: The Queerness of Creedal Christianity* (Eugene, OR: Cascade Books, 2015), 72.

elements of all as they exist being themselves. If only a memorial as Zwingli asserts, how are we, united into Christ, to become his body? And are the barriers really broken and do the divisions remain?

In the bread and wine united with Christ's presence, being at the Table unites us to Christ. In this unity, Christ gives forgiveness of sin. His self-sacrificing through his body is told to us in the Words of Institution in the Holy Eucharist: This is my body for you. In the giving of his body, Jesus shows the example of loving self-sacrifice. Jesus invites his disciples to imitate him. Marriage presents the opportunity for Black LGBTQ to give themselves to another in mutual love and self-sacrifice.[24] The Eucharist reveals the giving and self-sacrifice that welcomes us all to partake in through Christ regardless of our differences.

Many in the Black church will use the mantle of scripture as a justification to exclude Black LGBTQ believers from the Table. Scripture texts such as Leviticus 18:22 and 20:13 are used as reasons to keep the Black LGBTQ believers from being at the Table as their "open" selves, administering the sacrament as an "open" clergy, or being married. Even if you hold on to the biblicist approach in scripture, Luther's consubstantiation through ubiquitous presence welcomes all to receive and be at the Table.

Luther and Martin Bucer engaged one another about whether an unbeliever could receive Christ's body and blood in the meal. Faith was at the center of the controversy: if a person had no faith, did they receive the body and blood of Christ or just bread and wine?[25] Luther indicated that Christ was present in the bread and wine regardless of the recipient's faith. Concerned that such a position might lead to a mechanistic understanding of the sacrament, Bucer sent a letter to Luther and wrote that the sacramental union was not extended to everyone; not all received the bread and wine into salvation and he broke it into categories. Unbelievers received bread and wine, but not the body and blood of Christ. It could be given to all, but would not aid all.[26] However, Bucer added a third category of recipients called the unworthy (*indigni*). He said that the pious and the unworthy received Christ in the bread and wine, but not the ungodly. Luther accepted that because he believed that because we are all sinners and justified, everyone was unworthy. He also believed the ungodly

---

24. Mark Achtemeier, *The Bible's YES to Same-Sex Marriage: An Evangelical's Change of Heart* (Louisville: Westminster John Knox Press, 2015), 52–54.

25. Jensen, "Sacrament of the Altar," 12.

26. Jensen, "Sacrament of the Altar," 12.

would not want to partake of the Lord's Supper. Improper taking of the sacraments was not neutral, but acted on the person (for the good or the bad).[27]

Even if one holds a biblicist view regarding the scriptures about homosexuality, the Lord's Supper is open to all who profess belief in Christ. In receiving the Eucharist as believers in Christ, the forgiveness of sin is administered to all. We are all qualified through the work of God through Christ at the Cross to receive forgiveness in Eucharist. We are all welcome at the Table. As believers in Christ, the Black LGBTQ community receives the same Christ's body and blood as everyone else.[28]

Just as the Black church has had to take scripture that had been used to justify slavery and oppression and examine it in the context of its liberation from oppression, it is time for it to do the same for its Black LGBTQ siblings in Christ. What the Bible means must take priority over what the Bible meant.[29] The story of liberation and welcoming all to God's Table must take precedent over the text.[30] The Black church has done this through the legacy of slavery and Jim Crow. It is time to do it again for its Black LGBTQ members so that all Black lives matter at the Table. Luther's consubstantiation through ubiquitous presence and its open table/open feast implications might be the vehicle to move us that way.

---

27. Jensen, "Sacrament of the Altar," 12.

28. Jensen, "Sacrament of the Altar," 12.

29. James H. Evans, *We Have Been Believers: An African American Systematic Theology* (Minneapolis: Fortress Press, 2014), 58–59.

30. Evans, *We Have Been Believers*, 58–59.

20

Leading as if Black Congregations Matter

Mariann Edgar Budde

Serving as bishop in the racially and culturally diverse context of Washington, DC, and four counties of Maryland is a tremendous blessing, but it requires a daily willingness on my part to be both humble and brave, to acknowledge mistakes and learn from them, and to bring my whole self into every situation while at the same time recognizing when my primary role is to listen, learn, and provide leadership opportunities for others. I realized almost immediately that in navigating the racial dynamics, challenges, and creativity of the diocese, my learning curve would be steep. I just didn't know how steep.

Among my many early missteps, I once showed up at a historical African American congregation to celebrate the feast day of Absalom Jones, the first African American to be ordained a priest in the Episcopal Church, with only simple choir vestments of rochette and chamire. That may not seem like a big deal—it certainly didn't to me—but the look of horror on the faces of those preparing to lead that worship made me realize I had made a dreadful mistake of etiquette with a deeper meaning I did not understand. I felt like the man in Jesus's parable who showed up to the wedding banquet in the wrong attire. Mercifully, I wasn't banished to the outer realms; instead the host priest kindly, yet firmly, suggested that I wear his celebratory vestments. Seeing my confusion, another one of the African American priests said, "Bishop, the majority of African American Episcopalians are quite formal in worship, and they like to see their bishops dressed in full regalia." I learned to show up with respect for that tradition.

Another misstep was to assume an informal, collegial relationship with the clergy of the diocese. "Call me by first name," I insisted. Most of the White clergy readily accepted a more casual leadership style, but almost none of the African American clergy did. I didn't understand the need for such formality, until it dawned on me how hard won such titles of respect are for those outside the dominant culture. It wasn't about my style, but about the need for respect. I pay attention to titles now, making sure I offer that same respect to clergy and lay leaders who have worked disproportionately hard to earn the titles of their positions.

Yet another stumble, this one with significant political implications, was about three years into my episcopate. I suggested what I thought was a modest change in our governance structure in order to promote more effective collaborative ministry. The resistance to the change was fierce, which surprised me, given how little the current structures served our mission and how few people engaged in it. Even more surprising, African American leaders led the fight against my proposal. What wasn't I seeing? Why didn't they trust me with a rather simple change in governance structure—to change the boundaries of the regions?

When, two years later, I dared to broach the subject of structural realignment again, I engaged clergy and lay leaders across the diocese in conversation. One memorable gathering was at my dining room table where for several hours, a small group of African American clergy and lay leaders educated me about the racial and economic realities of Washington, DC. Despite a gentrification boom, the lines of racial and economic segregation run north/south and across the Anacostia River, with stark implications for its residents of color. My initial proposals for diocesan restructuring would have reinforced those lines. No wonder they resisted! After much conversation across the city and the diocese as a whole, we agreed upon a new structure that cut across those lines, going east/west. While not a perfect structure, the new regional configuration is a great improvement. Again, I learned that my role serves a racially diverse diocese best when I ensure that people of color are at the tables where decisions are made.

I've lost count of the number of times I've been called to task for not remembering the importance of inclusion and representation—in photographs on the diocesan website, among those serving in roles of prominence on committees or leading worship. Those accountability conversations continue to challenge my assumptions and I'm grateful for those who have been willing to speak up. When we're at our best, the *first* question we ask whenever we're planning worship or an event is, "Who needs to be at the table?"

My primary responsibility as bishop is to serve the congregations and emerging worshiping communities of the Diocese of Washington during a time when the Episcopal Church is, in general, experiencing systemic decline. While some of the congregations I serve are thriving, many are not, and most are simply holding steady in contexts of rapid population growth. The historic African American congregations and those that are predominantly Black or multiracial due to White flight are struggling with the same trends of decline as the diocese as a whole. Most are surrounded by whole new populations, including the urban Black congregations whose members moved out of their neighborhoods years ago, but still return for Sunday worship. These congregations now find themselves in gentrifying neighborhoods with predominantly White new neighbors.

The racial dynamics are complex and intense. As the Rev. Dr. Gayle Fisher-Stewart says, "Racism created Black churches; racism maintains them, and racism will kill them."[1] Certainly, there is truth in her words. Yet some of the strategies needed to address and eventually reverse the congregational decline of Black and multiracial congregations are the same as predominantly White congregations. Any congregation, regardless of race, that is experiencing internal conflict, tepid in its expression of living the gospel, unwilling to adapt to engage the spiritual needs and aspirations of rising generations, and disconnected from its surrounding community, cannot thrive. But how those strategies are implemented and adapted varies dramatically, according to a given context. How the message is received depends on who is speaking. Who has the authority and credibility to lead the transformation of the Black church?

There are certain messages I can't effectively deliver to Black congregations. Thus, I've learned that the best thing I can do is to encourage opportunities for sharing as much power and authority with rising Black leaders as I can. I've also looked for models of thriving Black churches in other faith traditions and invited their leaders to address ours. There is no quick solution here, but there is hope for the future of Black churches in the Episcopal Church. God has planted seeds of possibility and new life in all of them—I see glimpses of the future in the faces of the faithful gathered; I hear it in the voices of those speaking with courage and love.

The societal context of the last eight years has both raised the stakes and sharpened the focus of what it looks like to lead as if Black congregations mattered. The election of Donald Trump; the rise of White supremacist groups and racially motivated violence; the number of African Americans lost to gun violence, including those killed by police; our national reckoning with symbols of the Confederacy; and the disproportionate number of African Americans imprisoned in this country all suggest that this is a time of reckoning for the

---

1. Gayle Fisher-Stewart, personal communication.

nation. I don't know where it will lead, but I am convinced that investing in the health of Black congregations has the greatest potential not only to reverse the trends of decline in our denomination, but release our most gifted leaders to be a force for greater good throughout the world.

Where is Jesus in the midst of all this turmoil, and where does he call us to follow? The answer, while not easy, is clear. We are called to move toward the struggle, not away from it; toward the cross, getting proximate, as Bryan Stevenson would say, to those who bear the brunt of our society's ills and be open to what only God can do through us, when we dare to show up. Black congregations matter because Black lives matter.

As bishop I must show up in the challenging conversations about race in this country and in our church. That requires me to be a lifelong student of history, politics, and theology, all through the lens of race. Among my many teachers are brilliant African American scholars of both past and present, including Frederick Douglas, W. E. B. Du Bois, Howard Thurman, Martin Luther King Jr., James Cone, James Baldwin, Michelle Alexander, Bryan Stevenson, and Kelly Brown Douglas.

Yet it's not only the Black experience that I need to come to terms with, but my own racial identity as a White person, with all the conscious and unconscious privilege of White supremacy. There are many default positions in such a reckoning: defensiveness, guilt, shame. No doubt I've circled through them all, which is the luxury of privilege. But I'm learning from rising thought leaders such as Robin D'Angelo, Katrina Browne, Peter Jarrett-Schell, and others who are calling all of us in the dominant culture to examine ourselves and the societal support structures that we take for granted.

My learning curve is still steep and will always be. But I am grateful for colleagues and friends of color who are willing to teach me, point out my missteps and blind spots, challenge my assumptions, and allow me to be their imperfect yet committed ally in the work of racial justice. Theirs are the voices to which we all must listen; theirs the lead we must follow.

21

I'm Searching

Kevin Burdet

It seems like the idea of an equal, diverse, loving Church has many barriers in the way of its fruition. I have attended a predominately Black episcopal church in the historic H Street Northeast area of Washington, DC, for the past two years, and my eyes have completely opened to the walls that we have all put up as a body of Christians. Growing up in rural Vermont, I was under the assumption that the only reason our rural church was all White was that there were only a handful of people of color in our town. I don't think the church itself was to blame for this since the local high school was 98 percent White. The lack of diversity allowed the media I absorbed and the images of Christian charitable organizations with depictions of starving Black children to paint a picture of what other races—especially Black people—were like, or at least what their general disposition was. When I think about it, besides one friend who was one of two Black kids in my grade, my church and other settings with Black people only told me that they were always asking for something, and that White people, as benevolent people, would either help or deny their requests. As a church, we funded kids in Africa and hung their pictures on our walls. During youth group, we passed a jar to collect coins and dollars for those kids, which became a practice of passing it around until it came back to the youth leader almost completely empty. We were all in middle school and none of us had money, but—if I'm honest—it may have done more harm to altruistic tendencies than it had helped. We learned how to deny the passive request of some kid like us whose life seemed alien to ours. Before I moved from Vermont, we had stopped funding these kids due to our lack of altruism.

There was a family from Africa that attended our church for a long time, and I think this was our first genuine experience with any Black people at the church. Although they were refugees and needed lots of aid, they began to grow a genuine relationship with people at the church. This family still perpetuated a certain idea of who Black people were and how they needed our help.

This lack of exposure did not stop at race. Our pastor was in the Burlington newspaper for his antihomosexual beliefs in comparison to a pro-rights activist because Vermont had just legalized same-sex marriage through its 2009 Marriage Equality Act. Although my mom, who was the main Christian role model in my life, did not agree with the pastor, I began to understand the exclusion that the church I had grown up in embodied. Did my Sunday school teacher who baked us cookies and loved us all as if we were her own children believe that homosexuals had no place in our church? Did my teenage peers at the church also believe that because their parents did?

Before I had any real conscious understanding of the rural church, my parents and I moved to South Carolina in 2009. We arrived in Clemson a week before my first year of high school began. My mom and I sat down with the counselor, who had no idea where I had come from or if I was a good student. He fooled me into joining ROTC and put me in the regular "college prep" classes rather than "honors" classes. I did not know what the labels meant, but I later realized that I was more of an honors student, but for my first year I was in class with everybody. I made a lot of friends who were from all sorts of backgrounds, and many of them were Black. It was a completely new cultural experience for my parents and me.

My dad was still back in Vermont, but my mom and I started attending the main Methodist church in Clemson, which had just built a huge new sanctuary in a new location. Even then, I didn't notice that none of my Black friends from class were at this church. Everybody other than one kid was White, and they were in the honors classes at school. I became close to these kids because they lived where I lived, and I related to their backgrounds more. I started to hang out with them more than with my initial friends; after my first year of high school, I moved to honors classes. I only saw my initial friends in the hallways, or hanging out at track and field practice. Within a year of moving to the South, I had become an active participant in my own racial division and a part of a process that seemed all but inherent. Nevertheless, I did learn more about White supremacy while in high school. I saw what blatant racism looked like, since everything in Vermont was subliminal. I saw the paradoxical relationships between Whites and Blacks, where a White person in an interracial relationship could still say they hated Black people.

When it came to same-sex rights, where my pastor in Vermont had been a dissenting opinion, I found a strong mission against homosexuality in South Carolina. My Methodist church seemed to be the only place that discussed homosexuality. By the time I left for college, they were one of the first to say that they welcomed everybody (and many members left for good). I did not know that it was a move, not by the entire denomination, but by the individual congregation. Methodists in South Carolina are still discussing whether to allow equal marriage and gay clergy.

The common thread I saw was that the acceptance of all people was blocked by historical divides that had been adopted as either familial common sense or denominational doctrine. At the University of South Carolina, I was jaded by churches that I was drawn toward, always finding something out of place with their level of inclusion: an all-White progressive church in the center of the diverse city of Columbia, a predominately White college-oriented church that was passively antihomosexual, a multilingual church whose pastor had a personal guard as he fought against LGBTQ organizations.

When I arrived in DC the fall after graduation, I was invited by a friend to go to a church in northern Virginia. It was the type of church that I had known throughout my time in South Carolina, with which I was comfortable: lots of new audio-visual equipment, a new building, and a new church body. Everybody was nice, and, in fact, the church was much more diverse than those in South Carolina, though the clergy was still mostly White. I drove forty minutes to get to the church, but that seemed natural to me.

After the service, I said goodbye to my friend who lived in northern Virginia, and drove back to DC. As I drove, I passed multiple churches, with churchgoers walking out as their services ended. Most of these churches were predominately Black. At that moment I realized I was being pulled back into the same sort of racial divisions I had been a part of in South Carolina and Vermont. If there was a point of my life to break this trend, it was that moment in DC as a new, young professional. My task was simple: I should search for churches in my area, which I was actively a part of gentrifying, and go to them.

I had had a good experience at an Episcopal church in Maine the summer between college and DC, and found their drive for community and inclusion was stronger than what I had experienced in other denominations, so I searched for the closest Episcopal churches in my part of town. Calvary Episcopal Church had a good website that showed me the members were active on social issues and wanted to make a change. That's where I went.

My experience at Calvary has been monumental in how I see my relationship to the body of Christ around me. Where I once pictured White congregations across the country, I now see a racially divided church body with minorities, segregation, and the overpowering of voices. I have been asked by people why I go to a predominately Black church, and I answer because it is in my neighborhood. The question makes me think people think I have an agenda; I must be trying to look better and show off about going to a church where I am a minority. In truth, I suppose there is selfishness because I know that my experience at Calvary allows me to grow. It is a predominately elderly congregation, so I have role models in my life I would have never met, as well as peers I might have never grown close to if I had met them on the street. I have been involved with the vestry of the church, celebrated birthdays, and mourned deaths. I have learned how to speak more openly about my own racism, and how to be more inclusive.

Even still, I am one person observing this racial division perpetuating itself. When a White family came to Calvary, I felt like it was my obligation to speak with them in hopes that they might stay. This was not necessary. It has been depressing to see, with the economic growth of H Street and as White people have moved into the area, that our historical, community-oriented church has struggled. White people came in as visitors, but they hardly ever showed up for a second service. I realized that even though I had grown close to the members of the church, I still felt like our home lives were separate, and meeting members at their house for dinner was something I only imagined. Maybe some of the White people who didn't come back felt the same way. I took a step of faith to join the church, but the societal and cultural differences still created a gap that I, and many other White people, needed to traverse.

After two years, I am moving once again. I'm leaving DC for Seattle, Washington, where I have heard good and bad stories when it comes to inclusion. I'm not worried about finding a church there; my girlfriend's friends all attend the same church in the city. It sounds big and welcoming. Still, I wonder where I will find a body of Christ that acknowledges the issues of inclusion our churches across the United States face. I hope that when a church realizes they are active in perpetuating racism, they would humbly seek to be more inclusive. If we are to live in a world where the Church is actively inclusive of all people, predominately White, heteronormative churches are going to need to lead because they are the ones who have kept barrier alive. They need to learn to listen, act, and speak with humility when it comes to race, gender, and sex. They must actively counteract the societal divides that pull us apart. They must listen to all its members, especially those who are minorities, and they must answer the call to fight injustice. It is not as complicated as it is made out to be. It is a matter of making a commonsense decision that everyone belongs. I think I have started letting my common sense get the best of me.

22

A Call for the Church to Embrace All, Unconditionally

Nicole D.

During my undergraduate years, I was often "that" student: the contrarian who eagerly called out teachable moments as the lessons were being taught (in the most respectful manner, of course). This was particularly on display in the fall of my senior year while taking a course focused on African Americans and religion. I felt a strong need to share with the class that I was raised a Catholic, which, I believed, set me apart from the others. By "others," I am referring to other Black students who attended our southern liberal arts predominantly White (PWI)[1] college; many of whom were raised in traditional Black faiths. Drawing attention to my experience, I often interrupted the professor to debunk a point he made, believing it required more zest. Why the need for my performance? Who was I trying to impress? Was it worth aggravating my patient professor? The quick answer to the latter question was a resounding, "No."

Of course, I now know there isn't anything particularly unique about being a Black Catholic. Additionally, relative to the environment, it also wasn't unique being one of only two Black students in that class. However, hailing from New Jersey and having not been raised Baptist, AME, or Pentecostal, I did feel slightly set apart. I was intensely aware of my differences. Upon reflection, the storytelling I insisted on sharing needed more maturity, appreciation to nuance, and a more appropriate audience. That said, I felt a strong desire to be seen. At that moment in life, I was intentionally and loudly "antireligion," as I had cast a large and wide net and believed religious denominations were basins of sexism and homophobia. Growth and experience helped adjust my perspective. And what of race? I hadn't paid much attention to the binary ways

---

1. Predominantly White Institution (PWI) in comparison to Historically Black Colleges and Universities (HBCUs).

in which church existed; however, I was fully aware of the history which led to those divisions.

Without necessarily going through an early/later adulthood tantrum stage, I think it is fair to assume we all want to feel welcomed, safe, and valued, and also have a place, an institution, as sacred as our churches or religious communities. My spiritual journal certainly documents such needs. My story is that of a Black woman raised Catholic, led by the faith of my grandmother and tied to the various Catholic institutions that existed throughout my upbringing and community. My story involves going a bit astray upon high school graduation, let loose from the grip of the Church and introduced to Black Southern traditions. At the current moment in my spiritual journey, I am not associated with any specific religion, though I am open. My openness is guided by my faith that Christian denominations can serve as vessels for all people. The Church should recognize its significant potential and serve as a model institution that embraces all people regardless of race, gender, orientation, age, ability, income status, country of origin, or other identities.

Growing up I witnessed the importance and widespread impact of a religious institution. I saw firsthand how religious traditions and ideology permeate the wider society in both good and undesirable ways. Fortunately, the Church encompasses many devout followers who follow Jesus's teaching of love, respect, and grace. My grandmother led by such example. Most measures of respect and feelings of nostalgia I have for the Catholic Church stem from my beloved late grandmother. While she was still with us, she showed that unconditional love was feasible despite theological, cultural, political, or other differences. She—a quiet, modest individual—symbolizes the hope I have for the institution.

My grandmother was a well-respected leader of the church she attended for decades. She was a warm presence for those who encountered her and she made people feel safe. Similarly, the Church should serve as a safe space for the marginalized. It should hold space for those who don't always abide by certain rules or dogmas. For instance, the Church is an institution that offers renowned education opportunities, but it could consider more progressive means of disciplinary actions. Young Black children in Catholic elementary schools could benefit from several of the meditative methods practiced by clergy and laypeople rather than stark disciplinary measures that reinforce stereotypes.

On a broader scale, the Church should increase participation in outward displays of unity by showing up and speaking out against White supremacy and all forms of bigotry. I know there are brave clergypersons doing so. I just wish it weren't considered an act of bravery and was considered more common-place. During the civil rights movement of the 1960s, nuns and priests marched alongside civil rights activists. Members of other faith communities did so as well. Indeed, we know that major aspects of the movement were led and car-ried out by Black religious figures. However, success required that those who did not face the daily terror of White supremacy (e.g., White clergy) find the courage and use their privilege to speak out. This need has not gone away. It is still required of all those with power and privilege, and particularly the Church, given its influence and stature. It is no secret that the Catholic Church has sev-eral issues to resolve—particularly, issues related to child abuse, sexual abuse, sexism, and homophobia. The Church should actively work on those ills while also showing full support for the many diverse communities that sustain it.

At age eighteen, I left the comfort of home and ended regular Mass atten-dance to go to college in South Carolina. The move opened my eyes to the Black Southern experience, including historical Black faith practices, which I was not familiar with at that point. I was exposed to Black Southern culture and learned that faith traditions were key components of individual and com-munal identities. I was taken aback. I also came into my identity as a Black feminist and felt affronted. Rather than hold an openness to learn about the faith traditions, I was antagonistic and, as illustrated in the beginning of this essay, I lashed out. I sadly believed that historically Black faith traditions were antiwomen and anti-LGBTQA+. I, of course, was short-sighted since many denominations and faith traditions have exhibited homophobia and sexism, not just Black churches. I was also extremely disrespectful to the ancestors, my own included, considering the profound impact churches had on the journey toward freedom. While significant strides have been made, I believe we are still on that journey. For Black lives to matter in the Church, all Black lives must be valued whether they be trans, cis, straight, or not. However, the responsibility for valuing all Black lives does not lie solely on the backs of Black churches. All denominations should strive to be safe communities.

Currently, I do not regularly attend a specific church nor practice my faith in alignment with a specific religion. I believe in God. I am Christian. I just haven't been able to reestablish the connection I had to the Church growing up. With the passing of my grandmother last year, reconnecting has proven quite difficult. Nonetheless, I strongly believe that there is value in attending church—specifically, to be in fellowship, in community, a body in oneness coming before the Lord. I believe this is a necessity in my life as I am heal-ing. As such, I have "courted" several churches in my area. Those that haven't worked out have felt exclusionary in one way or the other and did not make me feel comfortable. I yearn to find one that feels like home. A takeaway: churches should accept the challenge of offering welcome and love without conditions, as Jesus did. They must show that they believe all are invited; they should make all who attend or visit feel seen and valued as God created them.

I have been fortunate to encounter and engage with churches that embrace all. The leaders and membership of those churches have also typically been at the forefront of social justice. I encourage these strong clergypersons and their members to invite other clergypersons and congregations to do the work as well. It may require hard conversations, perhaps even analysis of theology and the duty of church. From my own observation and experience, I believe there is a correlation between churches that preach and practice social equity and those same churches feeling like home.

23

Multicultural or Multiracial?

Gayle Fisher-Stewart

Multicultural, multiracial, interracial, culturally diverse: these and other terms have been used in the attempt to describe congregations with members from more than one race or ethnic group. Yet, a congregation can be multiracial and not multicultural. The faces may look different, but the style of worship can be seen as requiring the worshiper to leave their background and culture at the door. As we strive to evangelize, to bring others to Christ and into our congregations, our liturgies must actually reflect the work and lives of the people so that those in our pews can see themselves in the worship of the church.

It was Good Friday. As I walked into the narthex, I smelled the sweet aroma of Copal incense from Ethiopia burning in preparation for the service. It was the first time I had participated in the "Liturgy of the Burial of the Icon" (*Liturgia para el Enterramiento Del Icono*) and I was not quite sure of what to expect. As I entered the sanctuary of St. Stephen and the Incarnation Church in Washington, DC—a multiracial and multicultural congregation—I saw the icon of Jesus Christ on the table, reminiscent of a body waiting preparation for burial. I took my place in one of the seats placed in a circle around the labyrinth on the floor; the pews had long been removed. In the center was another table with the cross behind it. Soft cello music was playing. People from Mexico, El Salvador, Honduras, Guatemala had gathered, along with Anglos, African Americans, and Africans. We all filed in and found seats.

As the service began, the icon of Jesus's body, having been taken down from the cross and given to Joseph of Arimathea, was carried into the sanctuary by four members of the congregation and placed in the center.

> The journey to Resurrection begins. We recognize the pain and the suffering marked in Jesus's own body. We hear the Holy Scriptures and pray for all Creation, all peoples and societies, all religions, and recognize that in the solitude of this Vigil, God weeps with us, over such injustice. The crime—of the death of an innocent—echoes through the centuries, and is still happening in our

own day. The cry of God is not stuck in the past but is ongoing whenever our brothers and sisters are killed unjustly.[1]

There were prayers, recitations, music, and the reading of the Gospel of John. The readings, the music, the lighting engaged the entire body; all of our senses were needed to experience worship. The music spanned European anthems, Black spirituals, and Latino hymns. The readings and prayers were spoken in both English and Spanish. A Tibetan singing bowl announced the beginning and end of the periods of meditation.

According to the senior priest, the Rev. Sam Dessordi Leite, "The liturgy of the Burial is very touching, and visceral. I love the fact that it challenges our bodies. It makes us walk, stand, kneel, prostrate, and touch different textures. And the smells of incense, fresh bread, all the bodily senses are in use for acknowledging God's presence and pain."[2]

As the service came to an end, each person was given a tulip and the icon was carried to the table on the altar that would serve as the tomb. We gathered around and "buried" the icon with our flowers. We approached, pondered, and touched the icon one last time. Then we prostrated ourselves three times and left the sanctuary in silence, collecting our hot cross buns as we left.

While the service lifted up Latin, Central, and South American traditions, I also saw touches of the African tradition in the burial rite. When we prostrated ourselves, some took the prayer position of Muslims. It was a service where you "saw, felt, or heard" yourself regardless of tradition or culture. It was truly multicultural in that no one who attended felt left out. It was Episcopal—the framework of the Eucharist was there—however, a liturgy—the work of the people—enfleshed the bones of tradition. The procession to the altar of repose (the tomb) evoked visions of a New Orleans funeral procession. Everyone laid their tulips on the icon, gathering around the body and tomb as a final act of respect, saying goodbye, and also physically participating in the burial as those who prepared and buried the body of Christ. What a radical welcome for a first-time visitor: to experience worship that lifted up the familiar—a smell, a song, a prayer, a custom.

Anyone who attends an Episcopal service should be able to "see" themselves. They should not have to leave who they are in the narthex. They should not have to assimilate to worship. The preface to the 1979 Book of Common

---

1. Information concerning the service can be found at *https://spark.adobe.com/page/NRdsRMF2LeYFu/?w=0_4812*.

2. Sam Dessordi Leite, personal communication.

Prayer reads, "It is a most invaluable part of that blessed 'liberty wherewith Christ hath made us free,' that in his worship different forms and usages may without offence be allowed, provided the substance of the Faith be kept entire."[3] The Book of Common Prayer permits flexibility in worship and that flexibility will permit us to be both multiracial and multicultural, and above all else, welcoming. What a way to experience worship and to evangelize!

---

3. The Episcopal Church, *The Book of Common Prayer* (New York: Church Publishing, 1979), 9.

24

Drinking the Kool-Aid

Morgan G. Harding

As a teenager, I had two parents running two different households who had two different reasons for going to church. My mother eventually stopped going to church, though Christian values still rule her way of life. My father continues to be a faithful member of his church through today. When I visited his house every other weekend, my way of rebelling was watching music videos while getting ready for Sunday service. Once I graduated from high school, I made the choice to stop my every-other weekend visits with him and I stopped going to church. I still visit my dad, but I do not visit his church. I do not regret my decision.

The stories of my parents and their relationship with Christianity are no different than the other Christians I have met. I have seen how certain teachings affect the lives of those who choose to sit in the sanctuary every Sunday. Through Christianity, God and Jesus become the answer to everything and anything despite how illogical it may seem. If someone is rich, it is because they are blessed. If someone is sick, it is because they are being punished. If someone has not found the right partner yet, it is because they haven't prayed for the right prayer yet; none of this makes sense. I believe there are certain parts of life that cannot be explained by science; however, climate change is a direct result of how humans abuse the planet that God made and it is not a result of the United States legalizing gay marriage. It is such an understanding of Christianity and the Bible that I want to stay away from. That is why I stay away from church. I do not plan on returning.

During my freshman year of college, I did try to attend church again. I had a close friend who grew up near school and their family welcomed me with open arms and took me to church with them. I went a few times and enjoyed my experience, but I eventually stopped going again. While I enjoyed the sermon and, most of all, spending time with my friend and her family, spending three to four hours in church on Sunday did not appeal to me. I did not feel connected to the overall message of salvation, which was the main reason I always found myself trying to stay in the pews. Like those around me, I was afraid of death and the idea of going to hell, yet I was never convinced that everything a pastor said was really the truth. Much of my need for church was fueled by fear and guilt. I felt guilty that many of my curiosities and beliefs were allegedly sinful. Church was supposed to fix that, but it never did. I feared that if I did not go to church, I would eventually go to hell. I love music, especially rap and R&B, which were considered sinful. I liked to dance in ways that some would consider sinful as well, but moving my hips along with the beat is in my DNA as a Black woman. And, of course, there was the issue of sex before marriage. It was easy to wait for sex until marriage in the Bible when girls and women in the Bible were married off during their teenage years. Getting married so young now is taboo, so why is sex before marriage still an issue? Many could not give me a logical answer other than waiting for your husband. But what if I never married? What if someone did not want a husband? Too many churches are still encouraging women to "find their Boaz" as part of their Christian duty.

Once I went to college, the answers—or nonanswers—the Church and Christians gave to my questions did not suffice. I no longer needed church when my professors, textbooks, and social justice organizations provided the solace I needed in a community that I never found at church. Unlike the Church, my professors, many who still believed in God or considered themselves a part of a faith community, provided answers that addressed the sacred and the secular. My professors and textbooks encouraged me to challenge everything around me. They encouraged me to think for myself, which is something the Church did not do, nor do I think the average congregation wants to do, particularly when it comes to issues that face Black people in this country.

While I realize the adults around me were doing the best they can with the resources they had at the time, this no longer works for me as an adult who makes her own decisions. When conversations about homosexuality come up and a person's response starts with, "The Bible says . . . ," I immediately stop listening, because I know they will support their own bigotry with the teachings from the Church. And while I believe everyone is accountable for their own beliefs, I believe the Church, as an institution, needs to be held accountable as well. We live in a time where there is ample information available, yet many of the leaders of the Church do not suggest or encourage their congregations to ask questions or to seek answers from outside of their priest or pastor. They do not encourage reading past the King James version of the Bible or suggest that their congregations take new approaches on how to apply Bible verses to what is happening today, such as—again—issues that face Black people.

An institution that provides the ammunition for other's bigotry is not an institution I want to be a part of. I am interested in saving the world, not the Church. While I think the Church can be saved, that will not happen in its current state. Until the Church confronts its part in racism, homophobia, sexism, and ableism while making their congregations confront their biases as well, you will not see me listed as a member of anyone's congregation.

I believe in God and Jesus Christ. I can still fulfill my role on this planet outside of the sanctuary. When a family member or friend invites me to the church picnic, I will accept their invite, but I will refuse to drink the Kool-Aid. I have tried many churches and I still respect those who find that sitting in a pew every Sunday is an integral part of their lives; however, I know that it is not for me. I am at peace with that. I rather spend my time working with nonprofit organizations who give back to their communities and who are actively trying to fight against systems of oppression than isolate myself in church by refusing to see how the Church plays a part in the very oppression it thinks it is protecting people from.

25

From the Protest Line

WHY ARE YOU THERE?

James C. Harrington

In May 2019, fifty-two of us, organized under the aegis of the DC Chapter of the Union of Black Episcopalians, traveled to Alabama for a civil rights pilgrimage. It was powerful and moving and holy. Upon our return, our UBE organizer, the Rev. Gayle Fisher-Stewart, asked me to write a reflection on my experience as a White civil rights attorney and suggested various topics. "From the protest line—why are you there?" resonated. The phrasing of the question has an interesting ambiguity as to who is addressing whom. I will start with why I have been there and let readers consider why they are there as well, or should be.

During my three-quarters century on the planet, I have walked in too many protest lines to reliably count (probably pushing two hundred). My first was in high school. Since then, I've joined or helped organize protests of all kinds: civil rights, police brutality and killings, antiwar, prounion, proimmigrant, women's rights, United Farm Workers (UFW), and LGBTQ. I still have my UFW flag from the 1966 march on the capitol of Michigan, where I grew up. (My grandma joined me on a UFW line in her late 70s and loved it.) In a broader context, I have always considered my work as being in "the protest line." So Gayle's question is a good one: Why have I been there?

For me, human rights work is about right relation with each other and with God; it is deeply gospel work. A great deal of theology would be involved to unpack this contention—too much for the scope of this writing, but hopefully I can show some of its contours. As my sainted grandmother taught me, if you believe in the gospel, you do the gospel; gospel is a verb. And like any spiritual journey, doing the gospel evolves and hopefully deepens over time.

Sometimes there's a flash of lightning along the journey that changes its trajectory and deepens its meaning, For me, like many in my generation, that lightning bolt was President John Kennedy's call to "ask not what your country can do for you, but what you can do for your country." It moved me in the direction of community service and eventually toward civil rights, which, as a movement, was galvanizing at the time.

I had just entered the Roman Catholic seminary in Columbus, Ohio, as a high school freshman. The Pontifical College Josephinum was a conservative place, directly under papal control, but the Second Vatican Council was getting underway. Its progressive social action agenda meshed with Kennedy's call to action. Civil rights burst onto the scene, propelled by the violence sadistically inflicted by its opponents, which television news relayed across the nation.

We watched shocking brutality on the Huntley-Brinkley Report: the fierce violence against the Freedom Riders (1961); the White mob riots when James Meredith enrolled in the University of Mississippi (1962); the vicious reaction to the 1963 Birmingham Campaign against segregated businesses (1963); the assassination of Medgar Evers for registering voters (1963); the Birmingham Children's Crusade when police used water cannons and snarling dogs to attack the kids (1963); the Sunday morning bombing of Birmingham's 16th Street Baptist Church that killed four little girls (1963); the murders of James Chaney, Andrew Goodman, and Michael Schwerner as part of the violent pushback against Freedom Summer in Mississippi (1964); Bloody Sunday in Selma (1965), including the murders of the Rev. James Reeb, seminarian Johnathan Daniels (now a saint in the Episcopal Church since 1991), and Viola Liuzzo; and the near-fatal shooting of James Meredith in Tennessee on the second day of his March Against Fear (1966).

Personally visiting many of the Alabama sites on the UBE pilgrimage, places that I had only seen on television or in print, was profoundly moving and often painful. It was also a journey of hope, since it showed how much progress had occurred because of people's struggle, suffering, and even death.

Between 1955 and 1968 more than forty civil rights leaders were murdered, including seven clergy members, mostly by police officials or the Ku Klux Klan. Others gave their lives to the cause as well. Houses and churches were regularly firebombed. KKK violence was rampant and fierce. J. Edgar Hoover's FBI and COINTELPRO ran covert smear and disinformation campaigns and even facilitated some Klan aggression.

The nation paused to watch the riveting March on Washington in 1963 and hear the soaring speech of the Rev. Martin Luther King Jr., who himself would be assassinated five years later.

All of this greatly impacted me. I became intent on heading to the South as a priest to work with the civil rights movement and wanted to sign up for the Archdiocese of Atlanta. One of those life-changing quirks of fate (or providence), however, changed this trajectory: the seminary assigned me to study Spanish in high school and college, which led me to doing church work for five summers and then legal work for two summers in southwestern Michigan with 30,000 or so seasonal farm workers who had migrated mostly from the Rio Grande Valley in south Texas. All were of Mexican descent.

Gradually, I became more involved in working against the exploitation and oppression of farm laborers and the Hispanic community generally and moved from activities like church visits to migrant camps to more direct action, such as pushing wage law enforcement and pressuring the governor to enforce the state health code in migrant camps. We marched in Lansing to the capitol and actually caught the governor in a stairwell, trying to sneak out of the building. Since he couldn't get away, he had to address the crowd and promise to do better things, some of which actually came to pass.

By the time I finished college, I was convinced that church authorities would not let me do the human rights work that I felt called to do, whether in Georgia or in Texas—even with Vatican II. A two-week "civil rights" stint at the Catholic Church in Columbus, Mississippi, in the mid-1960s helped cement my view. The pastor was one of those "go slow" clerics (which meant "no go"), like the ones Martin Luther King wrote about in his Letter from a Birmingham Jail. My guess was that the pastor took us there to show us that things weren't actually as bad in Mississippi as the media portrayed.

So I left the seminary, and did a two-year stint in graduate school to pick up a master's in philosophy. I literally had an early Saturday morning wake-up call to abandon my PhD quest, go to law school, and then head to south Texas border, where I landed in 1973 at the South Texas Water Rights Project, associated with the United Farm Workers AFL-CIO, in San Juan.

Texas was violently pried loose from Mexico by Anglo immigrants from the South intent on establishing slavery there. By 1860, one-third of the population of the new state was enslaved, especially in the cotton-producing and farming areas of east and central Texas. The state's sordid history for much of the next ninety years involved widespread lynchings and violence against African Americans in east and central Texas and against *Mexicanos* in south and west Texas—and massive disenfranchisement of both communities.

The historical violence against people of Mexican descent in Texas and the Southwest was as brutal and fierce as that against African Americans. The *Mexicano* community suffered lynchings proportionate to those of Black Americans (somewhere around 4,000 by some accounts) and extrajudicial murders, especially by the likes of the notorious Texas Rangers, who essentially were Klan terrorists with badges instead of robes and hoods. *Mexicanos* were spared the scourge and brutality of slavery, but not segregation ("Juan Crow," it was sometimes called). They worked farmlands at home and around the country at an economic level only slightly better than that of indentured servants or sharecroppers.

By the time I arrived in south Texas, the civil rights movement was already underway, led by the Raza Unida organization, the Farm Workers, and a few other groups. I joined them on the protest lines and did what I could as a lawyer to support their efforts and use the law to give them space to do their organizing. I was always conscious that the growers and other members of the establishment preferred to deal with an Anglo lawyer rather than the Mexican organizers and leaders. It was a delicate dance to make sure our foes had to deal with the community leaders and not short-circuit them by just dealing with the attorney. I learned to take a community leader or two with me to each meeting and support the leader, rather than becoming the leader myself, but always making sure that the other side would find themselves in court that week, if they didn't come around. If already in court, I wanted them to know we were going to mobilize people for the trial.

After ten years along the border, I moved to Austin to serve as the Texas ACLU Legal Director. However, we had a falling out precisely about whether we should be in the community and in the protest line. So I founded the Texas Civil Rights Project in 1990. We eventually ended up with field offices in San Juan, El Paso, Odessa, Houston, and Dallas. We always took direction from the community and supported legally whatever they were doing. Sometimes, we had to encourage them; that we could help them move forward with their goals and programs to the protest line.

There's a long story here, but suffice it to say that organizing and litigation make a good team. Litigation can strengthen community action and solidify the social change brought about. Lawyers need to be on the protest line not only as present-day allies for community support, but also to honor those over the past two centuries who brought us this far through their work and sacrifice—those who have been beaten, ostracized, and have even given their blood for the cause of human rights. We are beneficiaries of their sacrifice; our responsibility is to move the cause forward with our sacrifice.

James Cone, the Black liberation theologian, described how the Anglo and African American communities tend to view the cross differently. For the White community, the cross is too often a symbol of status quo and sometimes even more direct oppression over others. For Blacks, the cross is a symbol of liberation through suffering and sacrifice, even death, that leads to resurrection. Christians, as a matter of doing the gospel, must to be in the latter camp. Our pilgrimage affirmed and honored the journey of so many people and called us into deeper relationship with the Cross, into the suffering of the Cross, into deep solidarity, gospel solidarity, with human rights issues that people continue to suffer through.

On the pilgrimage we concentrated on three cities: Birmingham, Montgomery, and Selma. In each city, we assembled in a church that had been key to the civil rights movement for a presentation by a church representative who had been connected with the civil rights movement in some fashion.

The visit to Birmingham offered a sobering and reflective experience. The city's name is almost synonymous with the civil rights movement. Birmingham was the site of much bloodshed and strife as civil rights leaders faced ferocious opposition and the attempted destruction of their churches and meeting places. Yet, the city has transformed itself to shed the stigma of violence and injustice. We flew into the airport named after civil rights activist Rev. Fred Shuttlesworth.

Our first pilgrimage stop was the Birmingham Civil Rights National Monument, a four-block area of downtown that includes:

- 16th Street Baptist Church, a still-active congregation and the target of the September 1963 bombing that killed four young girls who were preparing for Sunday school. This act of domestic terrorism became a galvanizing force for the passage of the 1964 Civil Rights Act.

- Kelly Ingram Park, where people gathered to begin their demonstrations and where peaceful protesters, including many children, were violently attacked with unleashed police dogs and powerful high-pressure water cannons. Images of the brutal police aggression shocked the nation and the world. Powerful sculptures throughout the park depict police violence against the peaceful demonstrators. Also in the park are two water cannons used against the kids.

- The Birmingham Civil Rights Institute, an interpretive museum.

The visit to 16th Street Baptist Church was especially poignant because of the horrific violence against the young girls. Our presenter at the church had known three of them. The fourth had been visiting the church with a friend. We also saw the large stained glass window of Jesus. His face had been blown out by the blast, but was otherwise intact. It was quite a symbolic statement. It was a place to pray and remember when I first heard the news of the bombing.

Birmingham also has a self-guided civil rights heritage trail that winds through downtown streets, marking actual civil rights events that occurred at various locations and singling out the many celebrities who came to Birmingham to support the economic boycott. It is didactic with reflections from famous people and leaders. I saw one teacher leading her young students on part of the route and discussing the markers, perhaps talking about the question: from the protest line, where are you?

In Montgomery, we visited the National Memorial for Peace and Justice, informally known as the National Lynching Memorial. It was created by the Equal Justice Initiative (EJI), to commemorate the approximately 4,400 African American lynching victims around the country. Walking through the memorial was almost overwhelming. Eight hundred six-foot-long corten steel tiles hang from the ceiling for different counties around the country where lynchings had occurred, with the names of the victims inscribed on each county's tile.

Six million Black people fled the South as refugees and exiles as a result of racist terrorism. In 1919, in what became known as Red Summer, anti-Black White supremacist terrorist attacks rampaged in more than three dozen cities across the United States, causing hundreds of deaths, thousands of casualties, countless burned homes, and profound economic destruction in their wake. The 1921 Tulsa Massacre took three hundred lives and completely levelled the city's Greenwood District, or "Black Wall Street," which was recognized nationally for its affluent African American community.

A historical irony is that the Lynching Memorial in Montgomery sits on a hill above the city, which was once the slavery center of the nation and a staunch perpetrator of segregation and racial violence. I wondered what Montgomery residents and visitors, both Black and White, thought when they looked up toward the stark memorial.

As powerful as the memorial is, even more powerful for me was the Legacy Museum: From Enslavement to Mass Incarceration, also created by EJI. The 11,000-square-foot museum is built on the site of a former warehouse where enslaved Black people were imprisoned. It is midway between an historic slave market and the main river dock and train station where tens of thousands of enslaved people were trafficked during the height of the domestic slave trade. Montgomery became the capitol of the domestic slave trade in Alabama, one of the two largest slave-owning states in America. I walked that distance and again wondered what Black and White Montgomery residents and visitors each thought when they were on that short street.

This interpretive slavery museum is stunning. Its holograms, interactive media, sculpture, videography, and exhibits immerse visitors in the sights and sounds of the domestic slave trade, racial terrorism, the Jim Crow South, and connects them to the American prison system—the world's largest. It underlines America's history of racial injustice and the legacy that remains strong today (the "New Jim Crow," as people sometimes put it).

I was surprised how close Dr. King's church, Dexter Avenue Baptist Church, was to the state capitol—virtually at the end of the capitol parkway slope. I wondered how many times George Wallace looked out his window at the church with disdain and anger.

Dr. King's parsonage was a typical 1950s home, except for the library attached to the back of the house. The important room, though, was the kitchen. It was there, on January 27, 1956, after receiving yet another late night death threat by phone, King got up, made a cup of coffee in the kitchen, buried his face in his hands, and prayed, "Lord, I'm down here trying to do what's right. . . . But . . . I must confess . . . I'm losing my courage." King said he heard "an inner voice saying, 'Martin Luther, stand up for truth. Stand up for justice. Stand up for righteousness.'"[1] He accepted his calling, fully aware that it, most likely, meant accepting his being killed. The fear ceased, but not the threats. Several evenings later, a bomb exploded on the front steps of the house. No one inside was hurt.

King's experience of doubt and trepidation is one shared by people doing civil rights work, although not as threatening as it had once been: how will I protect, support, and care for my family? Am I doing the right thing? What are the long-term consequences from friends and relatives? What kind of danger is out there for doing this? What would I have to anticipate from government surveillance? For me, what always moved me forward was trust in Jesus's "birds of the air" comment in Matthew (6:26) not to be overly concerned with taking care of ourselves and trust that God will provide for those with faith.

No doubt the piercing ambiguity of the question from the past is the same for the present "From the protest line—why are you there?"

In Selma, we gathered at Brown Chapel AME Church, which was the staging point for the Selma to Montgomery March in 1965. As the meeting place

---

1. Information is from the historical interpreter's presentation at the King parsonage.

and offices of the Southern Christian Leadership Conference (SCLC) during the Selma movement, it played a major role in the events that led to adoption of the 1965 Voting Rights Act. The nation's revulsion at Selma's "Bloody Sunday" on March 7, 1965, is widely credited with making the passage of the Voting Rights Act politically possible in the US Congress.

One of the people who marched with Dr. King from Selma to Montgomery was noted Jewish theologian Rabbi Abraham Joshua Heschel, who said, when asked if he had time to pray on the march, that he prayed with his feet. His marching, protesting, and speaking out for civil rights was his greatest prayer of all. Our speaker at Brown Chapel recounted how she, as a young school girl and despite her mother's instructions otherwise, snuck out of school to join the protest.

On March 7, 2015, President Barack Obama and Congressman John Lewis (whom the authorities nearly killed at the bridge in 1965) led 40,000 people across the Edmund Pettus Bridge, commemorating Bloody Sunday's fiftieth anniversary. We likewise followed in the footsteps of the original six hundred marchers—"foot soldiers" as Congress honored them. It was a quiet, sunny day for us; the calm beguiled the blood, chaos, fear, and fierce police aggression of five decades earlier. As Obama said, Selma was "a clarifying moment in US history," even as he acknowledged, "We know the march is not yet over"[2]—a call to the protest line again.

One thing that struck me about our visits to the three cities was that in each location people have organized for years, even decades, often around registering voters. This grassroots organizing laid the groundwork for what was to come in the 1950s and the 1960s. Rev. Fred Shuttlesworth in Birmingham was one of these gritty organizers. He was bombed, beaten, arrested more than thirty times, and involved in more cases as either a defendant or a plaintiff that reached the Supreme Court than any other person in history.

Local organizing matters. It's the tail that wags the dog. We too often think that change comes from on high, but it really comes from the ground up. The federal judges who ultimately helped integrate the South did not do so because they necessarily believed in what they were doing, but because of community pressure. We must keep that in the front of our minds.

I continue to reflect on four personal takeaways from the pilgrimage.

First is how absolutely horrendous and terrifying slavery was, as were the years of Jim Crow segregation that came after. Barbaric slavery was followed by almost a century of White terrorism.

Second, I better understand the importance and justice of reparations. Prior to the pilgrimage, I supported reparations intellectually, but the pilgrimage drew me into it empathetically. America, by law, ripped apart families in slavery, enforced poverty afterwards, denied tools of advancement (such as education), created Jim Crow to prevent advancement, and systematically prevented the accumulation of family wealth that allows upward mobility.

Third, I am awed by the bravery and courage of the tens of thousands of people—primarily people of color—who, for more than two hundred years, have fought back against America's systemic injustice, and many of whom have suffered greatly for their struggle, even to the point of giving their blood. We are the beneficiaries of their "blood, toil, tears, and sweat." We must honor their struggle going forward and answer that troublesome ambiguous question: From the protest line—why are you there?

Fourth, I appreciate more how much I have benefitted from White privilege. Although from a lower working-class background, I understand better, as I reflect on different phases of my life, how privilege helped move me forward. Becoming a lawyer in many respects accentuated that privilege. I have been aware of this for some time and have tried to deal with it, but I did not before understand how far back it went in my life, all the way to growing up on Clifford Street in Lansing. My job, as it has always been, is to use that privilege as an ally to help others move forward with their lives with the opportunity and dignity they deserve.

My life has come full circle. I retired three years ago so I could move forward with a call to eventually serve the Hispanic community as a priest, but still on the protest line, albeit with a different religious dimension. I work with a missional community at St. James' Episcopal Church in Austin. A friend guided me there fifteen years ago. St. James' is an amazing, diverse, multicultural community, formed seventy-six years ago in response to second-class treatment at the hands of the main Episcopal Church in Austin. A community leader in desegregating Austin, St. James' has often answered and still answers, with all its ambiguous possibilities: From the protest line—why are you there? Another way among many to put the question would be: We're on the protest line; where are you?

My gospel challenge now is to help continue and build the protest line in my new form of vocation.

26

Following Jesus While Black

Vincent Powell Harris

One of the most intriguing and thought-provoking stories in the Gospels is the account of Jesus cleansing the temple.

> The Passover of the Jews was near, and Jesus went up to Jerusalem. In the temple he found people selling cattle, sheep, and doves, and the money changers seated at their tables. Making a whip of cords, he drove all of them out of the temple, both the sheep and the cattle. He also poured out the coins of the money changers and overturned their tables. He told those who were selling the doves, "Take these things out of here! Stop making my Father's house a marketplace!" (John 2:13–16)

This incident occurs in all four Gospels, but there are differences in the accounts. In Matthew, Mark, and Luke, it occurs at the end of Jesus's public ministry. In John's Gospel, it occurs at the beginning. Only in John are we told that Jesus fashioned a whip of cords to drive out the money changers and the animal sellers.

Usually we think of Jesus as gentle and inoffensive; we water down his message and focus solely on the meek and mild Jesus. What we sometimes forget is "the revolutionary Jesus" who came into Jerusalem, spoke truth to power, and upset the institutional religious and political systems of his day. Even then, for some reason, we still look for that "gentle and inoffensive" Jesus and, in doing so, we create a modern Jesus who fits that image: a Jesus who challenges nothing, upsets no one, and is not a danger to the status quo. We create a Jesus who comforts us and never disturbs us.

By today's standards, Jesus wouldn't have made a very good politician. Truth be told, he wasn't a good politician in the first century either. A politician has to say things people want to hear to survive in the political arena. Jesus had the habit of saying things that upset people, that challenged their thinking and their attitudes and actions. Many politicians try to win votes by making promises that often twist the truth and bring together people around their own self-interests. Jesus tried to win people by telling and doing the truth. Jesus's cleansing of the temple illustrates this point.

Why did Jesus react so violently against the money changers and animal sellers? To answer that question, we must examine what was going on in the temple at the time.

Every male Jew was required to pay the temple tax of one-half shekel each year, which amounted to nearly two days of pay for a working person. There were many currencies in circulation at the time: Greek, Roman, Tyrian, Syrian, Egyptian; all were considered equally valid. But the tax had to be paid in the half-shekels of the sanctuary, or in ordinary Galilean shekels. The money changers demanded enormous fees to change a coin of equal value. If a larger coin was offered, they charged a commission for the required half-shekel and again for making change. They made huge profits in a deliberate swindle to separate poor people from their money.

Temple vendors who were selling animals for the ritual sacrifices sold their animals for ten or fifteen times more than the vendors on the outside of the temple. They could do so because they were in collusion with the temple animal inspectors who decided whether or not an animal was worthy of sacrifice. Most people felt it was safer to buy animals from the temple vendors because those animals seemed to pass inspection more readily than those bought from the outside vendors. Again, we find an organized, institutionalized victimization of poor people trying to fulfill their religious obligations. The temple animal vendors, in collusion with the temple inspectors, legally robbed poor religious pilgrims. In addition, all the booths where these corrupt practices were taking place belonged to family of the high priest.

To add insult to injury, all of this occurred in what was known as the "Court of the Gentiles"—the only place that Gentiles and others who were considered not "clean" were allowed to worship. The "Court of the Gentiles" was also a good distance away from the "Holy of Holies" and served as a physical reminder of their distance from the God of Abraham, Isaac, and Jacob. Under the threat of the penalty of death, no Gentile dared risk going beyond the "Court of the Gentiles." Imagine the noise and the stench in the only place where Gentiles were allowed to assemble and worship. Jesus did much of his ministry in that area. Jesus was appalled at what was taking place in the temple, which was supposed to be a "House of Prayer for All People." Jesus saw that it had become "a marketplace" and a "den of robbers."

It was not just that the exchange of money or the buying and selling of animals interfered with the dignity and solemnity of worship that prompted such a violent reaction from Jesus. He was outraged that those who were supposed to lead the flock were instead engaged in fleecing and discriminating against them. Jesus saw powerless and vulnerable people being exploited. Jesus saw powerless and vulnerable people being excluded. Jesus cleansed the temple because it had become an affront to God.

For Jesus, it was a matter of religious disrespect and social justice injury. Through his actions in the temple, Jesus conveyed the message that those who commit injustice should not think that they could escape the judgment of God by preserving the outward symbols of religion. The religious establishment of Jesus's day did not accept his radical new direction in religious life, nor did it accept his criticism. Jesus was also a threat to their lucrative and corrupt commercial system and the prevailing religious and social norms to which they adhered.

While it is true that the meek might inherit the earth, it is also true that only the unafraid can carry out the work of the Church within the world. Only the courageous and fearless can put an end to the bitterness, fear, greed, hatred, prejudice, and violence that seem to dominate the world. We, as followers of Jesus, are not called to retreat into the status quo of the society in which we live, but to confront that society head on with what is often an unpopular and unsettling message. It's not always easy to stand on the side of the gospel because of what it might cost us. Yet this is what we are called to do as followers of Jesus.

One such follower of Jesus was a Syrian monk named Telemachus who, in the year 400 CE, was so disturbed at the gladiatorial contests taking place in the Coliseum of Rome that he jumped into the arena in the middle of the gladiators' combat and cried out, "This thing is not right! This thing must stop!"

The spectators, as well as the promoters of the gladiatorial contests, saw Telemachus's actions as interfering with their pleasure and their profits. As a result, Telemachus was run through with a sword and killed, but in dying he set an example that converted people's hearts and consciences. Because of Telemachus's heroic action, within a few months the gladiatorial combats began to decline and ended shortly thereafter. Telemachus, at the expense of his life, cleansed the Coliseum of Rome because he followed the example of Jesus.

Another follower of Jesus, the Rev. Dr. Martin Luther King Jr., was imprisoned in a Birmingham jail in 1963 for protesting racial segregation in that city. While incarcerated, Dr. King wrote an eloquent and profound letter in reply to eight White religious leaders who insisted that he stop all demonstrations against racial apartheid in their city. These leaders included two Methodist bishops, two Episcopal bishops, a Roman Catholic bishop, one Presbyterian minister, one rabbi, and one Baptist pastor. They thought that King's challenge to the segregated system in Birmingham was ill-conceived and ill-timed.

Dr. King's response evoked Jesus's response to what he saw in the temple that day:

In the midst of a mighty struggle to rid our nation of racial and economic injustice, I have heard so many ministers say, "Those are social issues which the gospel has nothing to do with," and I have watched so many churches commit themselves to a completely otherworldly religion which made a strange distinction between bodies and souls, the sacred and the secular.

There was a time when the church was very powerful. It was during that period that the early Christians rejoiced when they were deemed worthy to suffer for what they believed. In those days the church was not merely a thermometer that recorded the ideas and principles of popular opinion; it was the thermostat that transformed the mores of society. Wherever the early Christians entered a town the power structure got disturbed and immediately sought to convict them for being "disturbers of the peace" and "outside agitators." But they went on with the conviction that they were "a colony of heaven" and had to obey God rather than man. They were small in number but big in commitment. They were too God-intoxicated to be "astronomically intimidated." They brought an end to such ancient evils as infanticide and gladiatorial contest.

Things are different now. The contemporary church is so often a weak, ineffectual voice with an uncertain sound. It is so often the arch supporter of the status quo. Far from being disturbed by the presence of the church, the power structure of the average community is consoled by the church's often vocal sanction of things as they are.

But the judgment of God is upon the church as never before. If the church of today does not recapture the sacrificial spirit of the early church, it will lose its authentic ring, forfeit the loyalty of millions, and be dismissed as an irrelevant social club with no meaning for the twentieth century. I meet young people every day whose disappointment with the church has risen to outright disgust.[1]

Dr. King's critique of the Church is as relevant today as it was in 1963. Yet, despite his disappointment with the Church, Dr. King fearlessly and

---

1. Martin Luther King Jr., "Letter from a Birmingham Jail," August 1963, *https://web.cn.edu/kwheeler/documents/Letter_Birmingham_Jail.pdf*.

courageously fought Jim Crow segregation, opposed the Vietnam War, and championed the cause of poor people. He worked to cleanse the city of Birmingham of its segregationist practices because he was a follower of Jesus. His witness to the gospel eventually cost him his life.

Following Jesus may not mean losing our lives confronting the "principalities and powers of this world" like Telemachus and Dr. King. However, following Jesus can lead to occasions that require us to challenge the status quo at the risk of enmity and marginalization.

In the late fifties and early sixties there was a TV series called *The Naked City*. It was famous for the iconic line, "There are eight million stories in the Naked City and this is one of them." Well, there are 1.7 million stories in the "Naked Church," and I offer three from the perspective of an African American priest in the Episcopal Church who is trying to follow Jesus.

I was a newly ordained priest and a member of the Division of Social Ministry in my then diocese when a resolution was passed at our diocesan convention instructing the Division of Social Ministry to study the conditions of migrant workers in our area, most of whom were African American or Hispanic. We were asked to report back to the next diocesan convention. I suggested that, as the Division of Social Ministry, we should actually visit the migrant worker camps and document the conditions we found through interviews and photographs, in addition to reading and discussing books, reports, and papers on migrant worker conditions. After all, that was what we had been asked to do.

We scheduled interviews with people who provided support for migrant workers and we visited several camps. Before we could put together our report for the next diocesan convention, the chairperson of the Division of Social Ministry received a call from the Canon to the Ordinary who had received a call from one of the owners of a farm and a migrant camp where we had conducted our inquiry. This person, who was a member of an Episcopal Church in the area, asked the Canon to the Ordinary why the diocese, particularly the Division of Social Ministry, was asking questions about a situation that was not really the business of the Church. The Canon to the Ordinary obviously agreed with the caller because we were told to stop what we were doing and that our report would not be necessary. We had crossed a line we did not know about. Even one of my fellow White presbyters called me a communist because of my involvement in this undertaking.

Another incident was a meeting I attended at the Washington National Cathedral right after the collapse of the Soviet Union. We discussed the implications for the Church in what was called, at the time, the "New World Order."

Clerics, college professors, seminary professors, and State Department members attended the meeting. A discussion arose about the change in world power politics now that the Soviet Union had collapsed. One attendee asked what Jesus would say about power politics in a global context without a Cold War. The answer given by one of the priests who was present was interesting, if not surprising: "What could a first-century rabbi tell us about twentieth-century global power politics?"

The implication was that Jesus was of no help when it came to global politics. Jesus was relegated to the ethereal world rather than being intimately involved in the real world.

I had recently read an article about the "Theology of Letting Go" that talked about looking at the world from a different perspective because one had experienced a conversion. Such a perspective leads people who benefit from the way a society is structured to realize that a radical change is needed to that structure or people who are not benefitting from it will continue to suffer from an existential condition that is without predictability or security affecting their material and psychological well-being.[2]

The "Theology of Letting Go" voluntary relinquishes the privileges of power, control, and domination in order to free both the oppressed and the oppressor from the adversarial chains that pit them against each other, thus creating opportunity for new relationships to emerge where all members of a society enjoy freedom, dignity, security, respect, and access to the basic means of life.

I asked the group if a "Theology of Letting Go" could be part of this New World order we were discussing. I also remarked that I was aware of the oft-repeated observation that power is never given up; rather, it must be taken. A seminary professor who was sitting across from me and who had taught me ethics when I was a student leaned in my direction and said forcefully, "Now you are being a realist. No one voluntarily gives up power. You have to take it."

I took what he said to mean that he, a White man, would protect his power by any means necessary and I, a Black man, was naïve to think otherwise. End of discussion.

The meeting was revealing to say the least. It revealed how tangential Jesus's message was to some in providing solutions to world and societal issues and how the entrenched attitudes of White power and White privilege permeate not only the larger society, but the Church as well.

---

2. Elise Boulding, "A Socio-Theology of Letting Go: The Role of a First World Church Facing Third World Peoples," *Sociology of Religion* 39, no. 2 (Summer 1978): 187–88, *https://doi.org/10.2307/3710225*.

The third story is related to the second. As I was driving home from the meeting at the Cathedral, I remembered a previous encounter with the ethics professor as a member of my seminary's alumni association. In alternating years, there was a joint meeting of faculty and alumni to discuss contemporary issues in Church and society, as well as other topics. One year a faculty member would present, and the next year the presentation would come from the alumni.

At one of these gatherings, the ethics professor gave his presentation, and included a reference about Black people's deviant behavior. He talked about out-of-wedlock births, substance abuse, and crime as examples of the deviant behaviors that plagued the Black community and how they needed to be addressed. He even stated that Jesse Jackson Sr. agreed with what he was saying, as if that gave him permission to state this trope.

I was appalled. As an African American, I had heard the argument many times from well-heeled conservatives who would trot out these standard talking points to justify continued Black inequality. It was the classic blame the victim canard that is always intended to deny the role that systematic White racism plays in the unequal treatment Black people experience every day in this country.

My response to his irritating presentation was to point out that Marla Maples, who at the time was pregnant and in a relationship with Donald Trump, though not married, was on television asking the public to suggest names for her unborn child. Was that not deviant behavior? Or did having lots of money cover a multitude of sins? I also mentioned Michael Milken, the White Wall Street financier who was known for his role in the development of the market for high-yield bonds (junk bonds) and had pled guilty to felony charges of violating US securities laws. Ivan Boesky had also been convicted. Both men cost their investors, many of them pension fund investors, millions of dollars that affected the retirement income of thousands of people. Was that not deviant behavior? Or did having millions of dollars cover a multitude of sins? The professor did not respond and sat down.

There are 1.7 million stories in the "Naked Church." These have been just three of them.

The gospel is good news because it radically calls into question a world built without the recognition of the God whose inherent nature is justice and whose intrinsic nature does not value things that are contrary to God's will as revealed in the life and ministry of Jesus, who said that love of God and love of neighbor were the two commandments on which hung all the Law and the Prophets. When one believes in and proclaims this message, confrontation with the principalities and powers of this world is unavoidable. A gospel that bothers no one and questions nothing is no longer the gospel.

As we strive to follow the examples of Jesus, Telemachus, and Dr. King, we may feel at times that we are fighting a losing battle in a world that seems indifferent to the good news of God's reign. Even though we may be disparaged as dreamers or called agitators, we must not yield to the fear that leads to apathy, hopelessness, and indecision.

We cannot afford to forget that the unconquerable strength that is available to us is a gift from almighty God—the God who never abandons us despite all appearances to the contrary. And this strength is in proportion to the trust that we place in the one whose cause we have embraced. It is with full assurance of God's strength and power that we welcome and exercise our mission as witnesses to Christ proclaiming the good news in word and deed. We are joyful and confident to share with others the hope and trust that animate us without any form of arrogance or presumption because we know that our strength is not our own, for it is God in Christ Jesus who strengthens us.

Preaching from the Margins

F. Willis Johnson

But Peter said, "I have no silver or gold, but what I have I give you; in the name of Jesus Christ of Nazareth, stand up and walk." (Acts 3:6)

Humanity has become estranged from one another. Technology has advanced our means for greater connectivity and accessibility across time and geography, created cyber linkages that enable inexhaustible inquisitiveness, and fuels both a never-ending news cycle and an inextricable global economy, yet people are estranged from one another. Our history and practices have evolved, and still we return to inhumanness and injustice. My critique is not directed specifically at titans of industry, our democratic ideals and institutions, or global citizenship. It is, rather, an inclusive reference that speaks to all humanity.

The implied "them" in the term "humanity" actually means "us." The intellectual projection onto heartless and faceless examples of systems and culture is useful to create distance—distance between "here," our respective social location, and "there," where all that is not right or righteous exists. To say humanity is estranged simply means that each of us has turned away in feeling or affection. We have been unfriendly or hostile, and alienated ourselves from one another.

These exercises of indifference are not just what "they" do, but us—Christians—following along as well. Unjust acts elsewhere are unjust everywhere, near and here in the Church. Visible and proverbial walls, borders, gerrymandered and red lines, inner-city beltways, false social constructs of racial-ethnic-sexual-gender identity, nor interpretative and doctrinal positions, to name a few, are markings of marginalization; are signs of divide and indifference.

The biblical narrative in Acts 3 highlights an encounter at the Gates of Beautiful where the gospel message addresses matters of the margins. A man crippled from birth was carried and placed outside the entrance of the church, a common practice that easily identified persons needing help: prominently placed at a boundary close, yet distant, so as not to impede churchgoers.

Currently, the scarred, poor, busied, lonely, and those who need care are not as easily distinguishable, especially when historical precedents and social constructs are not employed. The uninsured reside both in center city slums and suburban condos. The drug epidemic is problematic for rural and rich and poor alike. More than ever more persons exist along some margin.

Therefore, it is important that the good news of Jesus Christ always searches and speaks to shared realities and responsibilities of all of us for those in the margins. Despite challenges of identifying with marginalized peoples, places, and predicaments while helping others, we ourselves remain answerable for ways our power fosters injustice. Practitioners who proclaim the gospel ought to operate in this spirit of expectation.

Whether you already preach or strive in solidarity with identified oppressed and vulnerable persons, there is an interrogative embedded in every homiletical and theological question: What does it mean to preach from the margins? What theological messages are more pertinent than others? How are we to connect the powerful and powerless through our preaching and so on? Inherent in these questions of challenge, mechanics, and aesthetics of preaching is this summative interrogative: "How do we help people be more human to the satisfaction of the divine expectation?"

A paradigm shift is required, a transition from seeing "others" as objects. Instead, we must respect others as subjects of God's grace-filled story of collective liberation. This commences with demystifying preaching focused on marginal subjects.

Preaching concentrated on marginal subjects should not further relational toxicity, engender piety or reliance, nor lead to gentrifying of others' experiences and spaces. Preaching at its core is a message of liberation and the promise of shalom.

Like Peter and John, everyone has a tradition that informs them. Examples and experiences that frame their worldview or give lyrics to their song. The Black church was my tradition of formation. The Black church is more diverse today than any other period. Diversity within African American and diaspora communities presents unique queries regarding preaching in an ever-changing setting. This conundrum not only challenges historically marginalized experiences, it is phenomena transcending race, politics, denomination, and geography.

Redress of marginal subjects requires all practitioners to attend to expectations similar to the Gates of Beautiful encounter. Our preaching must meet and speak to persons on the outside looking in while modeling for people inside peeping out. In other words, how do we meet people in their condition with unconditional love? Hence the practice of preaching focused on marginal subjects encourages reflection on one's own understanding of privilege, pronouncements, and power.

Practitioners must account for their respective privilege of position. Likewise, invitations need to be extended for others to note their respective social locations, taking inventory of their advantages, assurances, autonomy, and inalienable rightness accessible to them.

A central focus of preachment is God's present action in human life purposed toward change in hearers. Immersion in the life and situations of those we are privileged to preach and do life with is paramount. Also, alignment of biblical text to their contextual existence is nonnegotiable. Biblical interpretations must meet people where they are.

Peter and John offered nothing less than they possessed. They offered no more than they were willing to personally sacrifice. It is incumbent that practitioners remain answerable to the critiques, commentary, and strategies they raise. Prophetic pronouncements can be evaluated by this rubric: Are our efforts deployed toward the ends of help and hope or hurt and harm? Are these assets and actions liberating or further debilitating of others? Is our involvement fueled by means of grace and gratitude or grievance and greed? Is this an exercise inviting collective activation and employing our faith?

Lastly, practitioners concentrating on the margins respect that their posits, interpretations, and models are not absolute. Rather, we operate as those graced with permission to invite persons into the purpose and promises of God. The encouragement and strategies given are divinely inspired and sanctioned. We dare invite others to cross over, go beyond, imagine, confess, forgive, and love. It is by divine permission that we empower others to becoming and receiving what is on the other side of the Beautiful Gate.

28

Why Are You Throwing Yourself on This Fire?

Mike Kinman

It was early November 2014, and I was hiking in Northern California with my colleague group, eight brothers with whom thirteen years before I had covenanted to be in lifelong sacred community. We were learning how to love each other so deeply that we could ask each other the questions no one else dared. So, it was no surprise that one of my brothers, Dan, was the first person to ask me the question I knew so many others had wanted to ask, "Why are you throwing yourself on this fire?"

It had been nearly three months since Ferguson police officer Darren Wilson had murdered eighteen-year-old Michael Brown Jr. Nearly three months since Brown's body had laid in the street for four and a half hours. Nearly three months since the community that gathered in grief and lamentation had been met with tear gas, police dogs, and rubber bullets. Nearly three months since an uprising that started on the streets of Ferguson had become the longest sustained American civil rights protest since the Montgomery Bus Boycott.

In those three months, I had been challenged to be a part of that uprising. I had been challenged to acknowledge my privilege as a cis-gender, straight, White, male faith leader of the Episcopal Cathedral in one of the most segregated cities in America. To acknowledge my privilege, not as an act of shame, but to claim the gift of using it not as a leader but as a follower, not as someone who took up space for myself but who held and protected space for others, not as someone who filled the air with the sound of my own voice but as an amplifier of the prophetic voices coming from the young, Black, and often queer leaders who were midwifing the movement on the streets of our city.

In those three months, as I had tried to do these things haltingly and imperfectly, I had become one of the White people to whom the Episcopal Church looked to try to understand what was happening in what had become a global moment turned movement. In those three months, I had struggled with my own feelings of shame and guilt—and knew that journey was just beginning. In those three months, I had met Jesus again. A Jesus who is a revolutionary. A Jesus who, through my friend, the Rev. Traci Blackmon, looked me in the eye and told me I needed to "sit down in my discomfort." A Jesus whose body I experienced being re-membered on the street in front of the Ferguson Police Department through simple words I had said my entire life but now had new and infinite depths of meaning as I heard them being spoken by the young people gathered there: family, solidarity, love.

Through conversation with South African theologian Allan Boesak, I realized that I had indeed been radicalized—in the truest sense of that word. I was having an experience of *the root* of the movement that came from Jesus of Nazareth, a movement that had been co-opted and softened and changed from a movement of revolution to a chaplaincy of Empire. In those three months, people I loved and people who loved me—family, friends, colleagues, my congregation at Christ Church Cathedral—struggled with me as I struggled with this moment in history that was unfolding before us. Struggled with me as I struggled to find ways to explain the journey that Jesus was leading me on, convinced that they all were part of the journey as well. I struggled not to be absolutely insufferable in the process, for there is truly no zealot like a convert. I struggled with my responsibilities as a leader of an institution with major financial problems even as I came to understand the spiritual crisis and opportunity we were facing was so much greater.

I should have been ready when Dan asked, "Why are you throwing yourself on this fire?" I should have been ready, but I wasn't. And I'm glad I wasn't. Because instead of an intellectual argument, all I had to give was what my heart wanted to scream, "Because my friends are on that fire."

When Gayle approached me about writing an essay for this book, I hesitated. Did we really need one more White voice taking up space in this era where the backlash of White supremacy against movements for Black and Brown lives is so strong? Did we really need one more male voice taking up bandwidth when voices of women and gender nonconforming persons are struggling to be heard? What do you want me to write about?

"Why do you do it?" she asked. "You serve a predominantly White congregation. If you never mentioned race, it would probably be ok. You could have a very successful life without preaching about race or social justice. You could have a cushy job if you wanted to." (I'm not sure I agree with that.) "What drives you to preach and teach to a largely White congregation about White supremacy and racial equity?"

As she spoke, I heard Dan's question: "Why are you throwing yourself on this fire?"

I wrote this on the fifth anniversary of the Ferguson Uprising. I have since moved from where I had my initial Damascus experience in Ferguson and at Christ Church Cathedral in St. Louis to be rector of All Saints Church in Pasadena, a church with its own incredible history of following a revolutionary Jesus. As we as a nation experience more and more violent backlashes against the movements that sprung from the murders of Trayvon and Mike and Sandra and too many others, I know it is time for me to answer that question again. And this time, more deeply.

One of the biggest blessings of my eight years at Christ Church Cathedral was Kris. Kris is as faithful a person as I have ever known, and she found my involvement with the uprising in Ferguson deeply problematic. And she hung in with me and with the Cathedral because that's what faith and love look like.

Kris asked me out to lunch so I could talk about why I was doing what I was doing—why I was throwing myself and Christ Church Cathedral on this fire. As I stumbled through my story, seeking not to convert her but just to share what was happening to me, she didn't say a word. When I finished, Kris took a deep breath, looked at me with a smile and said, "I still don't agree with you, but I can tell that you are on a real journey."

In other words, "You are going through something real." I could not have imagined more healing words at that moment. I didn't need Kris to agree with me. I didn't even need her to understand me. I needed her to understand that something was happening to me. And what was happening to me was real.

That's what the rest of this essay is. A story of this journey as it continues to unfold. I am structuring it around four quotes that have shaped my journey. I share it understanding that it is an unfinished journey and that you are on a real journey along with your community of faith. We are all invited by a revolutionary Jesus to "sit down in our discomfort," to be a part of the Jesus movement that has never died and in fact is being reborn right now on our streets and in our communities. I pray our journeys can help each other.

"What do you want me to do for you?" —Jesus

"Stop killing us!" —Alexis Templeton

One of the scriptures that has guided me on this journey is the story of Bartimaeus in Mark 10. In fact, it has done more than that. The passage has reshaped my entire understanding of church. Jesus and his crew are heading for Jerusalem. They are on a mission. They have important people to see and important work to do. It is a march for justice, and justice will not be denied. On the way, Bartimaeus, a blind beggar who sits by the side of the road, one of the furthest outside in a world full of outsiders, cries out as Jesus passes by, "Jesus, Son of David, have mercy on me!"

In the timeless tradition of respectability politics, Jesus's disciples think they know what's really important. They are on their way for a big meeting and Bartimaeus is not the sort of person that someone who wants to be taken seriously by governors and kings needs to be associated with. So, the disciples, in the words of Darren Wilson to Mike Brown Jr., turn to Bartimaeus and say, "Get the f@*k out of the street."

I once heard my friend Amy Hunter ask, "How might Darren Wilson's encounter with Mike Brown had gone differently if he had just said something different? If he had just acknowledged his humanity?" The story tells us how. Bartimaeus refuses to be treated like less than human; scripture tells us "he shouted out all the more." And then something transformational happens: Jesus stops. And when Jesus stops, everybody stops. The entire Jesus movement stops in its tracks because a blind beggar is crying out.

The story doesn't end there. Jesus says, "Bring him to me." And the disciples, hustling to act like they hadn't just told Bartimaeus to get out of the street, tell Bartimaeus to come to Jesus. Bartimaeus throws off his cloak—he's completely naked now—and stands before Jesus, who asks, "What do you want me to do for you?"

Can you see what Jesus is doing here? Jesus stops everything to take the most marginalized person, put him at the center of the community, and let him set the agenda for the entire community. Why? Because it is those who among us who have been the most targeted, marginalized, and oppressed who know most clearly and deeply what healing needs to happen. Reconciliation and healing are the central mission of the Church. Paul tells us, "All this is from God, who reconciled us to the divine self through Christ and gave us the ministry of reconciliation" (2 Cor. 5:18).

When I was installed as rector of All Saints Church, Becca Stevens (who, with the women of Thistle Farms, has taught me more about what it means to be church than anyone else) reminded me to "practice the one sacrament of the Church with its seven prisms: healing."[1] How do we do that? Where do we

---

1. Personal communication.

start? Alice Walker writes, "Healing begins where the wound was made."[2] Bartimaeus knows what healing needs to happen because he is the one who carries the wound. Bartimaeus is the only one who can tell the church what our work is because he is the one who carries the wound that needs to be healed.

"What do you want me to do for you?"

"I want to see."

And Jesus heals. Scripture tells us that "Bartimaeus joined them on the way." That's the Church. Right there. Who is screaming in pain from the margins? Who are the prophets of the movement? Who are we not hearing? Who are the champions of respectability telling us to "get the f@*k out of the street?"

That's whose rightful place is in the center of the community.

That's who needs to be setting the agenda for the rest of the church.

That's who leads the march into the center of power.

That's the work of a revolutionary Jesus.

That's the gift of being Church.

In September 2014, I stood in the street in front of the Ferguson Police Department and met Bartimaeus. Her name was Brittany Ferrell. Their name was Alexis Templeton. They faced a line of police in riot gear, menacingly tapping their batons against their shin guards.

And Brittany cried out, "I am a person!" (Jesus, Son of David, have mercy on me!)

And the people asked Alexis, "What do you want?"

And Alexis cried out, "Stop killing us!"

Brittany and Alexis were not looking to the Church for help. They had seen us for who we were. We were truly the disciples of Jesus, more interested in preserving our respectability than in healing the wounds. We were no better than Darren Wilson. In some ways we were worse because the Church was standing with the police telling the protesters to get the hell off the street. My collar did not give me any authority. My collar made me suspect. For they saw the Church as the church that Jeremiah railed against, one that was preaching "peace, peace" when there was no peace. The only authority I would ever have in this movement would come if I decided actually to try to act like Jesus. If I actually decided to try to let Jesus act through me.

The only authority we will ever have in the Jesus movements that are happening all around us is if instead of ignoring them or trying to lead them,

---

2. Alice Walker, *The Way Forward Is with a Broken Heart* (New York: Ballentine Books, 2012), 217.

we use our privilege and authority to center the voices of those among us who are most marginalized and let them determine the agenda for healing for the Church. Those people have been out there for a long, long time. The people outside our churches know who they are. Those of us inside the Church will never know who they are until we get out of our churches and listen. And follow.

The church is being reborn. The church is always being reborn.

A month before I arrived in Pasadena, officers from the Pasadena Police Department killed an unarmed Black man, J. R. Thomas, a father of eight. Soon afterward, a brilliant young local Black theologian and activist, Andre Henry, began a gathering of lamentation every Thursday night at the Pasadena Police Department. He called it "subversive liturgy." It was subversive. And it was nothing new. It was Bartimaeus crying by the side of the road, "Jesus, Son of David, have mercy on me." It was Alexis Templeton crying, "Stop killing us." Easter Sunday 2019, at the central services of the liturgical year, Andre Henry and I preached together, side by side. Why? Because the prophets of the movement belong in the center of the community.

Who is it in your church? Who is crying from within and crying from without? Who is being silenced and yet is shouting out all the more? Who needs to claim their rightful place at the center of your church so Jesus can ask, "What do you want me to do for you?"

> "Reconciliation without equity is just telling the powerless to be reconciled to their fate." —The Rev. Dr. Starsky Wilson

Reconciliation. Healing. This is the central mission of the Church. Paul tells us this: "All this is from God, who reconciled us to the divine self through Christ and gave us the ministry of reconciliation" (2 Cor. 5:8). In our own Episcopal prayer book, the mission of the Church is "to restore all people to unity with God and each other in Christ."[3] Reconciliation. Healing. The central mission of the Church.

Since I was radicalized by Jesus the revolutionary, I have routinely been called divisive. I have been told I had no place in a church that is about reconciliation because I have clearly been standing with one side against another—and standing with people whose language is causing conflict and even inciting violence. For most of the first year of the Ferguson Uprising, I answered those charges by noting that I was not creating division; I was

---

3. The Episcopal Church, *The Book of Common Prayer* (New York: Church Publishing, 1979), 855.

merely standing with those whose cries revealed the division that already existed. I was standing with those who revealed the necessity of the church's mission of reconciliation.

On the one-year anniversary of Mike Brown's murder, I stood in the back of Greater St. Mark's Church in Ferguson while my friend, Starsky Wilson, spoke on a panel. Someone asked him why, as a pastor, he wasn't trying to lead the protesters into peace and reconciliation. Starsky didn't pause for a moment. Yes, the church's mission was reconciliation. And that was not the same as keeping the peace. In fact, in times like this, peace was the enemy of reconciliation. You see, Starsky said, you can't have reconciliation if you don't have equity. As long as there are oppressors and oppressed, what might look like reconciliation is truly a false unity, a false peace. "Reconciliation without equity is just telling the powerless to be reconciled to their fate."

There are massive inequities in our country. There are massive inequities in our Church. These inequities, more than anything else, divide us by race, gender, generation and orientation. These inequities create divisions of class. It has never been more important than today for the Church to embrace our mission of reconciliation. That means we have to name and heal the deep inequities in our church, in our nation, and in the world, which is, ultimately, deeply generative and joyful work.

But getting to that place of generativity and joy is a heavy lift, made all the more difficult by the Church's lack of understanding of and experience with the sacramental tool we already have that is our roadmap for the journey. Inequity is sin rooted in sin. Inequity is sin because it is death producing. Inequity is sin rooted in sin because the fertile ground in which inequity flourishes is what Paul Tillich rightly noted as the essence of sin: estrangement.

We are estranged from each other.

And because we are, we fear each other.

We do not hear or see or feel each other.

We are not moved by or care about each other.

We do not recognize how our past and present lives impact each other.

We are content to let some of us flourish and others of us drown.

Inequity, rooted in the historic and present estrangement from and denial of God's image in each other, is the barrier to the unity God dreams for us. And yet God has given us a sacramental gift to make that dream a reality. Estrangement? Inequity? Sin? We've got an app for that. Our sacramental theology of reconciliation gives us a way to overcome estrangement, dismantle systems of oppression, and achieve God's dream of true reconciliation—reconciliation with equity. The right tool for the job has been with us all along.

The sacrament of reconciliation has five stages, each of which must be engaged fully, lovingly, and prayerfully.

1. Self-examination. Listen. Listen deeply to one another. Listen to the cries of our hearts. Listen to the songs of our souls. Look deep into our lives now and into our histories. How have we allowed ourselves to become estranged from one another? How have our actions created inequities? How have some of us benefitted and others of us suffered from those inequities? What structures perpetuate that estrangement and those inequities? What are the stories of the wounds? Together, can we create safe, brave spaces to share those stories? To show the wounds? To speak and hear deep, deep truth of ourselves and our ancestors? Can we be truly, deeply, profoundly real with each other about how we have hurt and continue to hurt one another?

2. Confession. Speak. Once we have identified the estrangement, the inequity, the wound, the sin, say it. Say it out loud. It's liberating. We no longer need to hide it. We no longer need to be afraid of someone finding out. Once we say it, we can deal with it. Once we say it, the healing can happen. Once we say it, we can invite God's grace and love to do her stuff!

3. Repentance and Reparation. What does it mean to repair the damage that has been done? There is a price that needs to be paid, not because some of us are bad and unworthy but because it is our joy to bring healing to the nations and peoples. What breaches need to be repaired? What wrongs need to be righted? Reparation is not taking from one side and giving to another. It is recognizing that there are no sides and therefore it is an act of enrichment for us all, for when we hoard at the expense of another it is to all of our poverty.

4. Amendment of Life. How do we change the way we live so that we don't fall into old patterns of estrangement and inequity? How do we bind ourselves together in relationships of loving support and accountability so hurting one another would be so deeply painful as to be inconceivable? How do we truly maintain a eucharistic community—everyone gathered around Christ's table, offering our lives in full for God and one another, and receiving the new life of Christ and each other in return. What needs to be dismantled and destroyed forever? What needs to be built anew?

5. Absolution. God sings. God dances. God sculpts and paints and plays. And through it all, God says those words God has said throughout creation: This is very good. You are very good. Only, this time we believe it. We accept fully our own goodness and lovability because it is not just a concept but our way of life. The sin no longer exists because there is no more estrangement. No more inequity. All is blessing and all are blessed.

This is the work of the Church. Yet far from embracing it, the Church has for centuries in its participation in oppression, embrace of Empire, and fear of death and loss, convinced ourselves that segregation and inequity are actually tolerable if not outright divinely ordained. Why? Because our hearts know. And our hearts fear. We know that those of us who have power in Church and society have acquired and maintained that power through estrangement and inequity. We fear what will happen if we lose that power, if we lose that privilege. Because in those moments where we let ourselves truly see and hear, we quickly go to that place of shame and the discomfort that shuts us down because we are estranged from each other and from God. Because we do not have those relationships of deep, secure attachment from which courage comes, we become not those who have faith and preserve our souls but instead those who shrink back and perish.

Shame. I have come up against it in myself and in the communities of my White cousins where I have served. Shame is powerful. And yet shame can also be an amazing teacher. Shame can guide us into that first, transformative step of the process of reconciliation. Shame can be our teacher if we can invite it in, learn from it, and then let it go. Shame can be our teacher, if we can believe that shame can never define us. Only one thing can define us.

"Love without judgment." —Becca Stevens and the women of Thistle Farms

If my whole life fell apart, if all my secrets were told to all, if I was rejected by my church, my friends, my family, if I was despised and shamed before the world, I know where I would go. I would go to Thistle Farms.

Thistle Farms (formerly Magdalene) is a community of and for women who have survived sexual exploitation, prostitution, violence, and drug abuse. It was founded more than twenty years ago by the Rev. Becca Stevens. She and the women who make up the global Thistle Farms community are my spiritual guides. There are beautiful spiritual principles that undergird the Thistle Farms community:

Come together.

Remember you have been in the ditch.

Unite your sexuality and spirituality.

Forgive and feel freedom.

Love without judgment.

The most transformational for me has always been "Love without judgment."

Love without judgment is the essence of the Christ. Love without judgment means no matter what I have done, I am loved beyond measure. Love without judgment means I can be maximally courageous because I need never fear losing anything, because the only thing that matters—love—is the one thing I can never lose. Love without judgment means I can—we can—do the deep self-examination required for reconciliation because we know that, as Bryan Stevenson says, we are all more than the worst thing we have ever done. We can confess deeply because we know our sins do not define us. Love without judgment means that shame can be our teacher and then we can let it go. Love without judgment means that reconciliation is truly about liberation for everyone. When we trust that we are loved without judgment, there is nothing we can't do for love of God and one another and no reason not to do it. It is the perfect love that casts out fear. It is the perfect love that is perfect freedom. Love without judgment can heal the world. Love without judgment will save us all.

To stop what we are doing and bring the Bartimaeuses of the world into their rightful place in the center of the community and letting them define our mission is the hard work that will tempt us to fear. Doing the deep work of self-examination, confession, repentance, and reparation, and amendment of life that leads to the resurrection life of absolution is hard work that will tempt us to fear. Love without judgment is how we do it all. Love without judgment is how the work becomes not obligation but joy.

When we believe we are loved without judgment, we begin to love others without judgment too. When we believe we are loved without judgment, we stop looking at the person crying out in the road as a freak we need to speed past and start looking at them as a gift to be embraced because we have been that person crying out and we have been told not to "get the f@*k out of the street," but we have also been embraced with the nonjudgmental, eternal, exquisite, healing love of God.

Love without judgment is the key to it all. It is the fire that burns in the heart of the body of Christ, in the heart of all creation. It is the essence of the Spirit that God continually breathes into each and all of us. It is why we speak of the Holy Spirit as fire.

I can still hear Dan asking me, "Why are you throwing yourself on that fire?" I am learning that my answer to him was true, but not the whole truth. Yes, my friends were on that fire. Yes, my friends are on that fire. And I am on that fire too—as are you, and the Church, and all of creation. For the fire is not a fire that consumes, but the burning bush that will never be consumed. The fire is the fire of love. The fire is where the love is.

Love without judgment.

Love without blindness.

Love without estrangement.

Love without inequity.

Why am I still trying to throw myself and the church on this fire?

Because the fire is the Church.

The fire is the love.

The love that will heal the world.

The love that will save us all.

29

I Am a White Guy[1]

Steve Lawler

I am a White guy. It is nothing I was told. I rarely have to explain it. For most of my life, I would say I haven't had to talk about what being White means. I am also male, educated, ordained, and privileged in a host of ways. Those things matter, but not as much as being White has in these past few months. Since I am giving context and descriptors of my identity, I have to mention Ferguson, Missouri. Since the end of 2001, I have been rector of St. Stephen's and the Vine in Ferguson, Missouri. Before Michael Brown was killed, I knew I worked in a multiracial community. The parish includes Black, White, and multiracial members. Neighborhoods, schools, stores, and occasional parades in Ferguson are various iterations of Blackness and Whiteness, but rarely exclusively one or the other. I grew up in a multiracial parish and live in a neighborhood that is majority African American. My experience with being in racially diverse communities is not new. Talking about being White with more and more White people is what's new.

After Michael Brown was killed, I felt my being White was inescapably and explicitly in everything I experienced like Blackness is for some of my African American friends and colleagues. I am tempted to say something about my experience being unique or particular, except that I increasingly see how the idea of a particular and unique legacy of a way of being White that operates in the background, slightly underneath the surface, is new. It is not something of which I am conscious most of the time. Unique and individualistic turns into being special and it also turns into ideas about all people being the same—uniquely created in the image of God, and probably unconsciously, like me. I find myself wondering more and more about what isn't unique to me, but is, instead, part and parcel of being White. I am learning how to speak about being White, sometimes with people who are used to talking about racial identity and sometimes with people who fidget and deflect.

---

1. Editor's note: This was written in the aftermath of the 2014 killing of Black teenager, Michael Brown by Ferguson, Missouri, police officer Darren Wilson.

As priest and professor, I talk a lot and not without some depth of knowledge and experience. But in these last few months, I am becoming increasingly aware of how rudimentary my abilities to talk about my experience of being White are. I can talk and write about being a priest. I have written academic and popular pieces on ethics, life in modern and postmodern frameworks, and have preached and taught about spiritual and religious matters. I have not had to focus on being articulate about being White. I am not saying I couldn't or didn't talk about being White. Often, I simply did it in jokey way, or sometimes in intellectual ways. I revved up for St. Patrick's Day, being proudly Irish American. My musical, art, and literary references are White even when they are not, like enjoying comics who are Black cracking on White people and then feeling as if I am in the know; that I am not like *those* White people. I am a White person who Black people like, or at least I think I am. For a long time, that was the best I could do. Now, I need to do better.

Lest this all be too ephemeral, let me offer an example. Early on, after Michael Brown was killed, reporters were everywhere—on the phone, at my door, e-mailing, looking for someone who could answer questions about what was really going on. I was full on. The Canadian Broadcast Corporation, *The Takeaway*, the *LA Times*, and *Time* magazine quoted my take on what was happening. Then an Australian journalist said to me, "I would really like to talk to someone Black about what Black youth are facing." Boom. I was a White guy who was consciously and, dare I say, clearly speaking from the one racial experience I have: being a White guy. So I started to speak differently. And I started keeping my mouth shut. I would say I listened better, but really, it was more introverted than that. What happened was, I waited. I paused to gut check. Guts are messy and mine started an anxious, messy, emotional, and vulnerable percolation. Nothing on par with conversation or an existential crisis, just the growing awareness of how, as a White guy, a part of my preferred game was just flat out over. I could not be in Ferguson, the parish, or my own skin without a lot more awareness. And honestly, I barely had game. And sitting this one out was not an option.

At this writing, six months after Michael Brown's shooting, I find myself being explicit in conversations, saying things like, "As a White guy . . . ," and "What I think White people are doing is . . ." It is awkward and I am not sure what impact it is having on some of my conversations; still, I know that I am doing it more.

I say these new things in conversations with other White people. Or I introduce questions like, "What I wonder is how we as White people can respond?" Or, "I wonder how I'd see this if I wasn't White?" It has not made me any better or worse as a family member, friend, priest, or community member. And it is something that Black friends either engage, indulge, or rib me about. Still, it is part of what living into the now is like. And it is, I think, a better way to live in right relationship, as I become more honest and clearer about what has never been in doubt: I am, as I said, a White guy.

30

Church and Trauma

Charles Michael Livingston Jr.

The Church and trauma have been synonymous for centuries. From the time of Jesus to the present, the Church has both imposed and been on the receiving end of trauma—especially for those of us with marginalized identities—that is, not White, male, wealthy, cisgender, heterosexual, nonimmigrant, Christian, or able-bodied. For those of us not of these often centered and idealized identities, understanding and navigating what the Church has become can be traumatic. More often than we would like to admit, people experience some form of bigotry from members of the Church who misunderstand what it truly means to be Christian.

From my perspective as a Black gay man, I've experienced some of this trauma firsthand. Members of clergy will say something either intentionally or overtly homophobic, or Church members will make ignorant comments they think the Bible is directing them to say. It's always "well meaning" and never intentionally malicious (so they think), but it is off-putting and hurtful to hear and experience when the entire basis of Christianity calls for us to be accepting of people of all identities as human beings who need love and spiritual community and not condemnation and marginalization. As I have largely attended majority Black churches, I've not frequently felt the effects of racism in Church but, when I have attended a church with a largely White congregation, I've felt acutely aware of both my race and my skin color: racism and it's sibling, colorism.

Church, ideally, should be a place where any and all people feel welcomed for who they are. So often I feel it is necessary in some church settings to conceal or not disclose certain aspects of my identity for fear of bigotry. The Church should be a place where social justice begins and is organized, much like the civil rights era where much of the organizing was done in the Church. Today, we have social media and the internet to help organize folks, but that doesn't mean the Church does not still have a place. Modernizing communication efforts, making it easier for us to feel in community even if we're not always physically present, can go a long way in helping the world become a better, more accepting, more loving place for all of us.

The Church has to become more representative of those of us with the most marginalized of identities and intersections. Black Lives Matter has to be a lived affirmation from the body of the Christ. Not just Black men or Black heterosexual folks. Not just Black non-Latinx folks or Black nonimmigrants or Black primarily English speakers. Not just Black cisgender folks or gender-conforming folks. Every Black life needs to matter and feel uplifted, loved, celebrated, and welcome for Black lives to matter.

One day, I hope our church homes will all resemble this.

31

Between the Pews

Monai Lowe

Going to church was not a matter of choice in my household as a child. It didn't matter the day of the week, plans you may have had, or even your personal opinion on whether or not church mattered: you were going to church. For Sunday service. Piano lessons. Choir rehearsal. Teen revival. Adult revival. *Revival* revival. Life was built around the church and that's just the way it was. I'm sure it was this way in many other Black, Southern households that chose to uphold Christian beliefs and practices. You were going to put on the proper clothes, pack your Bible, put on smile, bring your manners, and do the thing.

Church became a thing, at least that's the way I saw it as a child. It was fully ingrained in the routine of life—and not just the lives of my family and extended family, but everyone. Everyone I knew went to church. Saying that you did not go was almost shameful (sinful?) back then. It was the social framework for the community and how it revolved around the world. It gave people purpose and made them feel important, and some of those people actually were. Some of those people are still to this day the best people I've ever met. But you know what they say, "A few apples can spoil the bunch." The church can and does revolve *around* the world. There are specific ways in which the church functions that make it apparent that the church is not of the same world that exists beyond its doors. It was between the pews as a child that I came to see the dissimilarities of life in church versus life outside of it. Both spaces were filled with the same people, but these worlds were miles apart.

I didn't personally experience much discomfort growing up in the church, but that's definitely not to anyone's credit. To the church I presented as a nonthreat: a seemingly modest, obedient, heterosexual child who dressed appropriately. The church had no obvious reason to reign down on me. However, I know this was not the case for some people. To be clear: it should have been, but it was not. Every person who enters a church is not afforded the same convenience or luxury of feeling welcomed. It only took one unfamiliar face to walk down that center, carpeted aisle for me to realize that the church was not who it claimed to be. That we, as a church, as a spiritual community, were oftentimes more in need of the assistance and service than the communities we claimed to be helping.

On one particular Sunday a man who appeared to be homeless entered the church as the doors were opened in between prayers. He wore torn and ragged clothes, and had a strong smell that gave the impression that maybe he had slept outside for more than a few nights. As people watched this man walk down to the first pew of the church, they could barely contain themselves. The level of disdain and confusion on people's faces, and a few whispers in the back, indicated that this man had just committed a crime. What they didn't know (what also shouldn't have mattered) was that our pastor had invited this man to our church after meeting him on the street because our church had a homeless ministry that provided clothes and necessities to those in need. What I didn't see, and what disturbed me the most, was that after church, very few people made any attempt to approach and introduce themselves to our visiting worshiper. Most people just wanted to talk about who he was and how he knew the pastor.

That was the first of many Sundays I realized the gap between who the church was, and who the church was called to be. We simply weren't close to hitting the mark. And today we're still not hitting it. The intrinsic fault with the church is that it's made up of people. And obviously that's not something that can be helped considering the mission, but the innate nature of humans is painfully imperfect. We have free will, personal bias, and prejudices that present barriers to us living as true disciples. We have drama and trauma of our own that lowers our ability to be understanding of others. It's much easier to talk about accepting others than to practice that daily and consistently in our lives. It's comforting to talk about God forgiving us for our sins, but much more difficult to exercise that for our fellow human being. The teachings of the Bible have become more convenient to talk about than to live out: that's where the break in service lies.

What was intended as a place of worship and praise has actually deconstructed itself into a place of hurt and shame for people who don't fit the framework of what the church thinks a member *should* look like, act like, or possess. Members and visitors who present with trauma, illness, difficult social circumstances, poverty, or addiction are not always welcomed with the open arms we claim to have. Even those who come with an interest to learn more and dedicate their lives are appalled by the inner workings of the church and its members. Today, you can ask people if they go to church and most scoff at the idea. "Why would I go to church with people who don't even live up to their own morals?" "People in church are judgmental when the Bible clearly urges against it." "There's more immorality in the church than outside of it." These are a few of the responses I received when asking friends recently about their church attendance. The world is finding other ways to connect to God outside of the church because some feel like the church has lost its way.

So how does the Church get back to its purpose and regain the trust of the public to be what it's called to be? It would take an honest assessment of leadership and membership to uncover the weak spots, the touchy ones that seem suitable to skip over. The Church would have to address its own opinions of provocative, unpopular topics and dig into scripture for understanding as opposed to the personal feelings and beliefs of the general congregation. To salvage the relationship between the Church and humanity, the Church would have to admit where it's been wrong, how it's been wrong, and what was wrong about its position on those subject matters. The Church would also have to hold and remove those accountable for their wrongdoing. It's easy in theory, but would prove to be tough in practice. But ultimately, it's probably the most logical way to proceed. Scripture talks about removing the right hand if it causes you to sin (Matt. 5:30) and how the whole body with all of its many parts and organs still functions as one (Rom. 12:4–5). Applying these thought processes to the predicament of the Church is more than fitting and necessary to repair the Church and create less space between the empty pews.

32

Welcoming or What?

Sandra T. Montes

One of my first memories of being part of an Episcopal Church–wide service was hearing the speaker say, "We are part of the *Whiter* church." I was surprised that they would be so open about it, but I nodded as I said, "A-men" pretty loud. It was after a couple of more sentences that I realized the speaker meant we are part of the *wider* church. I thought, "Oh. That makes more sense." Not the part of wider vs. Whiter, but that the person was not calling out the obvious.

I came to the Episcopal Church in a dramatic and terrible way. My dad was delivering pizzas because his job as an evangelical pastor did not provide enough money to support a family of four. In one of his deliveries, he was beaten and left for dead. As he struggled to get to the hospital, he called his senior pastor to tell him his tragedy and the pastor told him to call him back when he was back home. My dad had met an Episcopal bishop, who lived in Houston, years before at an evangelism conference in New York City, and had his business card in his wallet. My dad was hurt, sad, and needed a pastor. He decided to call. The bishop was in the middle of a *quinceañera*, but as soon as he finished, he rushed to the hospital. My dad always remembers Bishop Pina, may he rise in glory, running into the hospital wearing his bishop garb.

My dad started working at St. Matthew's/San Mateo in gratitude and soon was teaching Bible study and leading the music ministry. The first time I went to St. Matthew's/San Mateo, I saw the huge cross with Jesus still hanging on it and I saw my dad wearing a dress (clerical vestments) and told my mom, "We are going to hell!" I had heard throughout my evangelical childhood that Roman Catholics were going to hell.

I have been in the Episcopal Church since then, over thirty years. During that time, I have not seen much progress in some areas and much in others. I am grateful for the opportunities the Episcopal Church has provided for me and my family and am saddened by the many signs of unwelcome that lurk behind many of our denomination's red doors.

When I am about to walk in a new Episcopal Church, as I often do because of work or life, I get a bit nervous. I have not lost my excitement for a good song or a good word. I have not lost my hope to be fed and to be able to be free during a service. I have not lost my wonder and curiosity about going into God's house. I have, however, wondered if I may lose all of this because of what I face almost every time I visit a new (to me) Episcopal church. I do visit other denominations, but I write mostly about the Episcopal Church because that is still, by choice, my spiritual home.

I am observant, curious, and what some call *criticona*—hypercritical—something church leaders don't usually like. Before I walk into a church, I notice things that are great and things that can be improved. The grass needs to be mowed, there are special parking spots for visitors (yay), there is a lot of clutter and dust, there are kids running around and making lots of noise (yay).

When I walk into a church, especially those that call themselves welcoming, I immediately try to find myself somehow. I notice if the people around me, especially those who are leading (ushers, greeters, lectors, people on the altar), look like me. I want to see myself in the leadership and in the church body. I want to belong and not feel left out or forgotten.

If I am visiting, especially where no one knows me, I notice everything: Did people around me give me the peace; is the Eucharist easy to navigate; do I know when I am supposed to stand or kneel; are there four books I have to juggle; are all the songs in English; is there a variety of music?

When I was a teacher, I had students with different learning needs and abilities or students from special populations (low socioeconomic, recent immigrants, students who have never been to school). I had to fill out different forms to document that I was doing certain things that were beneficial to ensure the student's success and specific for each student. I quickly noticed that these were best practices that all my students could benefit from: student sits near the teacher, student has extra time to finish difficult work, student assignments are divided into smaller chunks, tests are shorter, and test answers have fewer choices.

How does this translate into our church? As a Latina in the Episcopal Church, I am a person with different needs and from a special population. I am a foreign-born person who has attended mostly Spanish services throughout my life. That means I don't know *The Hymnal 1982* well, nor do I know all the prayers, nor can I find, rapidly, Morning Prayer, or the Psalms in the Book of Common Prayer. That means that there must be best practices that church leaders can use to ensure my success in church.

How can we do this in a welcoming, inclusive, sensitive, authentic way? By using our resources. For example, at a recent ordination we sang the hymn "In Christ there is no East or West." Great hymn. It is in *Lift Ev'ry Voice and Sing II*[1] and also in *The Hymnal 1982*. This cathedral had both hymnals in the pews. Guess which hymnal we were instructed to use? It would have been just as easy to use *Lift Ev'ry Voice and Sing II*, but only God knows why they chose to only use *The Hymnal 1982*. That says something to me. It says that the people who are putting together important liturgies and daily liturgies in this diocese and this cathedral, specifically, may not be sensitive to people who are not the *usual* Episcopalian. It tells me that the leadership probably does not look like me. It tells me that *Lift Ev'ry Voice and Sing II* is not on their radar. It tells me so many things that, if I did not love the Episcopal Church fiercely, I would never return.

"You're reading way too much into it!" I hear over and over again. Am I? As an outspoken person, I e-mail, call, text, and post on social media my criticism of our *Whiter* church. I have been criticized and ostracized because of it. I have also been thanked by the people who feel they can't speak up—as I felt at one time. And, even though it hurts and is exhausting to hear negative feedback on my constant challenge for the Episcopal Church to be wider not Whiter, up to this point it has been worth the tears and backlash.

If we, as a Church, believe in our baptism, and if we, as the Episcopal Church, believe our baptismal covenant, then we cannot forget what we promised:

- Will you seek and serve Christ in all persons, loving your neighbor as yourself?
- Will you strive for justice and peace among all people, and respect the dignity of every human being?[2]

If you answered "I will, with God's help," this is what that looks like:

- Having diversity in vestries and any other decision-making or influential bodies.
- Having an open commitment to diversity by the entire congregation.
- Reaching out to people of color, LGBTQI+, people with disabilities, and people of other diverse populations around our community and inviting

---

1. *Lift Ev'ry Voice and Sing II* is an African American hymnal, while *The Hymnal 1982* is the more traditional Anglican/Episcopal hymnal.

2. The Episcopal Church, *The Book of Common Prayer* (New York: Church Publishing, 1979), 305.

them to join our church for a special event, a meal, or anything that says they are welcome and truly loved.

- Asking the people in our pews what they hope for.
- Committing to justice and peace as a congregation by having many opportunities for growth in those areas: book studies, trips to important social justice sites, preachers from other traditions, panel discussion on hot topics.
- Committing to respecting the dignity of every human being as a congregation by participating in rallies and marches surrounding immigration, constantly singing music from different traditions and languages, becoming a sanctuary church or supporting one that is preparing meals and backpacks for people in need.
- Seeking and serving Christ in all persons and loving our neighbors no matter who they are by creating opportunities for our neighbors to be welcomed into our community—cookouts, fairs, Christmas pageant, Easter egg hunt, Halloween party, etc.

It is not so hard once we start. Being Jesus takes a daily decision and commitment. Let's commit to be wider, not Whiter.

33

Acknowledging White Privilege

Deniray Mueller

The words "White privilege" have been bandied around by pundits, the media, and in general conversation, and while many of us accept that it exists, we are not sure what it means. The best definition of "White privilege" I have found came from a class in women's studies at the University of Massachusetts:

> A set of advantages and/or immunities that white people benefit from on a daily basis beyond those common to all others. White privilege can exist without white people's conscious knowledge of its presence and it helps to maintain the racial hierarchy in this country.

The biggest problem with white privilege is the invisibility it maintains to those who benefit from it most. The inability to recognize that many of the advantages whites hold are a direct result of the disadvantages of other people, contributes to the unwillingness of white people, even those who are not overtly racist, to recognize their part in maintaining and benefiting from white supremacy.

White privilege is about not having to worry about being followed in a department store while shopping. It's about thinking that your clothes, manner of speech, and behavior in general, are racially neutral, when, in fact, they are white. It's seeing your image on television daily and knowing that you're being represented. It's people assuming that you lead a constructive life free from crime and off welfare. It's about not having to assume your daily interactions with people have racial overtones.

White privilege is having the freedom and luxury to fight racism one day and ignore it the next. White privilege exists on an individual, cultural, and institutional level.[1]

---

1. Arlene Avakian, "The Social Construction of Whiteness and Women," University of Massachusetts, Amherst, MA, accessed July 18, 2019, *https://www.academia.edu/2896838/SOCIAL_CONSTRUCTION_OF_WHITENESS_AND_WOMEN*. See also, "What Is White Privilege?" *https://www.mtholyoke.edu/org/wsar/intro.htm*.

To quote African American author, James Baldwin, "Being White means never having to think about it."[2] Many of us at Saint John's Episcopal Church benefit every day from our White privilege. We don't even acknowledge that we have it, and indeed, enjoy a life that people of color can only dream of but do not often attain. Life's path is smoothed for us; the entire world is set up to give us every advantage and allow us to come out on the top. Moreover, we don't want to talk about the fact that we are privileged, or even think that our privilege directly affects the lives of millions of people of color. We do not have to worry about whether our children will return safely as they walk home from school, or if they are driving, whether they will be stopped for the most minor of offenses and jailed. I have an African American friend who does not drive in Bexley because the police consider "driving while Black" a reason to stop him. We don't have that worry. And even if we are stopped by the police, we don't fear that we will be assaulted or shot. We don't have to teach our sons how to avoid harassment when they are doing nothing wrong. Other White people don't cross to the other side when we walk down the street, or hold tight to their purses when we pass by.

Racism is about much more than our feelings toward one another, or the differences we can fix with talk of tolerance or color-blindness. The story of race is an ideology of difference that shapes our understanding of ourselves, the world we inhabit, and the communities in which we live. Racial thinking assigns value to human beings who are grouped within artificial categories. We do not need to embrace contrived notions of racial differences in the name of inclusion, or to examine to the depth of our hearts how we really feel about people of color. Tolerance is not acceptable; we must search until we can truly look at any other person as equal to ourselves. By minimalizing another person, we are dehumanizing not only them, but ourselves.

In light of the murders and shootings of people of all colors, we may be appalled or anguished, but we also may not see these events are directly related to the long-standing racism in our nation stemming from slavery. Progress for people of color has been slow and halting; cultural attitudes and habits have changed at a glacial pace. We think we have made progress, but we have become so used to the racial divide in our nation, that in many cases, we do not even realize it is there. The sad and shocking thing is, these killings will continue. Too much of White America doesn't see the problem. Many subconsciously believe that the shooting victims "deserved it."

---

2. Avakian, "What Is White Privilege?"

None of this means the situation can't change. However, until the White people in America can see clearly the injustice and realize the freedoms and values that we as Americans believe in are not available to everyone, it will continue. Until it tugs at our own sense of fairness and justice, a lot of White people in America will remain unmoved to act. Denying the impact of White privilege on this country's judicial system creates more injustice, more inflamed rhetoric, more grief, more rage—and more deaths.

I saw a sign held by protester at a rally that said, "White Silence Is Violence." Truly, if we do not listen to others who are not like us, keep silent when disparaging words are spoken, or don't hold people accountable for their discriminatory conduct, we are just as complicit in racism as those who hold a gun or burn a cross or lynch a human being. White people are in a position of power in this country because of the long-standing power structure that they built and control. In the opinion of many, much of the political unrest that we are now experiencing stems from the fact that we fear we are losing that control. Are we brave enough to use our White privilege to correct that system or power structure? Are we, as White people, willing to do what it takes to stop the systemic murder of young Black men, combat the institutionalized school-to-prison pipeline, and heal the deep, bleeding wound that is racism in America? It is a hard pill to swallow that, in many ways, White people are the source of the problem and only we can change it. People of color may yell, scream, cry, plead, or demand justice, but until White people are willing to get really uncomfortable with our own participation in a racist society, nothing will change.

Let us not delude ourselves into thinking that we do not have the power. We may say, "I'm not racist—I have Black friends. I'm a good person." We may not be rich and we may truly struggle with daily aspects of our lives. We probably are good people, and we may have Black friends. But we still benefit from institutionalized racism. Andrew Rosenthal, a writer for the *New York Times*, writes:

> The point of the "Black Lives Matter" movement is not that the lives of African Americans matter more than those of White Americans, but that they matter equally, and that historically they have been treated as though they do not.[3]

It is time for White people to unlearn the racism that has been instilled in us by our country and our churches. It's time for White people in America—especially

---

3. Andrew Rosenthal, "The Real Story of Race and Police Killings," *New York Times*, September 4, 2015, *https://takingnote.blogs.nytimes.com/2015/09/04/the-real-story-of-race-and-police-killings/*.

the White American church—to start putting action behind our prayerful social media memes. The unfortunate reality is that America has a really big race problem and White people must take the leadership to fix it. We, who call ourselves followers of Jesus, should be leading the charge, not arguing about the semantics of whose lives matter.

I call on all congregations—especially White congregations—to unite in protest, to refuse to stand in silence, to speak out against racial injustice, to examine our individual lives and attitudes until we understand our participation in racism, and wipe it from our lives.

We must build a society where we no longer see people of color bloodied and broken or dead due to racial violence. We must ensure that our children do not take on the racial attitudes and habits that we were so subtly taught.

Join me in acknowledging, understanding, and shedding the mantle of our White privilege.

34

Books and Their Covers

Jamie Samilio

In contemplating this essay, I realized that to give an opinion on how I would preach to a Black congregation, you should first know part of my story. Otherwise, I fear my words would be added to the words of other privileged White folks, wanting to say the right thing. We are all at some point outsiders, and the more we share our stories, the closer we will get to respecting the dignity of all people.

We often assign the moniker of bravery to soldiers, but the bravest person I have ever known was a seven-year old Black girl—my friend, Belinda. I met Belinda in 1967 at the Villa Maria Academy, Elementary Division for Girls, in Erie, Pennsylvania. I see Belinda in my head as clearly as if I were in the school auditorium. Standing in rows are one hundred and thirty-nine young girls wearing heather blue uniforms, white blouses with peter pan collars, and navy-blue knee socks. One hundred and thirty-eight White faces and one Black—my friend Belinda. She knew she stood out in this body of White students, but she displayed confidence and was as proud as any of us to be a "Villa girl."

It was the turbulent 1960s and America was in the throes of the civil rights movement; Belinda was the first Black child to attend our fine Catholic school. Not that Blacks were kept out of the school: they just never imagined they would be welcomed—at least not until Mrs. Watson enrolled her daughter. Jane Watson was a nurse, a medical professional, skilled at what she did. Jane went to school in Pittsburgh, even though there were nursing schools in Erie. She would have been the only Black nursing student in Erie, and allowing Jane to have a private dorm room, or compelling a White student to share a room with Jane was not acceptable in the 1950s. But the times they were a changin' and Jane had enrolled her daughter in the finest school in the city.

This was a time when the headlines and the issues were as simple as black and white. I was privileged to attend a private school for girls, and Belinda, the only Black student, was viewed as privileged as well. My mother had made a point of meeting Belinda's mother. I remember them stopping to chat at a school open house. I had seen Black people before, and it did not strike me as odd that Belinda was Black. To me she was just another girl in my class, a girl whose home I would visit, a girl who would come to my house to play. But Belinda turned out to be more than that. Belinda became my first best friend. Our mothers arranged play dates for us. She would come to my house and we would play dolls, swing, and run through the yard. I would go to her house, where her mother and grandmother would cook while we played and listened to records. We would go to the basketball court across the street and hang with the other neighborhood kids. It seemed totally normal to me. I was a kid like any other kid and I watched cartoons like *Fat Albert and the Gang*—"Na, na, na, gonna have a good time." I loved visiting Belinda in the city where there was a basketball court and kids playing, just like in the cartoon.

Most of all, Belinda and I talked, laughed, and wondered what would become of us, imagining how our lives would unfold. About the only dis-agreement I ever had with Belinda was over Michael Jackson. All our friends were over the moon for Donny Osmond. His face was plastered on posters, book covers, and teen magazines. One day I told her I liked Michael Jackson better than Donny Osmond—that, in fact, I did not like Donny much at all. Well, *she* told me! Because I was White, I had to like Donny and I could *not* have Michael. I was mad. I did not want to be stuck with Donny Osmond. Who would? Even his sister Marie left him after a while. As it turns out, Jermaine Jackson was her real heartthrob, and Belinda cried the day his marriage announcement hit the newsstands.

It took many years for me to realize how brave Jane Watson was to put her daughter in an exclusive private school with all White children. It took me longer to realize how brave my mother was to greet Jane Watson, to arrange play dates for Belinda and me, and to let me spend time in Belinda's neighborhood playing with her friends.

I did not understand that my mother, who ran the ladies' golf league, belonged to the country club, and, with my dad, sent her children to private school, had decided to be color-blind and deaf to the White establishment. My mother and Mrs. Watson both took a step toward equality, a step they seemed to execute with ease. Sometimes, we do not recognize when we are being strong or brave, especially when we are just living in the moment and trying to do the right thing.

Years later, after many moves, college, and kids, when Belinda and I were reunited, we talked about how brave both our mothers had been to risk reaching out to each other. We realized that their small steps, combined with the steps of others, are what had helped to change the culture. I like to think that seeing my White face playing with all the kids in the Black neighborhood and seeing Belinda's Black face sitting in the Boston Store cafeteria where all the White shoppers gathered helped people accept the cultural shift of the civil rights movement. The world did not end when I played in the 'hood and no one died when Belinda had a milkshake in the department store. I do not know who saw us, but if they did and it moved them to accept, communicate, and include in their lives someone of a different race, then let us give thanks to God for the bravery of our two mothers in 1967.

My mother formed some of her opinions about prejudice from an experience in 1945, on Labor Day weekend, when she and my Aunt Irene went by train to Washington, DC, and then boarded a bus to Raleigh, North Carolina. They passed many half-filled seats and made their way to the back where they could sit together. The bus did not move. They sat for more than fifteen minutes with everyone looking at them. Finally, two Marines who were seated toward the front came to the back and said, "Do not say a word, just come and sit with us." The Marines explained that the bus driver would have sat there all night; the whole back could be empty, but Whites could not sit there. My mother would have none of it—and neither would her children.

My father, on the other hand, grew up in a household where they were skeptical about people of color. My dad was a first-generation American and was considered an outsider. I guess being near the bottom of the social ladder, feeling like they were at least one step above someone, is what drove my grandparents to hold prejudiced views. How we are raised and what we are taught to believe impacts our view of the world. My dad, however, liked to form his own opinions of people and, although it took him a while to shake the language of his childhood, he shut the door to ignorance and intolerance that his parents had opened for him. We are all one race, the human race. Humanity is divided by racism not by race; we are all colors created as individuals, not as clones.

My social education was grounded in the school community I experienced with the Sisters of Saint Joseph. I was an obedient child and I believed that what I was taught in school was true and should be followed. I was taught to treat others as I want to be treated, to have humility, to love everyone as brothers and sisters, to forgive, and to turn the other cheek when offended. The lesson that influenced me the most was that we are all equal in the eyes of God. I came to understand that each of us has different gifts and talents, that it takes all of us to create the rich, diverse, and interesting world we live in, and that all life has value. God is love, and love is what we must do, and loving others means respecting the dignity of all people.

I can never truly understand what it is like to be Black, to have my skin color be an outward and visible sign that my ancestors did not come here of their own free will. What I have experienced, however, is people assuming that, as a White person, I shared their point of view on race. As a gay woman, my personal experience includes people assuming that I share their views on sexual orientation. Numerous people, assuming I was straight, have confided in me their belief that homosexuals are sinners who choose to live a queer and disgusting lifestyle. Telling me—because I am a Christian—that all of "those people" (LGBTQ+) are going to hell. And furthermore, all "those" people should be locked up or eliminated. Those conversations had interesting outcomes when I told them that I was one of "those" people.

Being part of a subculture, I have learned a few things about what it means to be family. Some people do not have parents or siblings. Some have families, but have cut ties with them for one painful reason or another. Family are the people who come into relationship with each other and form a bond of love that can never break. In any family, there are fights and disagreements, but in the end, their love and support for each other stands firm. My wife, Sylvia, and I have been together since our freshman year in college. Thirty-five years later, we were married in Washington, DC, by a priest in an Episcopal church, surrounded by our families. When Belinda and I rekindled our friendship, she was excited to meet Sylvia, and even brought her daughter and grandchild over to dinner at our home. Belinda and I were family, and happy to have our other family members meet each other. A couple years after our reunification, I received a call from Belinda's daughter, who told me her mother had lost her battle with cancer and asked me if I would give the eulogy at her funeral. Sylvia and I found ourselves, along with one other White person, in a room filled with a couple hundred Black people. As I stood in front of the group and looked out at the crowd of family and friends gathered, I realized what Belinda must have felt like that day in 1967 when she walked into school and stood with us. I am forever grateful for my sister, Belinda.

Culturally, my wife, Sylvia, and I are members of the gay family, and we share a bond with other gay people. Interestingly, we have more friends who support us who are straight, and we are comforted that, as much as we belong to a subculture, we also belong to a large, diverse family of people who love, appreciate, and accept each other just as we are. Many of these friends have held up our marriage and relationship as something they strive for in their own lives—we are blessed.

I feel that my gay siblings who wore pink triangles in the German concentration camps are my ancestors, and my little siblings who have been thrown out of their homes because of their homosexuality are directly related to me.

It took me a long time to become a priest, but not because I was busy doing something else. I was denied a seminary education because I refused to lie about who I was as a person. The dean said, "We regret that we will be unable to allow you to attend Virginia Theological Seminary (VTS) because your psychological profile states that you are a practicing homosexual." I asked if he thought there were other homosexuals enrolled in the institution, and he said he was positive there were several, but their paperwork was *clean*. I then asked if he was fine with the institution's engraving the words of Jesus on its walls, "I am the truth, the life, and the way," yet admitting students who either lied directly or by omission about their sexuality. Would Jesus, the "Truth," approve of admitting only homosexuals who lied? Would he approve of a religious institution that felt it was right to accept people who told lies of omission? There was a long silence. It took another decade until VTS changed its policies and I was finally able to attend seminary as an openly gay woman.

I know what it means for society to view me differently, to be hated by some and condemned by others, but I can hide my homosexuality. I can even deny it. Being gay does not carry with it any outward or visible signs. I can hide in plain sight and enjoy the privilege of blending in. People make assumptions and judgments based on the way people look—rightly or wrongly. That is the way it works, until people take the time to get to know each other. What I cannot imagine is living in a world where my skin color is the determining factor in being stopped by a cop, given a loan, watched while shopping, or assumed to be uneducated or a troublemaker. Knowing what it means to be viewed differently makes me keenly aware that as a White person I am compelled to reach out, welcome, and connect with people who do not look like me because on the inside, I am them. I am their sister, a fellow human just trying to make my way through life.

I said that the bravest person I have ever known was a seven-year-old Black girl. I see Belinda in my head as clearly as if I were in the auditorium yesterday, 138 White faces, and one Black one—my friend Belinda. To me, this memory represents all of us when we find ourselves the "other" in a group.

When the Episcopal Church finally figured out there was a place for me, I was ordained a priest. I serve a predominantly White congregation. When I look out from the chancel into the faces of my parish family, I note the faces of people who are different from me. Some are Black, some are Asian, Indian,

Middle Eastern, gay, and more. I long to see more faces of people who are not like me. I want to welcome especially those who are church shopping and have come to see if we are a welcoming parish. When I see a new person of color, I look around and I am disappointed if I don't see our members who are people of color at that service. I want to say to all the brave people of color who attend predominantly White parishes that they are missed when they are not in church. Their presence in a "White" church is a huge gift of welcoming and evangelism to any non-White, non-heterosexual person who walks in the door, because those "other people" are looking for them. They are the outward and visible signs of a congregation that accepts, welcomes, and makes everyone feel safe as part of God's family in that place. There is a difference between saying we welcome everyone and people seeing for themselves how others like them are established in a church and welcomed. I have also experienced people of color making assumptions about our predominantly "White" congregation when they find themselves alone among our White faces. It is not like I can stand at the entrance greeting them as they leave saying, "Welcome, please stay and join us for coffee hour. I promise there are multiple people of other races and cultures who are members of our congregation; they were just all busy today. May we add you to our e-mail list?"

I realize what I do is not nearly as important as who I am, but who I am has so much to do with what I do. I am who I am, a loving and welcoming child of God with siblings of every race, creed, nation, and pronoun. I can use all the friends, family, and allies I can get, and I have found that sometimes help comes from the most unexpected places and unexpected people—the shape, size, color, ability, or any other description matters not.

I am calling on all White people to reach out to those who do not look like them. I am calling on all heterosexual people to realize how they act and what they say to members of the LGBTQ+ family matters. It is the duty of every person who identifies as a Christian to respect the dignity of all people; it is the Baptismal Covenant. And, if we are Christians, then we are known by our love and respect for everyone, including those who believe in a God of their understanding, and love even those who are not Christians. Period. Ultimately, love is the answer to the meaning of life because brilliance requires creativity, wisdom requires patience, love requires nothing, and gives everything in return.

Psychiatrist and Holocaust survivor Viktor Frankl said there are only two races: the race of decent people and the race of indecent people.[1] "Stay woke"

---

1. Viktor Frankl, *Man's Search for Meaning*, gift edition (Boston: Beacon Press, 2015), 70.

to the "others" in the world, those who stand out in a crowd, and those who are hiding in plain sight. Perhaps I should say this in a way everyone can understand. Be kind to everyone, love God, love your neighbors, and respect and uphold the dignity of all people—all the time —no exceptions!

Building relationships is at the foundation of building a life or a congregation, and breaking down barriers and making people feel welcome is a top priority. In my work on a diocesan staff, I often encountered vision and mission statements naming "diversity" as a goal to be achieved. Each time I encountered this language I had to carefully walk the group through the process of understanding that diversity in itself is not a goal to be set, but a byproduct of being a truly open and welcoming community. In my current congregation we make a statement before every Eucharist and at many gatherings. It is on our website and as much as possible on the minds and hearts of the people in the pews. "Whoever you are and wherever you are on your journey of faith, you are welcome here to receive God's love, freely given." My words from the pulpit support this statement when I tell people that what we do in the world matters and has an impact on other people. We need to stand with and for each other. I cannot stress enough how important this statement is to me and for the welcoming of people into our congregation.

As a Christian, I am aware that Jesus was a storyteller, reconciler, redeemer, healer, teacher, brother, son, savior, and more. Jesus stood up for those who could not adequately defend themselves, and Jesus told us to feed the hungry, clothe the naked, house the homeless, and stand up to oppressive forces. As Christians, this is what we are called to do for everyone, no exceptions. So put out a rainbow flag, post a Black Lives Matter sign, post words that let our neighbors know that we respect them just as they are. Speak using words that show love for those not like you, and walk in support of those who need support. We need to do all of these things if we are to create a welcoming community that will naturally become a melting pot of people, different from each other, but united by love.

One thing I think every preacher might consider is that people who have been discriminated against, had family members enslaved, live or have lived in poverty, hear the messages of scripture with very different ears than those of us who have been privileged and do not directly experience discrimination, poverty, and rejection in our daily lives. While I try to relate the scripture to my own story and experience, I think I do my best work when I can reach beyond myself and empathize with those who are unlike myself. I think it makes the message broader, and I think it helps to keep me humble.

Martin Niemöller is perhaps most famous for his words on standing up with and for each other:

First they came for the socialists, and I did not speak out—because I was not a socialist. Then they came for the trade unionists, and I did not speak out—because I was not a trade unionist. Then they came for the Jews, and I did not speak out—because I was not a Jew. Then they came for me—and there was no one left to speak for me.[2]

"They" also came for the Communists and the gays (the connection between homosexuals and pink triangles comes from the German concentration camp designations). The thing Martin said that I think every congregation can benefit from came in an interview when he was asked why he had initially supported Hitler. Martin listened to Hitler and believed him when he said that the Church would be supported and protected and that no real harm would come to the Jews. In the end, Martin deeply regretted his initial support of Hitler. He said he had paid for his mistake, but so had thousands of others; he was not alone in his sorrow or regret. What Martin had to do was look past the words being spoken to him and search his heart and his Christian identity to see if what was being said and what was happening were true and following Jesus's command to love one another as he loved us.

How are we following Jesus's command to love each other? It is easier to ignore and hate than to show respect and love. I think most of us naturally gravitate toward the easy way out. When we are anywhere in a group of other people, we naturally look for and speak to people who are most like us. If we are going to lead open and welcoming congregations, then we need to retrain our brains and learn to love each other. We need to practice. The next time you are at an event or even a grocery store where you do not know other people, seek out the other. Strike up a conversation with someone who does not look like you. Greet a stranger, be the first to smile. This may seem like a tall order, and emotionally costly, but the price of not reaching out in love to those not like us, comes at a greater expense—perhaps as high as the price of our souls. American journalist Dorothy Day said it well, "I really only love God as much as I love the person I love the least."[3]

---

2. US Holocaust Museum, "Martin Niemöller: 'First They Came for the Socialists . . . ,'" Washington, DC, *https://encyclopedia.ushmm.org/content/en/article/martin-niemoeller-first-they-came-for-the-socialists.*

3. Dorothy Day, in Allison Beatty, "The Person I Love the Least," February 27, 2018, *http://www.aggie catholicblog.org/2018/02/the-person-i-love-the-least/.*

35

From Blackface to Black Panther

THE IMPACT OF POP CULTURE IN THE BLACK LIVES MATTER MOVEMENT

Shayna J. Watson

We cannot enter into conversation about Black Lives Matter without first examining the lingering effects of blackface minstrelsy in the United States and its negative reflection on Black life in America. Minstrelsy, despite its negative effects, was still considered a part of popular culture. From "Jump Jim Crow" to "Amos and Andy" to "Tom and Jerry" cartoons, all of America has ingested destructive stereotypes about people of African descent, and it plays out in racial terrorist violence, racial prejudice, and internalized racial inferiority and hatred. The following examines how contemporary popular culture seeks to usurp the damaging roots of racial stereotypes sown by blackface minstrelsy during the nineteenth century. Blackface might have started it, but T'Challa, the hero of Wakanda, Black Panther will end it.

Every night before a performance, Thomas Dartmouth (T. D.) "Daddy" Rice would blacken his face and whiten his lips in imitation and mockery of what he observed to be the physical appearance of someone of African descent; thus, the term "blackface" was born. In the 1830s, blackface was popularized in the United States and became the expectation of both White and later Black performers. Rice gave rise to what became known as American minstrelsy. His embodied caricature of enslaved Africans perpetuated and commercialized stereotypes of people of African descent. Various stereotypes included the Happy Darky; the Lazy Negro; Noble Savage; the oversexualization of Black men and women, placing extra emphasis on certain body parts; and the perversion and twisting of Black vernacular. Enslaved Africans were experiencing the brutality of enslavement; the beatings, the breaking up of families, the bounding of movement, and overall dehumanization that would affect generations to come.

Although these mistreatments would destroy the physical body, blackface minstrelsy would destroy our character.

Although Thomas "Daddy Rice" Dartmouth died shortly before the Emancipation Proclamation in 1863, the damaging effects of minstrelsy continued and veined itself in the entertainment world, including films, novels, and of course comics. Portrayals of Black life through the lenses of White actors, writers, and illustrators served as the telescope of how Whites and the world would view people of darker hues and African descent.

The exploitation of Blacks in entertainment was prevalent in the mid-nineteenth century and remained intact well into the 1930s. During those seventy plus years, and for the following forty years, the United States underwent various political, social, and economic saturations that influenced pop culture, such as:

- Civil War and the Emancipation Proclamation 1863–1865;
- Reconstruction era, Jim Crow laws, and Black Codes;
- World Wars I and II; Korean War; Cold War;
- Brutal murder of Emmitt Till;
- Civil rights movement;
- *Brown v Board of Education*;
- Vietnam War;
- Assassinations of Pres. John F. Kennedy, Robert Kennedy, the Rev. Dr. Martin Luther King Jr., and El Hajj Malik Shabazz.

The world was indeed changing, and so in the spirit of "art reflecting life and life reflecting art," so did the popular culture world in the depiction of people of color. Writers and illustrators could no longer withstand the push for the minstrelsy stereotypes because the now-freed population was rising up and the pressures were on to see our people in a different light, with respect to Black life, community, and culture.

Enter, ΘeoCon (pronounced Thee-oh-con),[1] a one-day convention in which participants are introduced and invited to explore themes of theology and morality in pop culture, faith, and fiction. Pop culture mediums include, but are not limited to comic books, graphic novels, science-fiction (sci-fi) films, and gaming. With the popularity of the Marvel Comics film *Black Panther*, there is a seismic shift in how African Americans are being portrayed in the

---

1. Information concerning ΘeoCon can be found at *http://www.theocon.live/about/*.

media. Theaters were sold out. Black churches booked entire theaters and provided free tickets for children to see the movie with their parents or guardians. Black Panther curricula have been developed to explore the nature of Blackness in a world that has traditionally viewed Blackness as a detriment. Still, there is much work to do to ensure that African Americans are cast in a positive light in the media; the Church can lead the way by creating space for young people, youth, and young adults to explore ways to integrate their faith and pop culture.

Rather than seeing pop culture as being solely in the realm of the secular, there is something undeniable in ΘeoCon that captures the themes such as good versus evil or the triumph of the underdog as part of God's story. The safe space created permits participants to engage in intimate conversations that encourage crossing boundaries to create discussions about, for example, how *X-Men* explores issues of oppression, to the development of youth and Sunday school curricula that include *Christology and Superman*. Truth be told, ΘeoCon is church for those who might feel left out of traditional church culture and dogma. ΘeoCon encourages participants to bring their whole selves and also to explore the self that wants to be free; that wants to escape the battles of life for a little while.

36

Adventism and White Supremacy

Alissa Williams

I was seven years old the first and only time I've had a gun shoved in my face. The man wielding it was Marc. He was my Sabbath school teacher. I remember the vastness of the basement in Lamson Hall on the campus of Andrews University[1] where Pioneer Memorial Church's (PMC) Primary Sabbath school classes met at that time (before the expansion that brought us all under the PMC roof). I remember the room was filled with circular tables to accommodate the many kids, spanning several grade levels. My group's table was off to the right. Each table got its own Sabbath school teacher, just to ourselves.

I remember Marc was new that Sabbath. With the seminary literally in the shadows of PMC, children's Sabbath school meant being subjected to an endless revolving door of seminary students eager to mold young minds for Adventism. There were a lot of problematic Sabbath school teachers over the years, but Marc is the most memorable, for reasons that will become apparent. I remember he strayed off course from the Sabbath school lesson. He didn't care about our memory verses or lesson plan, which disappointed me because I had studied. He wanted to talk about the end-times. And he did.

Then he pulled out the gun.

I remember the gun being matte grey with a black rubber grip, and I remember my fear. My parents, in the tradition of the Adventist pioneers, were staunch pacifists. Guns are bad, my seven-year-old mind was screaming. I remember Marc pointing the gun at us, telling us it was unloaded, but that very soon we would have loaded ones in our faces and we would be forced to choose between dying for our faith or renouncing God. But, said Marc, that didn't mean we should go out without a fight. He proceeded to teach our merry band of seven year olds the proper technique for loading the gun, with the real ammo

---

1. Andrews University is a Seventh-day Adventist college in Berrien Springs, Michigan.

he'd brought. He passed the gun around our circle and encouraged us to hold it. Get a feel for the weight of it, the grip. A boy next to me grabbed it eagerly. His parents had guns at home. He had held one before.

"Good," said Marc, nodding encouragingly.

It was my turn. I refused. I didn't want to touch a gun. I didn't want to shoot anyone. I couldn't even conceive of such an idea. My face burned with embarrassment as Marc shook his head, clearly disappointed. Some of the kids held the gun, some touched it with one finger, others were just as eager as that first boy. I was still just trying to figure out how preparing for the end-times with guns jibed with the pacifism my parents believed in. I don't know how many of our group went home that afternoon and told our parents in varying levels of excitement and dread about Marc and the gun. My guess would be all of us. I can only speak to my parents' reaction, which was horror. I don't know which parents called campus safety (quite possibly mine). And I don't know if it was campus safety, armed with their pepper spray, or the Berrien Springs police, with their very real guns, who raided Marc's car. But I do know that my parents, both Andrews employees, learned the details later. His trunk was filled with an entire arsenal of guns and ammunition. He was prepared for the end-time battle he had described to our Sabbath school class.

He was prepared to die and take as many people out with him as possible. Instead, his weapons were seized, he was kicked out of seminary, and he was banned from campus for life. I don't know what happened to Marc after that. For all I know, he's holed up in a remote cabin on a mountaintop, hoarding his weapons and cans of veggie meat, still ready to kill for Christ. What I do know is that radicalized Adventism is real, it's scary, and it's all around us whether we recognize it for what it is or not. Maybe this is why the Adventist Church has had such a difficult time denouncing White supremacy: because same recognizes same.

Radicalized Adventism stems from the same ideology as White supremacy: fear of the "other" and feelings of superiority toward those we've marked as different. Marc was so terrified by the "other" that is preached against from Adventist pulpits that he couldn't see them as human beings anymore. They were, in his mind, coming after him and his people and therefore his job was to take them out first. To take out as many as he could.

Sound familiar? It should. Because that is the exact same type of radicalized ideology the White supremacist who killed almost two dozen people in El Paso subscribed to. Our "other" looks different: radicalized Adventism is terrified of the pope, the Catholics who live next door, and politicians who might one day usher in Sunday laws. We demonize and dehumanize those "others" through our preaching, our seminars, our pamphlets. But not *all* Adventism you might be thinking. To which I'd respond, no one is saying *all* Adventism, just as no one is saying *all* White people are White supremacists.

But that doesn't stop this radicalized thinking from infecting the entire church. And we're quite comfortable as a church living with this infection. Because these fear-based tactics bring people in. It fills them with a burning passion that we falsely equate with faith. We've so perfected an 1800s-style fire-and-brimstone message of fear and trembling that when we hear the message of Jesus's love, that is what sounds radical to our ears. That is what sounds false.

Here's the thing: because we evangelize through fear, the people who are attracted to our message are often those who have already been radicalized in other ways. Let me put this plainly. Our fear-based evangelism attracts White supremacists. The overlap in the Venn diagram of White supremacy and Adventism is larger than we'd like to admit, and it all stems from that same place of radicalized ideology against those who are somehow different from us. This is why the Adventist Church is so uncomfortable denouncing the cancer that is White supremacy. It's our cancer too. We can't denounce it without admitting the infection is in us as well.

These are the questions on my mind as time after time our church is complicit with its silence. The answer is pretty simple. We must denounce White supremacy from our pulpits and our pews, whether an Adventist with a huge platform or no platform at all. And in the process of denouncing this evil, maybe we'll also be better equipped to recognize the ways our own religion has radicalized us toward hate and fear.

Only then can we move toward the radical love of Jesus.

Reflection Questions

1. What is your story? How have you advocated to have all Black lives matter in the Church and in the broader society?

2. For several of the contributors, their essays were confession, how they have been treated by the Church, for example. When reading these essays, what was your initial reaction? How could you advocate for congregations to be more inclusive of Black lives?

3. Is your congregation multicultural, or is it multiracial with a dominant culture that overlays worship and liturgy?

4. Which essay most resonated with you? Why?

5. Are you willing to put your body on the line to make Black lives matter?

PART III

Teaching
for Black Lives

37

Can I Be Black and Episcopalian?

Gayle Fisher-Stewart

Is it possible for Black people to maintain integrity and identity within a "White" church?

—The Rt. Rev. John T. Walker[1]

All of us must learn to honor our whole selves just as we come, just as we are. We can do this by just living, just doing, just Being Black.

—Rev. Angel Kyodo Williams, Being Black[2]

The purpose of education . . . is to create in a person the ability to look at the world for himself, to make his own decisions, to say to himself that this is black or this is white, to decide for himself whether there is a God in heaven or not. To ask questions of the universe, and then learn to live with those questions, is the way he achieves his own identity. But no society is really anxious to have that kind of person around. What societies really, ideally, want is a citizenry which will obey the rules of society.

—James Baldwin, "A Talk to Teachers"[3]

Ignorance allied with power is the most ferocious enemy justice can have.

—James Baldwin, "No Name in the Street"[4]

It is difficult being Black in a culture that values, treasures, and promotes Whiteness and White privilege. It takes work and determination to be comfortable in the Black skin God has given us, especially as Moni McIntyre has

---

1. Harold T. Lewis, *Yet with a Steady Beat: The African American Struggle for Recognition in the Episcopal Church* (Valley Forge, PA: Trinity Press, 1996), 1.

2. Angel Kyodo Williams, *Being Black: Zen and the Art of Living with Fearlessness and Grace* (New York: Penguin Compass, 2000), 9.

3. James Baldwin, "A Talk to Teachers," in *Teaching for Black Lives*, ed. Dyan Watson, Jesse Hagopian, and Wayne Au (Milwaukee: Thinking Schools Publication, 2018), 287.

4. James Baldwin, "No Name in the Street," in *Collected Essays* (New York: Library Classics of the United States, 1998), 349.

written, "Whiteness embodies the raw power that proclaims and implies that 'I, who am white (and male), am better than you because you are not white (and male).'"[5] For McIntyre, and others who understand how Whiteness works, Whiteness is the antithesis of biblical love.[6] While Whiteness may be the antithesis of biblical love, it is, however, a strong determinant of how those created in the image of God view themselves, particularly when the Church is part of that process. Traci C. West asks, "How does anti-Black, White racism impact the actions and psyches of Black Christians?"[7] One impact is internalized racial oppression in which the Church can play a role in eradicating. To eradicate it, self-hatred must first be understood because the Church has a role in supporting it and can, through its teachings, through Christian formation, as in any educational process, make it normative.

I had the task of developing and teaching the section on internalized racial oppression (self-hate) in the antiracism training for the Episcopal Diocese of Washington. Rather than talk about it, I used the following spoken word. It was painful writing it, remembering, and reliving it, and even more painful *performing* it.

Why I Hate Myself—Internalized Racial Oppression

I am American—a brown-skinned, nappy-haired, infinitive-splitting descendant of Sub-Saharan Africans and the British.

Yet, for all too many years—to assimilate—I tried to become White—because in these United States, to be American, to be seen as fully American, is to be White—not Caucasian, but White.

That concocted, fear-derived, nonexistent, but real social construct—Whiteness—held aloft by so-called American values.

> I've suffered the trauma of being Black in America, while trying to be White.

> But I am not the only one.

> A couple of years ago, at the beginning of the school year, my friend's daughter,

---

5. Moni McIntyre, "The Black Church and Whiteness," in *Christology and Whiteness: What Would Jesus Do?*, ed. George Yancy (London: Routlege, 2012), 78.

6. McIntyre, "Black Church and Whiteness," 79.

7. Traci C. West, "When a White Man-God is the Truth and the Way for Black Christians," in George Yancy, ed., *Christology and Whiteness: What Would Jesus Do?* (New York: Routledge, 2012), 115.

She's eight.

First day of school, she comes home; something's wrong.

"The kids won't play with me," she says.

My friend, her mother, begins to comfort her daughter.

Probably just first day of school, who's in, who's out, who's new.

"They say, I'm too dark."

Her mother now frowns, careful not to let her daughter see her face—thinking.

Before she can say anything, her daughter asks,

"Do you think if I paint myself white, they will play with me?"

Eight years old. Traumatized. The trauma of being Black in America.

If you're white, you're all right.

If you're yellow, you're mellow.

If you're brown, stick around.

If you're black, get back.

I learned that rhyme as a child. We used to jump rope to it.

In fact, I also learned about the brown paper bag and ruler test.

For a certain Black social organization in DC, to be admitted, you couldn't be darker than a brown paper bag and your hair had to be as straight as a ruler.

I passed the first, failed the second. I didn't get in.

My mother was upset. But she couldn't pass either test. I could care less.

The beautiful Black women of my youth—Lena Horne and Dorothy Dandridge. "Lena Horne's nostrils flare; they do not spread. The bridge of her nose is thin and exact. The nose of Dorothy Dandridge is a little bit fuller, but it's not *full*. And she had a dimple right above her lips. Cupid's bow lips. Maidenly lips. Lena's smile is wide, but her lips are not. She has high, wide Indian cheekbones, so she needs a wide smile."[8] They both were married to White men. Would White men eliminate the racism they experienced? No.

Truth be told, most Blacks have or have had some form of internalized racial oppression or self-hatred.

---

8. Margo Jefferson, *Negroland: A Memoir* (New York: Pantheon Books, 2015), 66.

Ibram X. Kendi, the author of *Stamped from the Beginning: The Definitive History of Racist Ideas* and *How to Be an Anti-Racist* and now a professor at American University, says that he had to come to grips with some of the ideas he held about Black people because he, like me, was born into a world of racist ideas, many of which we held about Black people, people like us, people like me, people like him.[9]

Imagine being taken from your country—your homeland—taken from everything and everyone you know. Kidnapped, stolen, sometimes sold by your own people.

In a new land, a strange land, if you make it through the middle passage; you stand on an auction block, stripped naked.

White hands in your mouth, between your legs, your price is set—like a wagon, or a pig, or a nothing. Daina Berry in her book, *The Price for Their Pound of Flesh*,[10] writes about the value of the enslaved from the womb to the tomb in the building of this nation. How much am I worth?

You are nothing, not a person, but a thing.

You are owned; you are property. You have no rights, not even the right to defend yourself. You are dehumanized. Blacks could be whipped for lifting up a hand against any Christian, Christian meaning White—beginning in the colony of Virginia—regardless of the provocation. The dehumanization process was complete in 1680 because Blacks were legally precluded from responding in a manner thought normal for Whites or most other human beings.[11]

You are to work, work until you drop and you are to breed; increasing the master's stock.

Your language, your customs, your history—means nothing—your people contributed nothing to civilization—or so, they say . . .

You are heathen, a savage. Not created in the image of God, how could you be? God is White. You are Black. Enslavement was ordained by God and justified as a method of civilizing us.

"Slaves obey your masters!" God has sentenced you to serve the White man. If you do it well, one day, you will get to heaven; but there is fence in heaven and there is hole in that fence and you will be able to look over to the

---

9. Ibram X. Kendi, *How to Be an Anti-Racist* (New York: One World, 2019), 4–11.

10. Daina Ramey Berry, *The Price for Their Pound of Flesh: The Value of the Enslaved, from Womb to the Grave in the Building of a Nation* (Boston: Beacon Press, 2017).

11. A. Leon Higginbotham Jr., *In the Matter of Color: Race and the American Legal Process, The Colonial Period* (Oxford: Oxford University Press, 1978), 39.

White heaven through the hole in the fence. That's where God is—on the White side of heaven.

Black skin, big butt, nappy hair, thick lips, flat, broad nose—Beyonce likes her Negro nose with Jackson 5 nostrils—the old Jackson 5 nostrils, that is.

Saartjie "Sarah" Baartman, a South African woman was displayed—displayed naked—as a freak show attraction in nineteenth-century Europe under the name Hottentot Venus—she had a very big butt. Hottentot Venus . . .

Oogled at, laughed at. Displayed like an animal. Degraded for the enjoyment of White people.

But let us not forget our Native American brothers and sisters.

Forced off their land—considered savage because they did not rape the land and corral their animals.

They were not skilled in animal husbandry, so said the Europeans.

The only good Indian is a dead Indian, so said the president of the United States, Andrew Jackson, and he tried to make it so: the Trail of Tears.

Forced off the land, placed on reservations—children taken from them—for the good of the children, mind you, and placed in Indian schools.

Not really Indian schools, but White schools for Indians—stripped of their language, punished for speaking their language.

Stripped of their customs, made to wear European clothes because their clothing was—uncivilized.

Kill the Indian. Save the man: the "White" man . . .

Why was it when the Indians won a battle, it was a great massacre; and when the US army won, it was a great victory?

And what about all those laws that said we—Black people—were inferior, that we had no rights a White man is bound to respect?

But one day, you find yourself "free"?

But what is this freedom, and you want to prove that you love this land—have just as much right to be in this land—just as much right as the White man and so you want to become "American"?

After all, this is the only country you know.

But what is American? What does an American look like?

Open a picture dictionary. American? White skin, blue eyes, straight (good) hair.

And let's not forget the other "straight."

White, male, and straight. That is what it is to be American.

To be an American is to assimilate. Assimilate to what? To be White?

Others, to become American, can change their names, lose their accent; their skin color will get them through, but us?

So, we try—we straighten our bad hair to make it good.

We straighten it with hot combs; we straighten it. We straighten it with relaxers; perms that originally had lye; you know—lye, yes lye; if you left the perm on too long, it would burn your scalp, second degree burns, leaving it oozing for days.

The lye destroyed the natural curl pattern of our hair.

Something of us had to be destroyed to assimilate. Nappy hair, kinky hair brings shame. "Girl, you better do something with your hair." "You better 'fix' it." Fix it? Is my hair "broken"?

Some of us have never seen our natural hair. Mothers start perming it at age four.

The men, our men "conched" their hair—made it straight.

But it doesn't stay straight. Need to straighten, relax, and conch on a regular basis.

Can't let those roots reveal that you really have bad hair. Don't you want bouncing and behaving hair? And, oh, yes, and make it blonde, because blondes do have more fun.

Light skin, White skin, skin that has the mark of the rape of our women.

But it is prized.

Nadinola bleaching cream.

Now it's called Nadinola Skin Discoloration Fade Cream Extra Strength Formula and you can buy it at CVS.

There's also Porcelana skin lightening night cream and Daggett and Ramsdell lightening soap bar—you can buy it at Walgreen's. There's also Vantex by Fashion Fair.

Today it's marketed as skin tone; it is supposed to even out the skin tone but there was a time when it was used every day, every night, to get the skin lighter—maybe get it all the way to White.

After all, there are those of us who passed, who are passing, who have left their families and passed over to the White world never to return, but constantly living in fear that they might just be found out; that one day, there would be a knock at the door.

Whiteness has property value, and folks will mess with DNA to keep it light.

Shhh! Truth be told, if you're from DC and go back a few generations, you know families that intermarried just to keep the lightness, the Whiteness going.

Don't you bring home no dark-skinned boy. You ain't gonna marry him. What your children gonna look like? Red bone? Hi Yella? Café au lait? Better not be jet Black.

Folks went to court, all the way to the US Supreme Court to get certified, legally certified as White. Check out the book by Ian Lopez: *White by Law*.[12]

Crave the blue eyes. Toni Morrison. *The Bluest Eye*. Pecola is a young, Black girl who loves Shirley Temple, believing that Whiteness is beautiful and that she is ugly. Pecola is continually reminded of what an "ugly" girl she is, fueling her desire to be White with blue eyes. A poor Black girl, she believes she is ugly because she and her community base their ideals of beauty on "Whiteness." The title *The Bluest Eye* refers to Pecola's fatal desire for beautiful blue eyes. Her insanity at the end of the novel is her only way to escape the world where she cannot be beautiful and to get the blue eyes she craves from the beginning of the novel.[13]

There was a time: call somebody Black—you were asking—well, I'm going to tell it like it is—you were asking for an ass whipping.

Black: of the very darkest color owing to the absence of or complete absorption of light; the opposite of White.

dark, pitch-Black, jet-Black, coal-Black, ebony, sable, inky

Definition of Black for Students. 1 : the color of coal : the opposite of White.: a person belonging to a race of people having dark skin. 4 : an American having **Black** African ancestors : african-american.

Being of the color **Black**, producing or reflecting comparatively little light and having no predominant hue. Having little or no light: If Christ is the Light, then what are we with our absence of light—the absence of Christ?

Black—very wicked or evil—"my soul is steeped in the Blackest sin"—wicked, evil, villainous, "a Black deed." Blackball. Blackmail.

But then, we took the sting out of " Black" in the 1960s: "Say it loud, I'm Black and I'm proud." Can't hurt me no more. I've made it my own.

But stay out of the sun—not because of cancer, but because your grandmother didn't want you to get darker than you already are.

Back to hair. Imagine this, having to go to court to be permitted to wear your hair as God grows it out of your head—to wear it that way to work—because it is not professional? In the 1970s, went to court—had to sue to wear

---

12. Ian F. Haney Lopez, *White by Law: The Legal Construction of Race* (New York: New York University Press, 1996).

13. Toni Morrison, *The Bluest Eye* (New York: Alfred Knopf, 2000).

our hair the way it is. Natural. Sent home from work, disciplined because of our nappy hair. Who determines what is professional? Our children—today—are being sent home because of their hair. But California passed a law (this year?) that Black hair is legal. My hair had to be declared "legal."

Taught in now-integrated schools that our people contributed nothing to the history of this country—other than to be enslaved. We were meant to be enslaved; to serve White people.

The forefathers—the founders: all White, all male, all slaveholders. There was Negro History Week—Carter G. Woodson, Frederick Douglass—maybe a couple of more.

But not many.

Not in the regular history books. But in 2015 McGraw Hill published a history book that indicated that the enslaved were "workers" or "immigrants" who arrived in this country under "forced migration." Really? What year is this? Forced migration as opposed to shackled in the holds of slave ships.

Integration—necessary, but it hurt us as a people.

We left our communities where our children were disciplined by anyone who saw them misbehaving.

It takes a village to raise a child and we left the village because the White communities were, we thought, "better."

The schools we began because the government saw no reason to build schools for Blacks and which nourished and educated us are now languishing on the vine, closing because we want our children to go to the White schools because we think they are better.

We had a Black Wall Street. We had a couple of Black Wall Streets, but the one in Tulsa, Oklahoma, was destroyed by Whites, burned to the ground, and the others and Black businesses are struggling because we want to shop where the White folks shop because those businesses are better. White = better.

Industrial Bank was founded on August 20, 1934, and is the oldest and largest African American owned commercial bank in the metropolitan Washington, DC, region. How many of us bank there?

We left the Black church—our churches—where we didn't have to sit in the back or in the balcony or be preached at—by White ministers—we left them because they were too loud; don't need all that shouting, don't want to be slain in the spirit. Totally undignified.

Want to act like White folks; don't sing no Negro music in here. We praise the Lord, but do it quietly. And don't you touch my White Jesus, right beside Martin, John, and Robert.

But White folks are getting butt implants, collagen lip injections, lying on the beach to get darker and risking cancer on those tanning beds.

Bo Derek made news in 1979, in the movie *10* when she wore cornrows, as if Black folks had never worn them. She popularized cornrows when Black women were being sent home from work for wearing them because they were unprofessional.

May 2016, Belton, Texas—A Black mother recommended administrators at Belton Independent School District undergo diversity training after they told her nine-year-old daughter her hair was unacceptable. The assistant principal said it looked like a Mohawk and was not in compliance with the school dress code and pulled her out of class.

Her mother said, "She cried and said no one was going to want to be her friend because her hair was not as pretty as the (White) assistant principal's." As a parent, that's heartbreaking because that's just what God naturally gave her.

The child is questioning her natural, God-given image.

We can straighten our hair, we can bleach our skin, we can speak the king's or queen's English, we can live where White folks live, we can even elect a Black president, but all too many of us cannot assimilate, because we cannot BE White.

And—there is always the one-drop rule; we didn't make up that rule either. W. E. B. Du Bois wrote:

> The Negro is a sort of seventh son, born with a veil, and gifted with second sight in this American world—a world which yields him no true self-consciousness, but only lets him see himself through the revelation of the other world. It is a peculiar sensation, this double-consciousness, this sense of always looking at one's self through the eyes of others, of measuring one's soul by the tape of a world that looks on in amused contempt and pity. One ever feels his two-ness—an American, a Negro; two souls, two thoughts, two unreconciled strivings; two warring ideals in one dark body whose dogged strength alone keeps it from being torn asunder.[14]

I, like many African Americans who have been socialized in a racist society, was confused, totally confused. I had internalized Whites' view of Black people—my people—me. Internalized racial oppression is alive and well today.

---

14. W. E. Burghardt Du Bois, *The Souls of Black Folk: Essays and Sketches* (Chicago: A.C. McClurg & Co., 1920), 3.

I was speaking with a church member and she said, "Well, you know how Black people are."

I responded, "No, I don't, tell me."

She went on stating how Blacks are lazy, don't want to work for anything, are on welfare.

I listened and then I said, "Black people, like you?"

She looked at me, "No, not like me."

I wanted to say, "You have a problem"; however, I told her, "It's unfair to categorize an entire group of people when your knowledge is limited."

In the Church, Jesus is also co-opted by Whiteness, ". . . the truth and transformative power reflect norms of White dominance, human well-being, imagination, and potential are held captive."[15] Both the sacred and the secular upheld Whiteness, so I was caught between a rock and a hard place. Everywhere I turned, Whiteness reigned supreme. I saw myself through the eyes of Whites. I color-shamed myself. I hair-shamed myself. On the one hand, I craved Whiteness, at least the hair part; long, straight, lightened hair—hair that was not naturally mine. But there was something about dark skin.

What is it to be Black and how can the Church assist those of us who reflect the image of God in wonderful shades of Black and Brown? If we follow the one-drop rule, most of the world is probably Black. We are the racial chameleons of the world. We are like the universal donor of race. We are the O+ of racial categories. We mix well with everyone and the results are simply breathtaking. In order to be fully human and fully Black, it is critical that the Church, White and Black, create safe space to have these difficult conversations about throwing off the shackles of racial self-oppression, colorism, and colonization. We must emancipate ourselves of self-hatred, understanding that it has taken over four hundred years to arrive at this point and all these forms of racism will take time to fade. We must acknowledge that colorism, in particular, was used by the enslavers to divide us, to keep us hating ourselves and each other. Colorism also affected the Church—the Black church—and it must still be asked and there will be some who will be offended: do we have Black churches that are really White churches in blackface that eschew all things Black?

I love the sound of African drums as we process at the opening of the service. I love the look of African fabrics used as altar, pulpit, and lectern paraments (hangings). I love services, liturgies, where we begin by pouring

---

15. West, "When a White Man-God," 115.

libations to the ancestors. I love the sound of Negro spirituals, although I know they are, as pastor emeritus of Trinity United Church of Christ in Chicago, the Rev. Dr. Jeremiah Wright describes, "classically arranged anthemic renditions"[16] and not how they actually sounded in the fields and brush harbors. I just wish the Holy Spirit would just take hold of every single person sitting in our pews and do her thing. In a talk given in 2014, Rev. Wright told of a "hundred years war" between 1868 and 1968 when Negro spirituals were forbidden to be played or sung on Black college campuses; they were not considered sacred music. While I find joy in ancestral religions, I look at the faces of those in our pews who believe unless the liturgy is straight out of the Book of Common Prayer, it is not proper worship—it is not *Anglican*.[17] Who makes the determination of proper worship? It would seem that the Lord would be that judge.

What is it to be a member or adherent of any faith tradition? Can you bring your whole self or are there some parts of yourself that must be left behind, changed, altered, destroyed? Can I be Christian, Episcopalian, and Black? Regardless of a person's ethnicity (or gender identity), are they able to see themselves in the worship service or are they provided an image into which they must fit; an image that denies the image of God? Can worship services, coupled with church art, cause trauma? If God is White, then White must be God. Formation begins and continues as we step into the sanctuary.

Knowing the history of Christianity and the Episcopal Church particularly in America, the question probably should be, why would I want to be Christian and Episcopalian? In the nineteenth century, because of the history and role of the Episcopal Church as the church of the enslaver, Harold Lewis said there was "something incongruous about being Black and Episcopalian;" that the term "Black Episcopalian . . . 'approaches the status of oxymoron,'" however, here we are, Black and Episcopalian.[18] In 1977, the Rt. Rev. John T. Walker, the first and only African American diocesan bishop of the Episcopal Diocese of Washington, DC, my diocese, asked, "Is it possible for Black people to maintain integrity and identity within a 'White' church?"[19] Dr. Van Bird, an attendee at the same conference of Black clergy where Walker asked

---

16. The Rev. Dr. Jeremiah A. Wright Jr., "Slavery to Freedom Lecture Series," Michigan State University College of Osteopathic Medicine, March 27, 2014, *https://www.youtube.com/watch?v=f8fTYcl5f3Y&t=623s*.

17. Michigan State University College of Osteopathic Medicine.

18. Harold T. Lewis, *Yet With a Steady Beat: The African American Struggle for Recognition in the Episcopal Church* (Valley Forge, PA: Trinity Press, 1996), 1.

19. Lewis, *Yet With a Steady Beat*, 5.

his question, queried, "What does it mean to be a Christian witness in a racist church?"[20] Dr. Bird proclaimed that the Episcopal Church was racist; it mirrored the society into which it was born. How could it not be racist? James H. Cone also posed the same question, "Is it possible for me to be *really* Black and still feel any identity with the biblical tradition expressed in the Old and New Testaments? Is it possible to strip the gospel as it has been interpreted of its 'Whiteness,' so that its real message will become a live option for radical advocates of Black consciousness?"[21]

As Lewis writes, these were not new issues being brought up by Walker and Bird; they were issues that had dogged Black Episcopalians ever since Absalom Jones, the first Black man ordained priest in the Episcopal Church, split from Richard Allen after they and others were to be relegated to the balcony at St. George Methodist Church in Philadelphia, Pennsylvania. Richard Allen went on to form the Mother Bethel African Methodist Episcopal Church (AME). However, even as Dr. Bird was claiming it was possible to be Black and Episcopal, to combine Black and Anglican traditions, is that really possible when Blackness is seen by society in general as a deficit and it is neither lifted up in the tradition or in the educational process that *makes disciples*? While Harold Lewis writes that Black Episcopalians have been able to distinguish the gospel message from how Whiteness has packaged it, does that mean that traditions that have empowered and nurtured Blacks in America are wanted in what it is to be Episcopalian?[22]

Does Christian formation take into consideration the cultures, the ethnicities, the religious traditions of those who are to be molded, first into Christians, and then into a member of a particular denomination? Or is Christian formation akin to Marine boot camp where every aspect of personality is stripped away, the self is broken down, and then something else, someone else is created. A *someone* who fits into a prescribed mold of what it is to be, in my instance, an Episcopalian with an Anglican underpinning? Simply tanning up the characters on the covers of curricula or books used in the formation process or participating in Black History month does not create an inclusive and relevant process.

Nine years after graduating from Wesley Theological Seminary in Washington, DC, I was, sitting in Dr. Beverly Mitchell's seminar class, "Jesus Christ

---

20. Lewis, *Yet With a Steady Beat*, 5.

21. James H. Cone, *Black Theology and Black Power* (New York: Orbis Books, 2003), 33.

22. Lewis, *Yet With a Steady Beat*, 175.

in African American Christianity." I had wanted to return since graduation and I was auditing. The texts: *The Color of Christ: The Son of God and the Saga of Race in America* by Edward J. Blum and Paul Harvey; *The Cross and the Lynching Tree* by James Cone; *Power in the Blood?: The Cross in the African American Experience* by JoAnne Marie Terrell; *Jesus and the Disinherited* by Howard Thurman; and *The Soul of Hip Hop: Rims, Timbs, and a Cultural Theology* by Daniel White Hodge, all proved to be challenging.

The discussions were lively and Dr. Mitchell pushed and prodded; however, as I was sitting there, taking in the glory that is Black theology and intellectualism, I was dismayed by the number of students in the class. Wesley is no small school by seminary standards. There were two hundred and thirteen graduates in my class of 2010. For some seminaries that number would be the entire student population. This class began with all of seven students, two of them White, and two (including me) who were graduates and auditing the class. Two of the students dropped, one White and one Black. When a seminary employee also joined us to audit, the class was comprised of six students. Why were so few students taking culturally based classes?

As I thought back over my seminary experience, I recalled the number of Black-focused courses that had fewer than the normal seminar size registration and lacked White students. I also recalled my experience in 2015 at Virginia Theological Seminary, an Episcopal school, where I spent a year during my ordination process. All seminarians were required to participate in a weekly formation session held at the home of a faculty member. All of us in the Anglican Studies program were assigned to the same faculty member. We would meet two hours a week for the entire year. I can attest that it didn't make me more Anglican or more Episcopalian, and I am not any more community oriented than I was before I began the process. As an introvert, forced community is exasperating.

There were eight of us in this cohort: one Latina and me, the only African American. We were in our second and final semester. We had spent the first semester together with the same faculty member. On this particular day, the faculty member began by saying, "We are all White people here . . ."

I don't remember what followed.

I'm not even sure his opening salvo had anything to do with the words that came after. All I remember is feeling the pressure of my classmate's nails as they dug into my flesh, keeping me quiet. Before I could regroup and say anything, she said, "Gayle's here." I'm not even sure he heard her because he went on with whatever he was saying and I heard absolutely nothing. All I wanted was out.

One of my classmates must have either spoken to him or e-mailed him about the incident because I received an e-mail from him:

> Apparently, I must have said something to offend you. If I did and you would like to chat, stop by my office.

I pressed "delete." I was invisible. I was sixty-three years old, long-retired from the Washington, DC Metropolitan Police Department, and being ordained to the priesthood at a time when many of my soon-to-be clergy colleagues were either retired or considering retirement. I was too old for this s***.

While I know the Church is not perfect, the foundation upon which clergy are prepared is as racist as the society from which the Church was birthed. In the short time I spent at VTS, I did not have the opportunity to take classes that focused on the Black experience; at Wesley, I did. Still, the lack of diversity in those classes was alarming. Rethinking Christopher Emdin's critique of the racist educational system that divested this country's indigenous people of their language and culture (*Kill the Indian and save the man*), a vast divide exists between traditional, in this case, Episcopal seminaries, in which Black Episcopalians receive their formation and acculturation and their identity as African Americans.[23]

To have my Blackness valued and considered, must I attend a Black seminary? When will Black theology, womanist theology, liberation theology, and queer theology become part of the requirements for graduation, instead of electives or afterthoughts? When will White seminarians begin to take these courses as a matter of becoming well-rounded theologians? When will Black-oriented programs draw White students as a matter of course? When will Katie Geneva Cannon, Jacqueline Grant, Beverly Eileen Mitchell, Kelly Brown Douglas, Renita Weems, James Cone, Josiah U. Young III, J. DeLotis Roberts, Michael Battle, Frank Thomas, and other Black theologians be studied alongside of Acquinas, Bonhoeffer, Bruggemann, Luther, Barth, Tertullian, and other White males? I wonder how many seminaries focus on the fact that some Church fathers were not White, but North African: Tertulian, Origen, and Augustine. No, they were not Black sub-Saharan Africans, but they were certainly not European Whites. The answer: not until being Black is not seen as being deficient, and out of the mainstream of what is seen as being American, Christian, or Episcopalian.

The Episcopal Church has nine seminaries across the country. It is difficult without reviewing specific lesson plans to see which courses lift up Black

---

23. Christopher Emdin, *For White Folks Who Teach in the Hood . . . and the Rest of Y'all Too: Reality Pedagogy and Urban Education* (Boston: Beacon Press, 2016), 2.

history, culture, and theology. More research would have to be conducted to determine if courses that bring in cultures other than White or Anglican are required courses. Some seminaries provide programs in a specific cultural context, such as the Ministry in Latino Context program at Church Divinity School of the Pacific (CDSP). The Seminary of the Southwest has a master of divinity program with a Latino/Hispanic studies concentration. There are also courses, such as Multiculturalism and Diversity Issues in Pastoral Care, Latinx Theologies, Liberation Theologies, Womanist Theological Ethics, Liturgical Celebration in Latino Context, and African American Preaching. The School of Theology, University of the South offers these courses: History of Spirituality (which includes Martin Luther King Jr.), The Parish Priest as Public Theologian (which includes such voices as Martin Luther King Jr., Cornel West, Desmond Tutu, Oscar Romero, and Augustine), and North African Christianity. Still, the question is how many White students take these courses and which courses, if any, are required for all students?

How do Episcopal African Americans find their voices in a sea of White voices? Should we expect the church to lift up a black *imago Dei*? Do our curricula take into account the Black experience in America and perpetuate Whiteness? Our curricula are not color-blind. The fact that color or race is not mentioned does not mean it is absent. Whiteness is normative in this country and in the Episcopal Church. Stained glass windows, where they still exist in the traditional manner, tell the stories of the Bible in Whiteness. Children of color do not see themselves in those stories. A White Jesus looks down from the cross and perpetuates Whiteness. Simply colorizing characters on the covers or pages of Sunday school books and formation materials does not undue the racism and trauma that undergirds how God is taught. The White Church perpetuates internalized racial oppression. Eurocentric worship styles abound and Black worship styles and preaching are frowned on, by both Blacks and Whites, except for special occasions, such as Black History Month and Absalom Jones Sunday. Black worship is not deficient; it is just different.

Unfortunately, the Church can be a captive of the world, particularly as it relates to education. In the 2010 introduction to Carter G. Woodson's 1933 masterpiece, *The Miseducation of the Negro*, Charles H. Wesley and Thelma D. Perry write that miseducation of Black people stems from the failure to present "Negro history" in a way that does not negate our presence in and contribution to the growth and wealth of this country. Even the Church—and in particular the Anglican Church, which birthed the Episcopal Church—promoted Blacks as heathens and that slavery was a necessary tool to save the Black man and woman's soul. Never mind that the Church abused, exploited, and destroyed the Black body that reflected the *imago Dei*. The Church was the anti-Christ. Through the manipulation of history for the benefit of Whites, Blacks have been deprived of a history that provided uplift as opposed to a self-hatred.[24] As we look at the educational system in the country, Woodson's words in 1933 ring true today that Black Americans have been taught to view themselves through the lens of Whiteness.

> When you control a man's thinking, you do not have to worry about his actions. You do not have to tell him to stand here or go yonder. He will find his "proper" place and will stay in it. You do not have to tell him to go to the back door. He will go without being told. In fact, if there is no back door, he will cut one for his special benefit. His education makes it necessary.[25]

Becoming a Christian disciple and by inference, becoming Episcopalian, is a process. It begins with seeking and ends when God stops sharing God's breath with us. Formation is a lifelong process from the womb to the tomb. What follows is not a critique of the various curricula and programs; rather, what follows is a plea to understand that people learn differently, that our curricula and programs must be flexible enough to take into account these differences and the effects of an educational system, and a Christian formation process that has been and continues to be Eurocentric. In her critique of the formation process for Episcopal priests, the Rev. Rachel K. Taber-Hamilton blogged, "The 'Anglican' in Anglican identity is at its core White history and White identity," and that the board that assessed her suitability to become a priest, the commission on ministry, was concerned when she shared that she incorporated her "indigenous practices of burning sacred herbs and indigenous traditions of interacting with nature as important aspects of [her] spiritual practice and formation."[26]

What happens when formation collides with cultural differences brought to the process by those who are seeking to become Christian and Episcopalian? Do non-Whites have to be stripped of who they are to become "sufficiently Anglican"? And just what is "sufficiently Anglican"?

In assessing whether one can be both Black and Episcopalian, questions posed by Angel Kyode Williams invite discussion. Is it possible to include

---

24. Charles H. Wesley and Thelma D. Perry, "Introduction," in Carter G. Woodson, *The Miseducation of the Negro* (Las Vegas: IAP Publishing, 2010), 5.

25. Woodson, *Miseducation of the Negro*, 15.

26. Rachel K. Taber-Hamilton, "The Measure of a Priest: Racial Bias and White Privilege in the Episcopal Church," posted December 3, 2019, *https://greeningspirit.com*.

aspects of African-inspired religions, such as Yoruba, Santeria, and Voodoo in learning to be who God has called us to be? Is it possible to learn from and include rituals from Sufism, Buddhism, Islam, and others as we navigate what it is to be a follower of a Palestinian Jew?[27]

Can practices that have meaning to us be included and used without being accused of syncretism? Isn't it all about relationship; a relationship with God and each other? Must we be limited to and proscribed to adhere to a liturgy and way of relating that uplifts Whiteness, at least a Eurocentric way of believing and worshiping? As stated above, it is more than colorizing curricula or sticking a Black fact into the process of formation to animate this discussion. Are we creating Christians who happen to be Black or are we creating White Christians who look Black or Brown?

Woodson's critique of the miseducation of the Negro provides fruit as we ask whether we are misforming Black Christians in a manner that causes them to hate their history and culture, to engage in internalized racial oppression, and to deny an African influence in Christianity? I consider the rise of Black Episcopal parishes in what would become the Episcopal Diocese of Washington and the two foundational Black churches, St. Mary's and St. Luke's. St. Mary's has been described as the "foster child of the fashionable St. John's (White) parish. According to tradition, it was the church of (Black) servants of wealthy (White) Washington Episcopalians."[28] St. John's provided financial backing for the fledging St. Mary's and is the church that is still in Lafayette Park, across from the White House. The Rev. Dr. Alexander Crummell was called as rector to St. Mary's; however, internal difficulties led him to lead half of that congregation to build St. Luke's. St. Luke's became home to the upper crust of Black Episcopalianism, the Black intelligentsia, yet colorism undergirded the culture and Crummell, who was the founding rector (pastor) of St. Luke's, found himself at odds with his own congregation because of the "inability of Black people at that time to accept the leadership of one of their own."[29] Black Episcopalians were proud that they

> had outgrown the crude and tumultuous religious systems of a former day. It
> is nothing but an act of mercy for the Church to step in front now, with her

---

27. Angel Kyodo Williams, *Being Black: Zen and the Art of Living with Fearlessness and Grace* (New York: Penguin Compass, 2000), 3.

28. Wilson Jeremiah Moses, *Alexander Crummell: A Study of Civilization and Discontent* (New York: Oxford University Press, 1989), 198.

29. Moses, *Alexander Crummell*, 199.

chaste, sober, yet warm, and elevating system, to meet the needs and to satisfy the stimulated cravings of these trained and anxious minds.[30]

In other words, the religious traditions of the brush harbor, the incantations that invoked the ancestors; the "rich tradition of folk belief and practice, that included conjure, herbalism, ghost lore, witchcraft, and fortune-telling"[31] that flourished on the plantations and helped the enslaved to make a way out of no way, were to be shunned as primitive and improper, not sufficiently White, and surely not sufficiently Anglican/Episcopalian.

Whatever formation processes are used by the Church, they must first dismantle the idol of White supremacy in the Church and society. Formation must strengthen Black dignity. Therefore, all curricula and processes must be assessed for how the Christian/Episcopalian is formed and whether that formation mirrors Whiteness. As Beverly Eileen Mitchell writes:

> The nature of slavery in North America was distinctively different from previous forms of slavery in other civilizations. Slavery in North America was designed, categorically and systematically, to *dehumanize* Blacks who were forced to serve under this system.[32]

Christianity was part and parcel of that process. The Church, in particular, the Anglican Church which gave birth to the Episcopal Church was at the root of this dehumanization and must admit its complicity with more than apologies. Every aspect of Christian formation must be assessed for how it continues to promote White Anglicanism, White supremacy, even though the words "race," "discrimination," and "White supremacy" are nowhere to be found. The words do not need to be obvious because they form the taproot of what it is to be Anglican/Episcopal. The evidence is before us, with every Black parish—those that are historically Black and those that have turned from White to Black—where Whites are unwilling to worship in sufficient numbers. Racism created Black parishes, racism maintains them, and racism will kill them. As a colleague stated, Black parishes are dying on the vine and rotting on the ground. Is there anyone who cares?

So where do we begin? What is the church's role? First, we need to begin with decolonizing our people and our churches. There are some Episcopalians,

---

30. Moses, *Alexander Crummell*, 198.

31. Albert J. Raboteau, *Slave Religion: The "Invisible" Institution in the Antebellum South* (New York: Oxford University Press, 2004), 275.

32. Beverly Eileen Mitchell, *Black Abolitionism: A Quest for Human Dignity* (New York: Orbis Books, 2005), 2.

including Black Episcopalians, who believe that to be truly Episcopalian is to adhere to the Book of Common Prayer and the *1982 Hymnal* with no deviations. I've watched and listened as Black Episcopalians turned up their noses and sneered that they did not want any of that "Negro music" in their church. Negro music? Have they looked in the mirror lately?

What Learning?

People learn differently. At all ages, people bring with them previous learning experiences. Every formation teacher/educator must be aware of these learning styles and experiences to be effective and ensure that learning uplifts culture. Something as benign as a tour of the sanctuary can send a powerful message. Stained glass windows, with their stories of the Bible, say more than chapter and verse. Are all the characters White with blonde hair and blue eyes? What message is being sent to the Black child who is attempting to discern their place in God's kingdom? Are there pictures in the Bibles in the pews? Who do those pictures lift up? Who is more "godly"?

Church is to be a place of refuge, a place of safety. Many of our Black children have come from school systems that see them as problems, regardless of their socioeconomic status. Some of our Christian educators, regardless of race, have also worked in those systems and they bring with them some of those biases and prejudices.

"He frightens me," the young White teacher said.

"Frightens you? What does that mean, he frightens you? Do you mean because he is Black and taller than you?" I pushed back. My clergy colleague, the Rev. Peter Jarrett-Schell, writes of me in his book *Seeing My Skin (A Story of Wrestling with Whiteness)* that I have "little patience for pretense."[33] He is correct; I have little patience for a system that dehumanizes my son and nieces and nephews, and me. I have no patience with a Church that seems to have little power or desire to change itself. Racism kills. Racism kills the soul, it kills the spirit, and it kills the body. Trayvon Martin is dead. Michael Brown is dead. Atatiana Jefferson is dead. Sandra Bland is dead. All killed by the police. Mary Turner was lynched. Gracy Blanton was lynched. Dora Baker was lynched. Jesse Hose was lynched. The list can go on and on, but these will suffice. They are dead because White society sees the Black body as a threat. 1 John 4:18 says

---

33. Peter Jarrett-Schell, *Seeing My Skin (A Story of Wrestling with Whiteness)* (New York: Church Publishing, 2019), 265.

"Perfect love casts out fear." God is perfect love and even God seems powerless to cast out the fear of the Black body in this country. Retired Methodist bishop William H. Willimon lifts up the mirror to the face of Whiteness so those who claim Whiteness can see how it "others." He calls for those who claim Whiteness to look at their reflection in the mirror and see themselves as the Other, the one who is a threat to both God and one's neighbor. He says that for him, the goal of Christian preaching is to render him, to see himself, as the Other.[34] In teaching, it is also the responsibility of those who cling to Whiteness to render themselves as the Other.

I return to my question of the teacher: "You are afraid of his Blackness? His Blackness frightens you?" My demeanor probably did not help. I am not a small woman, and I was at least five inches taller than the teacher as I stood up to my full height. It was my practice to visit my nephew's school and sit in his classes at least twice a month. For some reason his grades had slipped, he was getting into trouble, so his police officer aunt went to find out why. When I spent time with him, he read above grade level. He could explain how "Brown" became the name used in the 1954 landmark case *Brown v Board of Education of Topeka*. He was better in math than I was. I wanted to know why he was being placed in the disciplinary class at his middle school. I already knew the answer. I had not spent twenty years in policing and obtained degrees in criminal justice without knowing the answer; I wanted the teacher to tell me why. She was afraid because this middle schooler was a foot taller than she. He was a Brown-skinned man-child. I knew the answer because since slavery Black men have been seen as animals, less than human, criminals, who had to be controlled to save the purity of the White woman. In 1996, my colleague at the University of Maryland coined the term "criminal Blackman" stereotype.[35] That stereotype follows all Black men and boys to this day. I knew why she was afraid, unjustifiably so, but I knew why. I had consulted for the Department of Justice during the *superpredator* era and the Crime Control Bill, which really should have been the "Negro Control Bill." I knew because I had been in classes where we were being taught that private prisons were being built based on third grade reading levels, even though that urban myth was false. The young White teacher had been raised in the society and culture that would prefer to have Black males either in jail or back on the plantation. She was afraid of my

---

34. William H. Willimon, *Fear of the Other: No Fear in Love* (Nashville: Abingdon Press, 2016), 13.

35. Katheryn Russell-Brown, *The Color of Crime: Racial Hoaxes, White Fear, Black Protectionism, Police Harassment, and Other Macroaggressions* (New York: New York University Press, 1998).

nephew and I wanted her to be afraid of me. The school-to-prison pipeline is for real and a reality for all too many of our Black children who find their way, we hope, to our Sunday schools, confirmation classes, and acolyte preparation. We cannot afford to have our Black children seen as threats by those who are to help them become followers of a Palestinian Jew who was killed as an enemy of the state because he was the Other.

School resource officers are not the Officer Friendly of the 1950s and 1960s. Our schools are becoming prisons. They are on lockdown—not because of an active shooter drill (which traumatizes all children); our Black children are the inmates. We've seen the videos of police officers tackling our children in schools, arresting five- and six-year-old children for being, well, five- and six-year-olds. Dyan Watson writes that she worries about sending her Black son to schools that as a matter of course assign our Black boys into special education classes, criminalize their behavior at younger and younger ages, and view them as the statistics that are the result of systemic inequalities as opposed to biological deficiencies.[36] Our Black children are being traumatized and then they come to us on Sunday, to a sanctuary where they should learn that they carry the image of God and they are loved.

So they come into the Sunday school classroom and may be considered loud. Loud is an indicator that they will be problem students. They are too urban, too street, too not like us, the proper-acting Christians. They come for religious education; however, religion has become a defender of the racist status quo. We need to be careful of the pictures we use; they are not harmless:

> God, for all practical purposes, is imaged as an elderly, benign white man, seated on a white throne, with bright, white light emanating from his countenance. Angels are blonds and brunets suspended in the air around his throne to be his messengers and execute his purposes. Satan is viewed as being red with the glow of fire. But the imps, the messengers of the devil, are black. The phrase "black as an imp" is a stereotype.[37]

bell hooks reminds us that while integration was necessary, when our children left a world of Black teachers who believed in their potential, they found themselves in classrooms where racist stereotypes were reinforced. Education was no longer an opportunity to engage in the practice of freedom. In all too many

---

36. Dyan Watson, "A Message from a Black Mom to Her Son," in Watson, Hagopian, and Au, *Teaching for Black Lives*, 356.

37. Howard Thurman, *Jesus and the Disinherited* (Boston: Beacon Press, 1976), 43.

of our classrooms, domination was and is the main goal.[38] In all too many of our classrooms, Black children have their humanity stolen by stereotypes that exist in our society; stereotypes that are falsely placed on our children. Our children were to fit into a mold determined by those who saw them as problems as opposed to free spirits waiting to learn. That is why it is important to assess biases in the curricula we use in church. It is important to ensure that our manner of teaching and the materials used respect and care for the minds and souls of all our children in a way that creates the best learning environment.[39] If performed with the love that undergirds our belief, not only can our Christian educators participate in the creation of disciples, they can also be healers of the system that denies the true humanity of our children. No education, including Christian education, is politically neutral. We teach for a purpose and as we look at forming our children as Christians, followers of Jesus, which Jesus will be the model? A White Jesus who models a racist society or the Black Jesus, who as Howard Thurman offers, is with those who find themselves with their backs against the wall?[40]

We cannot assume that the secular school system and society at large will build them up, will enable them to see the *imago Dei* that resides in each and every one of them. Sunday school, Christian formation is more than busywork, making foam Jesuses, and watching the children until service is over. This is sacred work.

These young disciples are never too young to have discussions about differences. They are never too young to be taught to stand up for themselves and confront racism and ignorance. If they do not receive information concerning race in their schools and then come to Sunday school or Christian formation and do not receive what they need, they will fill in the blanks with what they see or hear. Rita Tenorio advises that we can have "real" conversations about the racism, power, and privilege they will all experience consciously or unconsciously and there is no age when they are "too" young.[41]

Children are not blank slates; they come to us full of experiences and many of those experiences are affected by what they hear and see in their families, what they see and hear in the media, what they are taught in their schools,

---

38. bell hooks, *Teaching to Transgress: Education as the Practice of Freedom* (New York: Routledge, 1994), 3–4.

39. bell hooks, *Teaching to Transgress*, 13.

40. Howard Thurman, *Jesus and the Disinherited*, ii.

41. Rita Tenorio, "Brown Kids Can't Be in Our Club: Teaching 6-Year-Olds about Skin Color, Race, Culture and Respect," in Watson, Hagopian, and Au, *Teaching for Black Lives*, 355.

and what their friends share with them. Tenorio writes that children "have an unstated but nonetheless sophisticated understanding of the issue of race and power."[42] If we are committed to building the beloved community, then we will want to help our children—all children—navigate race and provide them with effective strategies that will assist them to counteract racism. We must remember, millions of students have gone through our educational system, past and present, and many will come to us carrying heavy baggage about themselves and others to be formed as disciples. Education should not create or reinforce opportunities for racial self-hatred and the Church will be called to undo the harm that is our secular educational system.

For the Rest of Us

My clergy colleague, the Rev. Peter Jarrett-Schell, who is White (however, I believe he is *ontologically Black*),[43] was finishing the bulletin for the service. He was including the hymns. I looked at one of the selections and said, "I'm not singing that." He looked at me quizzically. "I'm not singing anything that washes me as white as snow." Peter is brilliant at many things. He went right to work and changed the verse. Problem solved. I'm still Black. Nothing can wash me as white as snow. Something as simple as a verse or word in a favorite hymn can contribute to self-hatred. Of course, there will be those who will attempt to justify the verse by saying, "That is not what it means." It might not have mattered when pen was put to paper; what matters is how it is interpreted and internalized now.

Too many of us grew up believing that our people contributed nothing to civilization, in fact, were not civilized, were heathens, savages; had no history that White people should acknowledge and that God and Jesus were White and the Bible was all about White people, even though geography told us differently. We know we come from great people. Yes, Africa is a continent of countries and for many of us, tracing our lineage to a specific country, a specific tribe is difficult; but what we do know is that Africa had great civilizations, different civilizations. Different is not deficient. We know that there were great universities and libraries in Timbuktu and many of the manuscripts survive to

---

42. Tenorio, in *Teaching for Black Lives*, 355.

43. JoAnne Marie Terrell writes, "Reconciliation is the result of God's initiative, which can only be realized with Whites affirming Blackness by becoming 'ontologically Black' (that is, by identifying with the oppressed), and by repudiating their own Whiteness (that is, by refusing to accept the benefits of Whiteness)." JoAnne Marie Terrell, *Power in the Blood? The Cross in the African American Experience* (Eugene, OR: Wipf & Stock, 2005), 95.

today.[44] We had been infantilized, negated, and erased. It is amazing, perhaps only by the grace of God herself, that Blacks are Christians. We could be followers of Jesus without being Christians; we could practice Howard Thurman's religion of Jesus without being Christians, even though Harold Lewis wrote that we were able to separate out the gospel of Jesus from the racism of Whites. How does a race's history, culture, and, in reality, its people become invisible? Erasure is a sin. Defacing is a sin. Defacement denies the respect and honor that comes from being created by and in the image of God. Defacement ignores or denies a person's full humanity. As we look at the treatment of Blacks by White Christians past and present, it is a failure to see the sacredness that God has imbued in Blacks.[45]

James H. Cone and Kelly Brown Douglas helped us to see that Christ is Black and Cain Hope Felder opened our eyes to see ourselves in the Bible. Felder counteracted White supremacist erasure of Black people, which created openings for racist readings of Scripture. He offered that even without looking for a Black presence in the Bible, there is nothing other than a White supremacist narrative that would lead anyone to believe that the original intent of the biblical narratives was to "negate the full humanity of Black people or to view Blacks in an unfavorable way."[46] Ibram X. Kendi has written in *Stamped from the Beginning* that self-interest, White self-interest undergirds the creation of racist policies and laws.[47] That same racist self-interest propelled White Christians to promote racist interpretations of the Bible. Interpretations that helped them justify racist treatment of God's Black children. Making reading illegal supported that self-interest because if the enslaved could not read the Bible for themselves, they were subject to interpretations provided them by racist Whites. The *Slave Bible* omitted portions that pointed toward freedom: for example, the Exodus account, or equality, "There is no longer Jew or Greek, there is no longer slave nor free . . . for all of you are one in Christ Jesus" (Gal. 3:28). To purposely co-opt the Bible points to the nefarious intent of Whites

---

44. Liberty Writers Africa, "700,000 Ancient African Books Have Survived in Mali's Timbuktu University," November 24, 2019, *https://libertywritersafrica.com/700000-ancient-african-books-have-survived-in-malis-timbuktu-university/?fbclid=IwAR0vNrpwA0EvrQ-OtotDuHpKyo3NKd5fo-iZ9YxPXu0PFHnjQpJz5a6Py2U*.

45. Beverly Eileen Mitchell, *Plantations and Death Camps: Religion, Ideology, and Human Dignity* (Minneapolis: Fortress Press, 2009), 50–51.

46. Cain Hope Felder, "Race, Racism, and the Biblical Narratives," in *Stoney the Road We Trod: African American Biblical Interpretation* (Minneapolis: Fortress Press, 1991), 127.

47. Ibram X. Kendi, *Stamped from the Beginning: The Definitive History of Racist Ideas in America* (London: Bodley Head, 2017).

who knew they were wrong, but were motivated by self-interest.[48] There has to be a reason for a people to hate and despise another, and Whites created those reasons for their own self-interest: cultural, political, and economic.[49]

A New Testament scholar and longtime professor at Howard Divinity School in Washington, DC, Felder researched ancient cultures of the Near East. He found that Zipporah, Moses's wife, was Black, although there is some disagreement between biblical scholars.[50] She certainly was not Israelite. In Numbers 12:1, Miriam and Aaron spoke against Moses because he married a Cushite (Ethiopian) woman, believed by some to be Zipporah. However, Moses was married at least twice; the second woman who is unnamed was also a non-Israelite, a Nubian.[51] So either one or both of Moses's wives were Black. What is important is that there is racial/ethnic diversity in the Bible as opposed to the White-washed supremacist co-optation of the Bible. Other researchers and theologians have offered that what we call the Middle East, to include the Holy Land, was part of Africa until the Suez Canal was completed in 1859. The Middle East had been referred to as North Africa for most of modern history.[52]

It is important that in our curricula and other materials the Black presence in the Bible is lifted up and made a focal point in our teaching. It is not enough to be color-blind. We don't create Black presence where there is none; however, where it does exist, emphasis must be given to negate the centuries of Black self-hate and oppression. We have too many pictures of White Jesus in Black homes, still hanging between Martin and John.

So What?

A self-described preacher's kid who found herself in a Christian bubble, Lisa Fields had never encountered anything that went against her faith until she took a class in New Testament and read a book by Bart Ehrman who argued

---

48. "The Slave Bible: Let the Story be Told," Museum of the Bible, accessed November 18, 2018, *https://www.museumofthebible.org/exhibits/slave-bible*.

49. Lonnae O'Neal, "Ibram Kendi, One of the Nation's Leading Scholars of Racism, Says Education and Love Are Not the Answer," The Undefeated, September 20, 2017, *https://theundefeated.com/features/ibram-kendi-leading-scholar-of-racism-says-education-and-love-are-not-the-answer/*.

50. Daniel Silliman, "Died: Cain Hope Felder, Scholar Who Lifted Up the Black People in the Bible," October 2, 2019, *https://www.christianitytoday.com/news/2019/october/died-cain-hope-felder-bible-scholar-african-american.html*.

51. Wilda C. Gafney, *Womanist Midrash: A Reintroduction to the Women of the Torah and the Throne* (Louisville: Westminster John Knox, 2017), 144.

52. Onleilove Alston, "The Black Presence in the Bible: Uncovering the Hidden Ones," *Sojourners*, February 19, 2014, *https://sojo.net/articles/faith-action/black-presence-bible-uncovering-hidden-ones*.

against the inerrancy of the Bible. She struggled in that class because her faith was challenged; however, that experience forced her to seriously consider what she believed and why. She realized she wasn't the only person who accepted their faith uncritically and she founded the Jude 3 Project[53] to address the unique "intellectual struggles of Christians of African descent in the United States and abroad."[54] She brings together primarily African American theologians, lay and ordained, across the religious spectrum in one-on-one interviews, conferences, seminars, and exciting panel discussions called "Courageous Conversations," where different views concerning a wide-ranging list of topics are discussed and debated—all with the focus to assist African Americans to defend what they believe. It is not a particular tradition promoted; rather, it is her belief that you ought to be able to defend whatever you believe; although in "Courageous Conversations," there will be pushback and the panelists defend their beliefs and challenge others.

While the focus is on millennials and assisting them in defending what they believe, the theologians who provide the commentary are across the board in age. Millennials are leaving the church and the belief they would return as they got older, married, and had children has not borne out.[55] Apologetics is important to Fields. She believes apologetics is important to Black millennials who believe that Christianity is the White man's religion and have difficulty dealing with the hypocrisy in the Church. She takes her apologetics tour to Historically Black Colleges and Universities (HBCUs), where students are eager to have their questions addressed and their doubts taken seriously.

Church must become safe space for these conversations to occur and millennials' questions addressed if we have any hope of stemming the hemorrhage. People, regardless of their age, should be able to explain why they believe what they believe. They ought to be able to provide an apology. To assist with this venture, Fields and Yana Conner have published a curriculum, *Through the Eyes of Color: A Contextualized Guide to Help You Know What You Believe and Why*.[56] The text sets the tone at the very beginning with the advisory

---

53. The Jude 3 Project at *https://jude3project.org*.

54. Jasmine Holmes, "Rethinking Apologetics for the Black Church," *Christianity Today*, July 18, 2018, *https://www.christianitytoday.com/women/2018/july/rethinking-apologetics-for- Black-church.html*.

55. Daniel Cox and Amelia Thomson-DeVeaux, "Millennials Are Leaving Religion and Not Coming Back," FiveThirtyEight, December 12, 2019, *https://fivethirtyeight.com/features/millennials-are-leaving-religion-and-not-coming-back/*.

56. Lisa Fields and Yana Conner, *Through the Eyes of Color: A Contextualized Guide to Help You Know What You Believe and Why* (Jacksonville: Jude3Project, 2019).

that God is big enough to take all our questions. Young people have difficulty with churches or denominations that fail to answer their questions. The Jude 3 Project understands that and provides ways for those questions to be answered in ways that are not judgmental. The guide deals with basics, a way to get people started in asking questions about what they have been taught in and out of Church. One section might surprise people who are uncomfortable with cults. In this section, the Nation of Islam, the Black Israelites, Kemeticism, and Pan-Africanism are discussed. What is surprising is that Christianity is also included in this section: Christianity as a cult. While the curriculum is geared toward African Americans, anyone can benefit from struggling with the information and gaining insight into African American beliefs. What could be learned if "Courageous Conversations" occurred in predominantly White seminaries?

At some point, aside from the issue of possible reparations for the role the Episcopal Church played in slavery, Jim Crow, segregation, and continuing discrimination, the ugliness of faith must be dealt with. What better place than during the process of formation in the church and seminaries? Let people have the information concerning the role of the Church and race and let them decide whether they are willing to follow Jesus in a way that repairs the breach that continues to affect relationships in the Church and the broader society.

Regardless of the number of books and curricula a seeker, veteran Episcopalian, or seminarian might have to take on this formation journey, at some point the Book of Common Prayer will be used. With roots all the way back to the first prayer book of 1547, the Book of Common Prayer is what makes many Episcopalians feel Episcopal—and any deviation can be tantamount to heresy. In this book, this guide, are the various services that take us through the Church year and life, prayers, and historical information. As one studies to become Episcopalian, or a better Episcopalian, one will turn to "An Outline of the Faith" also known as the Catechism.[57] The introduction provides,

> This catechism is primarily intended for use by parish priests, deacons, and
> lay catechists, to give an outline for instruction. It is a commentary on the
> creeds, but is not meant to be a complete statement of belief and practice;

---

57. The Episcopal Church, *The Book of Common Prayer* (New York: Church Publishing, 2007), 844–62 (hereafter BCP).

rather, it is a point of departure for the teacher, and it is cast in the traditional question and answer form for ease of reference. The second use of this catechism is to provide a brief summary of the Church's teaching for an inquiring stranger who picks up a Prayer Book.[58]

This outline of faith is in the form of questions and answers. Imagine, rather than questions and answers that affirm the sacredness of all human beings— "You shall love the Lord your God will all your heart, with all your soul, and with all your mind . . . [and] You shall love your neighbor as yourself"[59]— one finds questions and answers like these:

Q. 37   When Negroes become religious, how must they behave to their masters?

A.   The Scriptures in many places command them to be honest, diligent, and faithful in all things, and not to give saucy answers; and even when they are whipped for doing well, to take it patiently and look to God for their reward . . .

Q. 39   Which do you think is the happiest person, the master or the slave?

A.   When I rise on a cold morning, and make a fire, and my master in bed; or when I labour in the sun, on a hot day, and my master in the shade; then I think him happier than I.

Q. 40   Do you think you are happier than he?

A.   Yes. When I come in from my work; eat my hearty supper, worship my maker; lie down without care on my mind; sleep sound; get up in the morning strong and fresh; and hear that my master could not sleep, for thinking on his debts and taxes; and how he shall provide victuals and clothes for his family, or what he shall do for them when they are sick—then I bless God that he has placed me in my humble station; I pity my master, and feel myself happier than he is.

Q. 41   Then it seems everybody is best, just where God has placed them?

A.   Yes, the Scriptures say, if I am called being a slave, I am not to care for it; for every true Christian, is Christ's free man, whether he be bound or free in this world.

---

58. BCP, 844.

59. BCP, 851.

Q. 42   How can you be free and bound both?

A.   If Jesus Christ has broken the chain of sin, and freed me from the curse of the law, and the slavery of the devil, I am free indeed, although my body and services may be in the command of another.[60]

In another catechism developed for the enslaved, we find:

Who gave you a master and mistress?

God gave them to me.

Who says you must obey them?

God says I must.

What book tells you these things?

The Bible.[61]

Imagine using the catechism in the Book of Common Prayer alongside the slave catechism in formation and seminary classes. In addition to teaching the precepts of the Episcopal Church, there is also a requirement to participate in God's justice, to reconcile all of God's people to God and each other and to see how God's word has been perverted: how sin and evil have perverted the Church. This is a call for those with questions and those coming to the faith to fully understand the call to repentance, for the body of Christ to literally change its mind and go in another direction toward God in Christ Jesus.

Willie James Jennings writes that Christianity is a teaching faith. By teaching disciples are made; however, in delving deep into the historical faith we see how White hegemony found its way into Christian doctrine and practice.[62] Beaten, maimed, killed, raped, sold—Christian enslavers attributed their treatment of Blacks to God; God created them for the sole purpose of serving Whites. Enslavers created a distorted vision of God for the benefit of Whites; after all, God is White and if God had wanted Blacks to be equal to Whites, God would have created them White. The creator of the first catechism denoted was the Rev. Charles Colcock James. He was a Presbyterian minister, but his catechism was used by many denominations, including the Episcopal

---

60. Willie James Jennings, *The Christian Imagination: Theology and the Origins of Race* (New Haven: Yale University Press, 2010), 238–39.

61. Jennings, *Christian Imagination*, 239.

62. Jennings, *Christian Imagination*, 106.

Church. William Meade, the third bishop of Virginia (1841–1862) advocated for the instruction of the enslaved in his diocese and no doubt approved the use of all or some of James's catechism as James cites Meade's pastoral letter urging instruction using his book *The Religious Instruction of the Negroes in the United States*.[63] Christianity would come to the enslaved by rejecting any concern for this world, which is at the heart of African religion, and focusing on heaven and Whiteness.[64]

If we are open about the use and abuse of religion, seekers and seminarians will be encouraged to challenge the Church as they try to make sense of the theodic behavior on the part of Whites who control societal systems and structures. As questions are asked and answered, it will make sense why Black and White churches came into being and why they continue to exist today and how racial reconciliation in the Episcopal Church will be difficult to achieve if there is no reconciliation between the Black and White churches. There is a conflict that must be resolved if we continue to teach the *ekklesia* as the one body of Christ. As we delve into theodicy, why would God permit such treatment? We begin to understand why it was necessary to erase all past memory of the religion and culture of Africa and prohibit all expressions of African religion from the enslaved which led and leads, again, to racial and cultural self-hatred. This White supremacist-imposed self-hatred was evident in Blacks who championed racial uplift, such as W. E. B. Du Bois and Joseph Washington, who denigrated Black religion and worship styles.[65] It is on display in the Episcopal Church when we are told that our cultural expressions are *not Episcopalian*. According to Zora Neale Hurston, African or Black religious expression was about human agency and freedom. It was (and is) an artform and it could not be permitted.[66] Even today, assimilation to White supremacist ideas has been powerful enough that even the most "woke" Black person at some point looks down on non-Christian religions, practices, or anything that smacks of being African.[67] Jeremiah Wright, the pastor emeritus of Trinity United Church of Christ in Chicago, preaches that Blacks have been convinced of the inferiority of Black and African religious customs.[68] We have been convinced that there

---

63. Charles C. Jones, *The Religious Instruction of the Negroes in the United States* (Savannah: Thomas Purse, 1842), 143.

64. Cone, *Black Theology and Black Power*, 33.

65. Terrell, *Power in the Blood?*, 50–51.

66. Terrell, *Power in the Blood?*, 48–49.

67. Terrell, *Power in the Blood?*, 50.

68. Jeremiah Wright Jr., *Africans Who Shaped Our Faith* (Chicago: Urban Ministries, 1995).

is something inherently wrong with us and so we strive to be White; however, that has been tried and we have failed. It is time to be who God has created us to be. Rather than see our African heritage as something to be denied or brought out on special (Black) occasions, Christianity and the Episcopal Church will be spiritually and culturally enriched when we include the total package in worship, all forms of worship, as just something we do to be closer to God and each other.[69]

So what? The Episcopal Church was complicit in slavery, Jim Crow, segregation, and ongoing discrimination and defacing of God's children of ebony grace, yet we Black Episcopalians remain. The question is why? What difference do we make? What difference can we make? How do we make our voices heard to make this church one that follows Jesus, one that practices the religion of Jesus as opposed to the religion about Jesus?[70] One that affirms and lifts up the Black Jesus, because that Jesus understands how it is to be hunted, how it is to have to flee your country to live, how it is to be marginalized, hated, despised, and ultimately murdered because you are the ultimate outsider who challenges White space.[71]

In the Beginning

> God made the White man White because He wanted him White and to stay White. He made the Black man Black because He wanted him Black and wants him to stay Black. The Devil made the mulatto. . . . Remember the Negro is not much more than 150 years from cannibalism, while there is more than 6000 years behind the White race![72]

On October 3, 2008, at the historically Black St. Thomas African Episcopal Church, in Philadelphia, a public act of remorse was on display. A "Litany of Offense and Apology" began the service of repentance and detailed the ways the Episcopal Church has participated in slavery, segregation, and continued discrimination. Since that time, the Church has struggled to figure out what repentance looks like. There have been discussions around reparations. The General Conventions have put forth recommendations; however, as Karen

---

69. Terrell, *Power in the Blood?*, 52.

70. Thurman, *Jesus and the Disinherited*, 25.

71. Douglas, *Stand Your Ground*, 69.

72. Henry T. Egger, "'Created Equal' God's Truth or Man's Theory," in Robert T. Ingram, *Essays on Segregation* (Houston, TX: St. Thomas Press, 1960), 71.

Hardwick of the Episcopal Diocese of Washington lamented in 2008, "It's virtually impossible to measure injustice and the damages that flow from slavery."[73] While not addressing the Episcopal Church, James Cone's critique of apologies is relevant in that while apologies are important and often welcomed by those who suffer harm, the apology does not substitute for justice.[74] There is not the time nor the space to fully examine what needs to be done to repair the harm done to both the Church and her people; however, as Rev. Ed Rodman also offered in 2008, "Vision only comes when you learn your history"[75]—church history, the history of the Episcopal Church, the eldest daughter of the Church of England.[76] The Church of England that gave birth to the Episcopal Church was involved in the purchasing and owning of human beings. This is more than individual church members purchasing and owning the enslaved; rather, this was the church at the auction block. A search of various texts used to teach Church history revealed this fact had been omitted.

Jurist A. Leon Higginbotham's text, *In the Matter of Color—Race and the American Legal Process: The Colonial Period*,[77] revealed with seminary texts did not. In writing the book, Higginbotham wanted to assess "to what extent the law itself had created the mores of racial oppression. Did the law merely perpetuate old biases and prejudices? Or had it been an instrument first in establishing and only later in attacking the injustices based on color?"[78] Higginbotham assessed the use of the law in maintaining a racial caste system in the colonies of Virginia, Massachusetts, New York, South Carolina, Georgia, and Pennsylvania, but it is only in the section that deals with Virginia that the Anglican Church as an institution is implicated in enslavement. The laws were specific, and until the disestablishment of the Church of England, the Church was the state and the state was the Church. Churchwardens and vestries acted as agents of the state; vestries served as the local government. From the 1691 statute (Act XVI):

> And it is further enacted, that if any English (meaning White) woman being
> free shall have a bastard child by a Negro, she shall pay fifteen pounds to the

---

73. "Episcopalians Gather to Apologize for Slavery," The Episcopal Church, October 3, 2008, *https://episcopalchurch.org/library/article/episcopalians-gather-apologize-slavery*.

74. James H. Cone, *The Cross and the Lynching Tree* (New York: Orbis Books, 2011), 99.

75. "Episcopalians Gather to Apologize for Slavery."

76. Egger, "Created Equal," 61.

77. A. Leon Higginbotham, *In the Matter of Color—Race and the American Legal Process: The Colonial Period* (Oxford: Oxford University, 1978).

78. Higginbotham, *In the Matter of Color*, ix.

church wardens and in default of such payment, she shall be taken into possession by the church wardens and disposed of for five years and the amount she brings shall be paid one-third to their majesties for the support of the government, one-third to the parish where the offense was committed and the other third to the informer. The child shall be bound out by the church wardens until he is thirty years of age. In case the English woman that shall have a bastard is a servant she shall be sold by the church wardens (after her time is expired) for five years, and the child serve as aforesaid.[79]

It took a text on the law and others that dealt with enslavement, as opposed to the history of the Church, to make the connection between the ownership of the enslaved and the Church. The Church of England negated the command in Acts 17:26: "That God hath made [of one Blood] all Nations of Men, for to dwell all upon the face of the Earth."[80] Although there were other denominations represented in the Virginia colony, the Church of England was the established church and Anglican Christianity found its way into the laws, customs, practices, and court records.[81]

The year 1619 is given as the date when the first "twenty and odd Negroes" were brought to the colony of Virginia. The location was not Jamestown, but Port Comfort, which is modern-day Hampton, Virginia. The other significant act is that the first governmental structure, the House of Burgesses, was also formed in 1619.[82] To be a member of the House of Burgesses, a man had to be a member of the Anglican Church. With the establishment of select vestries in the parishes (churches), there was a comingling of function and since both vestries and the House of Burgesses were populated with slaveholders, it was inevitable that slavery would develop unchecked both in the colony and the church.[83] Anglicans had no problem with African enslavement because they believed the Bible supported it. In their interpretation of the Hebrew Bible, it was permissible to hold heathens, those presumed to be outside God's covenant, in bondage.[84] The line between the sacred and the secular was not blurred; it was eliminated.

---

79. Higginbotham, *In the Matter of Color*, 45.

80. *Holy Bible*, KJV.

81. Rebecca Anne Goetz, *The Baptism of Early Virginia: How Christianity Created Race* (Baltimore, MD: John Hopkins University Press, 2012), 7.

82. Goetz, *Baptism of Early Virginia*, 9.

83. Winthrop D. Jordan, *White Over Black: American Attitudes Toward the Negro*, 1550–1812 (Chapel Hill: University of North Carolina, 1968), 210.

84. Charles F. Irons, *The Origins of Proslavey Christianity* (Chapel Hill: University of North Carolina, 2008), 11.

There are several Episcopal dioceses currently involved in determining if reparations are in order as restitution for slavery in this country. Naturally, there is pushback with many Whites and some Blacks declaring that those who live today are not responsible for the actions of the slaveholders. However, the challenge as the discussions concerning reparations evolve is whether there is a direct line between the colonial Anglican Church and the Episcopal Church of today.

In the Virginia colony, vestries were responsible for calling ministers; the bishop of London exercised little authority over the American parishes, although each minister needed to be licensed by the bishop of London.[85] The calling of clergy could be difficult. Tobacco was the cash crop; ministers were paid in tobacco, and its cultivation was intensive and needed the labor of the enslaved.[86] Anglican racism without the official title, the need for ministers, the need for cheap and free labor on glebe land, created an environment where "Anglican parishes were the first institutions in Virginia to own slaves that were acquired initially through donations [from member slave-holders] and later through deliberate purchase.[87]

Anglican parishes, the Anglican Church in the colonies, became the model for other churches and denominations. This was a goal of James Blair who wanted Virginia parishes to provide the model for slaveholding.[88] The Anglican Church's success with enslavement gave permission to other denominations to engage in ownership of the enslaved. To attract ministers to the colony, the Anglican Church purchased enslaved Africans who were attached to the glebes, the land that surrounded the church and sometimes the rectory or parsonage. Ministers received payment in tobacco and other crops, which were grown on the glebe and tended by the enslaved. The clergy benefits package was enhanced with the addition of enslaved labor to be used for the benefit of clergy who had lifetime tenure.[89] Still, there is the connection between the Anglican Church before the Revolutionary War and the task of establishing institutional enslavement after disestablishment. According to Jennifer Oast, the change from the Church of England to the Episcopal Church did not stem the tide of purchasing and using enslaved labor. In fact, after disestablishment, with the church no longer being supported by mandatory tithes, glebe-slaves were even more

---

85. Nelson, *Blessed Company*, 122.

86. Willard J. Webb and Anne C. Webb, *The Glebe Houses of Colonial Virginia* (Westminster, MD.: Heritage Books, 2008), 28.

87. Jennifer Oast, *Institutional Slavery*, 14.

88. Oast, *Institutional Slavery*, 29.

89. Oast, *Institutional Slavery*, 15.

important in the quest to hire ministers.[90] Some parishes before the Revolution did not purchase the enslaved; however, after disestablishment, to support and/or attract ministers and maintain the glebe, these now-Episcopal parishes purchased the enslaved.[91]

The first commissary of the bishop of London to the colony, the Rev. James Blair, who also built the College of William and Mary (an Anglican institution which also purchased enslaved persons), was the first to suggest that vestries purchase the enslaved and attach them to parish glebes.[92] If there were vacant cures, parishes without ministers, the funds that were still accruing would be used to not only ensure that the vacant cure had sufficient enslaved persons and other necessities (cattle, library, seeds), but that the monies not used to pay a minister be used to supply other parishes until each parish in Virginia had all of what Blair called the "essentials," to include enslaved persons.[93]

Still, part of the difficulty in determining the holding of the enslaved by Anglican and Episcopal parishes is whether there are records to support the claim. In Williamsburg, Virginia, is a church, Bruton Parish, which is in the heart of historic Williamsburg. It was established in 1674, and is still in use. Parish records establish that in 1767, "Thomas" was born to "Molly," and that "Molly" belonged to Bruton Parish. What happened to Thomas and Molly or any other enslaved persons who might have been owned by Bruton Parish is unknown.[94]

Remembering that the Church and the state were one, the General Assembly regularly gave permission for parishes to sell parish properties that were unused and to purchase enslaved persons. The enslaved were purchased outright by individual parishes and also when directed by the General Assembly. In one case, the General Assembly was very specific that the vestry for Ware Parish in Glouester County, Virginia, was to purchase enslaved, one-half of whom were to be young females because females would reproduce and the children would add to the number of enslaved owned by the parish.[95] In the case of Lynnhaven Parish, the General Assembly had the parish purchase the enslaved for the purpose of breeding, thereby adding to the value of the glebe.[96]

---

90. Oast, *Institutional Slavery*, 15, 34.

91. Oast, *Institutional Slavery*, 34.

92. Oast, *Institutional Slavery*, 22.

93. Oast, *Institutional Slavery*, 23–24.

94. John Vogt, ed., *Bruton Parish, Virginia Register, 1662–1797* (Athens, GA: New Papyrus Co., 2004), 52. (Available at the Alexandria Library, noncirculating collection.)

95. Oast, *Institutional Slavery*, 25.

96. Oast, *Institutional Slavery*, 26.

The Revolutionary War and the disestablishment of the Church of England caused havoc for the parishes, the glebes, and ministers. Without mandatory taxes in the form of tithes, ministers were not being paid and the glebes could not be maintained. Some parishes (vestries) rented their glebes to private citizens and other vestries ordered their wardens to sell all church property.[97] Legislators promised to protect parish property, but that was difficult because there was no public money coming in to support the struggling church.[98] Public support of the church was all but ended and in 1784, the former House of Burgesses, now the General Assembly, granted a charter for the incorporation of the Protestant Episcopal Church. With that charter, all property under vestry control prior to the Revolution became the responsibility of the Episcopal Church. All property, to include the enslaved attached to the glebes, became the property of the Protestant Episcopal Church as opposed to being the property of individual parishes and vestries.[99] The Protestant Episcopal Church as the owner of the enslaved was short-lived, however. The final nail was placed in the coffin of establishment with the passage of Thomas Jefferson's Statute of Religious Liberty in 1785. The charter establishing the Protestant Episcopal Church was also repealed, so there was still the question of who owned parish property, to include the enslaved.[100]

This history of the colonial Anglican Church and the Episcopal Church after the Revolution is different than most students, seminary, and parish-level receive. Suppose as part of the seminary formation processes, members were challenged to research the history of their parish and race. Of course, this would be done with assistance and the groundwork would have already been begun by catechists and instructors.

Can I be Black and Episcopalian? I must be. What follows is a glimpse of what inclusive formation and education could be.

---

97. Webb and Webb, *Glebe Houses of Colonial Virginia*, 31.

98. Alan Taylor, *Thomas Jefferson's Education* (New York: W.W. Norton, 2019), 50–51.

99. Nelson, *Blessed Company*, 298.

100. Nelson, *Blessed Company*, 298–99.

38

Transformative Theological Education When Race Matters

THE WORK OUR SOUL MUST DO

Kelly Brown Douglas

It was a hot Wednesday afternoon in August. My brother, two sisters, and I were playing in our bedrooms while my parents were sitting on the living room couch watching something on TV. Out of nowhere, with a sense of urgency, my mother called the four of us to come to see what they were watching. We ran in, not quite knowing what to expect. When we got there, my parents told us to sit down and watch because history was being made. I did not know what they meant by that, but I followed their instructions, as did my siblings—we sat and watched the "history that was being made" on the television screen.

I remember watching and wondering why so many people, especially Black people, were standing in the hot sun listening to a man give a speech. My then six-year-old mind was not taking in what he was saying. What I was taking in, however, was my parents' reactions to his words. Both were clearly moved by this man's speech. Occasionally one of them would utter, "That's right," or, "You tell them."

That "history making" day was August 28, 1963, when Martin Luther King Jr. seized the American imagination with his dream for this nation and its people. What I did not realize then was that for my parents the "history being made" on that screen was about their hope that the dream they had for their four children was coming closer to reality on that day at the Lincoln Memorial. They, too, wanted their four children to live in a world where they, as King said, "will not be judged for the color of their skin but by the content of their character." They, too, wanted, as King dreamed, a world where little Black boys and Black girls would be able to join hands with little White boys and White girls "as sisters and brothers." Their dream for my brother, sisters, and me was King's dream for our world.

What I also did not realize at that time was the sense of urgency that my parents felt as they listened to King. For they knew what I would come to know many years later: eight years prior, on that very day, another mother's dream for her child had come to a tragic end.

At 2:00 a.m. on August 28, 1955, Mamie Till's fourteen-year-old son, Emmett Louis Till, was dragged from his relatives' home where he was staying in Mississippi and lynched because he was accused of "flirting" with a twenty-two-year-old White woman. Over sixty years later, the woman admitted that she had "fabricated" parts of the story that led to Emmett's monstrous murder at the hands of her then husband and his half-brother, both now deceased—but both of whom, after being found innocent of Till's murder by an all-White jury, bragged in *Look* magazine about how they had indeed lynched Emmett and disposed of his body in the Tallahatchie River.

Why am I beginning an essay on theological education and racial justice with the importance of August 28 in our nation's history? Because that one August day reflects the challenging context in which we find ourselves as we think about theological education.

In his classic 1903 text, *The Souls of Black Folk*, W. E. B. Du Bois (who died on August 27, 1963—just one day before King's speech) speaks of the "warring" souls of African Americans, at once African, at once an American. This poignant image of warring souls provides an apt description of our nation, more than fifty years after Martin Luther King's speech and over sixty years after Emmett Till's lynching. Ours is a nation with a warring soul. Borrowing the words of Du Bois, we are a nation with "two thoughts, two un-reconciled strivings, two warring ideals."[1] We have yet to decide if we are going to be a nation and a people defined by Martin Luther King Jr.'s dream, or a nation and a people defined by Emmett Louis Till's lynching.

The warring soul of this nation is most recently manifest by the fact that though we have boldly declared that all are created equal and endowed with the inalienable rights of "life, liberty and the pursuit of happiness," we elected a "Make America Great Again" vision defined by a racially chauvinistic agenda and inhumane xenophobic policies, and one that also traffics in toxic misogynistic and LGBTQ-phobic realities. There is no getting around it: we are a nation with a warring soul.

Such a soul is intrinsic to our country's very identity. Thus, throughout our nation's history, we have been challenged by the reality of two

---

1. W. E. B. Du Bois, *The Souls of Black Folk* (New York: Barnes and Nobles Classics, 2003), 9.

unreconciled strivings, two warring ideas. Are we going to be a slave nation or a free nation? Are we going to be a Jim and Jane Crow nation or a just and equal nation? Are we going to be a xenophobic and intolerant nation or a multiracial, multiethnic, welcoming nation? Until we as a nation—as a people—make a decision, we will continually find ourselves in warring soul times of chaos and crisis.

That said, there *is* something new about this time: that new is us. This warring soul moment is ours. This is our time to have our say about what kind of nation and what kind of people we want to be. I am convinced that this time in which we are living is our *kairos* time. As so aptly stated by South African clergy and theologians in their 1985 Kairos Document in response to apartheid, this is for us a "moment of grace and opportunity, [a] favourable time in which God issues a challenge to decisive action." The document goes on to say, it is also "a dangerous time because, if this opportunity is missed, and allowed to pass by, the loss for the Church [and society] is immeasurable."[2]

In as much as this is our time of decision as a nation and as a people, it is even more so for the Church and for theological education. At Union, where I serve, this is a warring soul time that we must make a decision about who we are and what it means to be a theological seminary. For as convinced as I am of this being a *kairos* time, I am even more convinced that if our nation is going to settle its warring soul, then it will be churches and theological communities that must lead the way to the better impulses, "the better angels," of who we can be as a nation and a people. Why? Because by virtue of the fact that we are communities of faith, that the core of our identity and that which animates our very existence, our collective and institutional soul is not defined by the mercurial and compromising declarations of human beings and human societies, nor is it accountable to the frailties of human history. Rather our soul is inextricably bound to that transcendent "arc of the universe," as King would put it, that "bends toward justice"—that which is the good and loving justice of God.

There is even more significance for theological seminaries. For if we take seriously the root meaning of the word "seminary," they are to be "seedbeds," planting the seeds to do the work of God in the world. Paraphrasing the words of Episcopal theologian Vida Scudder, a theological seminary is to "evolve" a society "which bears some likeness to God's sublime nature" of love. And as

---

2. Gary S. D. Leonard, "The Moment of Truth: The Kairos Documents," Ujamaa Centre for Biblical and Theological Community Development and Research, University of KwaZulu-Natal, 2010, *http://ujamaa. ukzn.ac.za/Libraries/manuals/The_Kairos_Documents.sflb.ashx*.

liberation theologian Gustavo Guiterrez says, "To know the God (who is love) is to work for justice."[3]

What does all of this mean? It means in preparing students for their various ministries in the world, seminaries are to plant the seeds of justice; we are to plant the seeds for the evolving of a just earth. This is the work "our soul must have," as womanist ethicist Katie G. Cannon would say. This is transformative work that will help evolve a society, a world where Black lives truly do matter. What does that work look?

Moral Dialogue

This work begins with being a seminary that fosters *moral dialogue*, which is informed by two givens: first, affirming that each and every person, without exception, is a cherished and indispensable part of God's human family and, therefore, each and every person, without exception, is sacred and has sacred worth; second, recognizing that no person by virtue of their socially and historically privileged color, gender, sexual orientation, expression, or any other attribute has an indisputable corner on the "truth." Hence, to be a seminary that nurtures moral dialogue is to be a place energized by conversations in and out of the classroom that intentionally value the sacred dignity of all persons— even when those conversations are difficult and uncomfortable. Moreover, these conversations, characterized by a respectful and mutual exchange of ideas, are animated not by a desire to pronounce the right answers, but by a yearning to seek the right questions. They are questions that help free us from making an idol of our own perspectives, our own traditions, and casting them as "Truth."

Given the complexity of our very world and the complicated realities of injustice before us, it is absurd for us to think that any one cultural, faith, or religious perspective or tradition could even begin to possess all of the answers that would allow us to progress toward a more just way of being together on this earth—a place where all human beings are valued. Therefore, if a theological seminary is to even come close to being a seedbed for the justice that is God's, then it must be committed in all of its interactions to promoting the kind of dialogue that values the humanity of everyone engaged and incites thoughtfully hard questions about the assumptions we hold of ourselves, of one another, and of the truth that is God's loving justice, thereby opening us to new ways of seeing ourselves, others, and the world.

---

3. Gustavo Gutierrez, *A Theology of Liberation*, 15th anniv. ed. (Maryknoll, NY: Orbis Books), 156, Kindle.

Moral Memory

Moral memory is about nothing less than confronting the truth about our history as a people, as faith communities, and as seminaries. The truth-telling that is moral memory is not for the purpose of exonerating ourselves from the past. Rather, it is about recognizing the past we carry within us, the past we want to carry within us, and the past we need to make right. And righting the past is about more than facile apologies or easy reparations. Rather, to right the past is to acknowledge the ways in which our ecclesial systems, structures, and ways of being a church and seminaries are perhaps continuations of White supremacist myths, narratives, ideologies, and constructs that serve to demean, marginalize, and exclude Black and Brown people. Essentially, it is with the truth-telling that is moral memory that we can foster ministerial leadership that recognizes the ways in which our churches and seminaries have been shaped by and continue to benefit from the reality and legacy of White supremacy, even as they may also unwittingly perpetuate White supremacist realities, thereby suggesting that Black and Brown lives are not welcome and thus, do not matter.

Moral Proximity

If the work of seminaries is about planting the seeds for God's just future, then they must also be committed to being a community that prioritizes *moral proximity*, which is about helping students to be "proximate," to borrow from the words of Bryan Stevenson in *Just Mercy*, with those persons who are different from themselves.

Recent studies have revealed the harsh reality that 75 percent, that is three-fourths, of White Americans have no people of color within their intimate social circles. Furthermore, of the 25 percent that do, those social circles are still 91 percent White.[4] It is no wonder, therefore, that Black and White people have such widely different views of reality[5]—such as on the impact and presence of racism in the nation. Nevertheless, even with the difference that race makes in perceiving the world, most Americans agree that the racial divide[6] in this country is real and growing.

---

4. Jessica Ray, "75% of White People Can't Even Use the 'I'm Not Racist, I Have a Black Friend' Defense," NY Magazine, Intelligencer, August 26, 2014, *http://nymag.com/intelligencer/2014/08/race-friendship-study.html*.

5. Pew Research Center, "On Views of Race and Inequality, Blacks and Whites Are Worlds Apart," June 27, 2016, *https://www.pewsocialtrends.org/2016/06/27/on-views-of-race-and-inequality-Blacks-and-Whites-are-worlds-apart/*.

6. Julianna Menasce Horowitz, Anna Brown, and Kiana Cox, "Race in American 2019," Pew Research Center, April 9, 2019, *https://www.pewsocialtrends.org/2019/04/09/race-in-america-2019/*.

Seminaries must be intentional in leading the way to bridge the racial divide, which means nothing less than fostering opportunities for moral proximity. To be sure, it is only through moral proximity that we can discover that those who seem so different from us are indeed just like us—people with hearts that can be broken and need love, bodies that can be wounded and need healing, and souls that can be dispirited and need to be renewed. Moreover, it is only when we can look at another person and see ourselves, regardless of racial or other human differences, that true compassion can take place. This leads to a final aspect of transformative theological education.

Moral Participation

If doing the work of our soul means partnering with God to help mend the world, then seminaries are compelled to join God in mending the world of the injustice that is the division of race in this country. This is what moral participation is all about. Moral participation involves at least two things: being places of sanctuary and witness.

To be a sanctuary means no individual should feel diminished or unsafe because of who they are or are not within our communities. Hence, seminaries are to be spaces in which persons can thrive, feel connected, and discover their passions and their voice. They, therefore, must be free of bigotry or intolerance of any kind, not simply in the most overt ways, but perhaps in the ways we don't even readily notice—ways that may be embedded in the fabric of the buildings or even the fabric of programming and worship, not to speak of the curriculum.

Seminaries must ask hard questions of themselves. What are the images and icons in the buildings? What is the story they tell? What are the stories that are left out? What perspectives and experiences are centered in the curriculum? Has Anglican Studies become synonymous with Anglo-studies, or is the diverse racial, ethnic, and cultural realities and experiences central in all aspects of the Anglican Studies curriculum? The point of the matter is if seminaries want ministries where Black and Brown lives are held as sacred and matter, then they must matter and be regarded as sacred within every aspect of seminary life and programming.

Secondly, seminaries are called to be witnesses to the very vision that is God's for us, which means nothing less than calling out racism, xenophobia, and any other -ism or bigotry for what it is, even when it masks itself in the politically correct language of "greatness." But most importantly, being witnesses to God's just future means the very demographic of the seminary community, from students, to faculty, to administration should reflect the rich diversity of God's creation. And so, what difference does this make given the challenging times in which we find ourselves?

There is much at stake in our nation. It is not about being a Republican or Democrat, nor is it about conservative or progressive ideologies. The very soul of our nation is a stake. It is, therefore, in such a time as this that theological seminaries have a special responsibility in providing the kind of transformative moral leadership that can bring us closer to a just earth, where in fact Black lives matter in this world just as much as they do to God. To ignore that responsibility is to miss the opportunity that this *kairos* time brings us. But most of all it is to betray our very soul.

Let me end where I began—on August 28th. Even as I remember that fifty-six years ago King stood in front of the Lincoln Memorial calling for the nation to live beyond its biases and into its highest aspirations, we must also remember Emmett Till's lynching. Indeed, King spoke about a dream where Emmett Till's life would matter. Unfortunately, this nation's warring soul indicates that lives like Emmett Till's still do not matter, as poignantly revealed by the fact that sixty-four years after his murder the Mississippi memorial to him is continually desecrated by bullets and more.

This *is* our *kairos* time. Never before have theological seminaries had a more sacred opportunity to be a sign of God's just earth than today. This time in which seminaries are called to provide and nurture transformative moral leadership in order to create a world where all are free to live safely and fully into their created potential. This is the charge for theological education that matters. This is the work our souls must do.

39

Travel for Black Lives

Gayle Fisher-Stewart

Many seminaries and divinity schools provide opportunities for theological and cultural travel and immersions. The Holy Land, Greece, Turkey, Egypt, Latin and South America are popular destinations. These opportunities must be broadened to include locales that expand knowledge of Blacks in America, how we got here, and the events and locations that are important in the struggle for civil and human rights. What follows is not a discussion of those opportunities; rather, it is just to plant the seed and to share the experiences of some of the fifty-two pilgrims who traveled to Alabama in May 2019. This pilgrimage was the first for many to visit ground-zero of the 1960s civil rights struggle in Birmingham and Selma, and to experience the Equal Justice Initiative's Legacy Museum and the National Memorial for Peace and Justice in Montgomery. The pilgrims not only had the opportunity to visit and reflect on sites, they also spent time with several of the foot soldiers, many of whom were children during the 1960s. Some of the pilgrims have provided sermons or essays in earlier sections. What follows are reflections of others in various forms.

· · ·•••· ·

Four Days in Alabama

Staci L. Burkey

My first night in Birmingham, I was running an errand with the Rev. Gayle Fisher-Stewart, picking up water and snacks for the bus. She caught me off guard by asking why I came on the trip. It was a fair question; I had just not thought about it. When my neighbor, an Episcopalian, invited me, I accepted knowing only that I wanted to be better. Better for the little girl I mentor, my friends who I know not to ask to educate me about "being Black," and the people in my community to whom I want to be a better ally. I told Gayle that I mentored a little girl and I wanted to make sure I never seemed like an out-of-touch White lady or make her feel marginalized—not a great answer, if I am being honest. I was embarrassed to admit I didn't exactly know why I was there other than to be better.

Growing up in the Amish country of Ohio, nothing derogatory was ever said about people of color. My hometown was predominantly White and I honestly thought that the few children who were Black were tan or had a dark complexion. I was fifteen when I learned two of the kids were in fact from Africa, adopted by missionaries from my church. I then wondered if my assumptions about the other kids with dark complexions were way off. Did this mean our mailman, Kato, wasn't just tan from driving around delivering mail all day? While my story of childhood ignorance often makes people chuckle, it makes me ashamed. Not seeing people as different meant I didn't notice when they were treated differently or that I understood why.

To prepare for the trip, I read the history of Africa. I wanted to know who these people were who were kidnapped, lied to, and treated like anything but human. I read DeRay Mckesson's book *On the Other Side of Freedom: The Case for Hope* to learn more about the inequity in the justice system. I read *Barracoon: The Story of the Last "Black Cargo"* by Lorraine Hansbury, and other books that detailed vile things I still can't comprehend.

During the trip I expected to cry and feel shame, guilt, and anger. I had prepared myself for the overwhelming emotion I would feel at the Lynching Memorial the same way I prepared myself to see Emmett Till's empty casket at the Smithsonian National Museum of African American History and Culture in Washington, DC. Spoiler alert: there is no way to prepare for these moments.

My goal was to not be problematic: sit in the back, make sure I addressed men and women as "Sir" and "Miss," hold the door, and be respectful that there were emotions being felt I could never begin to comprehend. My perception was that this trip was not for me. It was for my fellow Brown and Browner pilgrims to hear their story told honestly. It was a privilege for me to be included and I would use the generous opportunity to fill in gaps from my public school education where I learned America had slaves and then a war because it was wrong. The North won and slaves were free. There was some resistance with Jim Crow laws, but those were unconstitutional, and then everyone got the right to vote. The end.

I failed on day one. We were dropped off on the corner of the Kelly Ingram Park in Birmingham, a staging area for protests during the civil rights movement. We were told to meet up at the Sixteenth Street Baptist Church on the opposite corner. Walking through the sculptures that recreate the experience of police dogs attacking protestors, children being jailed, a sculpture of Dr. King, and a memorial piece of four little girls who were killed, I was overwhelmed at how cruel people were "back then" to people seeking equality. To know it is one thing, to feel it is another. I sat near the sculpture of the four little girls who were murdered in the bombing of the Sixteenth Street Baptist Church, embracing the depiction of hope and promise the artist created for each lost life.

Once I crossed the street and entered the church, I immediately asked if there was a restroom I could use. Our host pointed to the door near the altar, "Down those stairs, the door is on the left." A fellow pilgrim led us in the songs of the civil rights era as we waited to hear the history of the church. Knowing those songs made me feel connected to the group, like it was okay that I was there. We were introduced to our speakers and they told us how four little girls had been murdered, the four little girls who were the subject of the statue in the park. Murdered by a bomb planted by members of the Ku Klux Klan just outside the bathroom of this church—the bathroom I had so callously asked to use upon entering this sacred space.

The next day was life-changing for me. We visited the Equal Justice Initiative Legacy Museum prior to the Lynching Memorial. I walked into that building armed only with my understanding of the Black experience in America based on my public school education, having never taken the time to understand that slavery, lynching, voting rights, segregation, Jim Crow, police brutality, and inequity in services were not just points in time: they were all connected in a timeline that continues to today. There never was an end.

Imprinted on the floor of the Legacy Museum is a timeline of the evolution of slavery beginning with the kidnapping of men, women, and children to be sold into slavery. Then it outlines the way they were terrorized after slavery supposedly ended, moving onto segregation, racial bias in law enforcement, and the mass incarceration of Black men, women, and children.

At the end of the timeline is a bench surrounded by pictures of Black leaders who have made change. I sat surrounded by people I should have been honoring and instead fought to keep my lunch down. Inside the site of warehouse that held human beings waiting to be auctioned off as slaves I struggled to comprehend how hundreds of years of slavery had never accurately been labeled as such, and was intentionally mislabeled to maintain control over people of color and deny them the freedom they had been promised.

A switch had been flipped. There has not been an increase in violence against people of color. I was ignorant in assuming that the brutality against Black people was escalating due to racists feeling emboldened by our current political environment. Retaliation for having a Black president for two terms prior. Everything I thought I knew was wrong.

Leaving the safety of my bench, I made my way toward the exit. Receiving another important lesson of how I benefit directly from the abuse of Black enslaved women. The "father" of gynecology was a slave owner who used Black women's bodies as medical test subjects because it was believed they didn't feel pain. He experimented on these women without their consent and with total disregard of their pain.

In the bookstore I sat alone in a corner of the coffee shop, flipping through children's books while my stomach churned and my thoughts raced, struggling to accept what I had not seen until that morning. It has *always* been legal to murder Black men, women, and children. Over time *we* have just changed how it's done. Black people have never truly been free.

I came on the trip thinking it was a privilege to tag along, but it was not for me.

I was wrong. The trip was for everyone. This is the trip eighth graders should be making instead of going to DC. This is where we truly learn the cost of freedom.

We spent our last morning together in Selma. Before we crossed the Edmund Pettus Bridge, we had the pleasure of meeting Miss Joanne Blackman Bland at the Selma Interpretive Center. She was eleven years old during the march from Selma to Montgomery. As she said her goodbyes, she made the statement that emboldened me the most. "They have been preventing us from voting from the very start because they know if we did, things would change. Look how important we are." She spoke softly and with frankness, not anger. Her parting words and the images of children fighting for the right to be equal when they supposedly were free, forced me to recognize that the fight for civil rights is something in which White people need to take responsibility. Black people have fought enough. They have given their lives. White people started this and we need to end it.

As I write, it has been almost three months since I visited Alabama. Anytime I am asked about the trip I respond that it was life-changing and say why. There hasn't been a single day since that I have not thought about what I learned during those four days. The weekend I came home I started crafting a nonprofit to raise awareness among other White people about racial bias. I hope to make this an annual trip, one that is free or at least discounted for pilgrims of color, and inclusive of White people whose education was as lacking as mine. I want to support Black women in their business ventures and am offering my business acumen to them at no cost. I want to confront the obstacles my little mentee and her family face as they try to live every day and support them every chance I get. Toni Morrison knew, "I tell my students, When you get these jobs that you have been so brilliantly trained for, just remember that your real job is that if you are free, you need to free somebody else. If you have some power, then your job is to empower somebody else."[1]

I will be better.

• • •••• •

A Reflection

Laura Evans

The pilgrimage was one of the most powerful experiences I have had. Powerful images and experiences from the pilgrimage come to me constantly. However, one word from our time in Alabama brings tears every time I recall it. The word is *No.*

Our first day in Birmingham we visited the Sixteenth Street Baptist Church. Mr. Bragg, a lifelong member of the church, spoke to us about September 15, 1963, the day four little girls were murdered by members of the KKK who bombed the church. Someone asked Mr. Bragg if White churches in Birmingham reached out and offered help after the bombing. In his quiet, gentle voice, Mr. Bragg said, "No."

From the people we met and from other pilgrims, I learned that I have been willfully complacent about the titanic and continuing battle African Americans fight against White racism in America. I learned how easy it has been for me to speak antiracist talk without taking any antiracist action.

Now I must act. I don't want to hear Mr. Bragg say, "No" again.

• • •••• •

1. Valerie Strass, "They Read Toni Morrison in School—And She Changed Their World," *Washington Post*, August 7, 2019, *https://www.washingtonpost.com/education/2019/08/07/they-read-toni-morrison-school-she-changed-their-world/.*

Reflections on Our Pilgrimage to Alabama

Ginny Klein

Being there. So many places and events I had heard about, read about, and seen on TV, during the 1960s. But they had faded from memory, somewhat, and I needed the immediacy of place to ground me again in the long, long struggle for freedom and rights.

Being present at the Sixteenth Street Baptist Church in Birmingham, the Dexter Avenue Baptist Church in Montgomery, and the Brown Chapel AME Church in Selma, and hearing firsthand from some who had witnessed those historical events was very powerful indeed.

Just as riveting was the Equal Justice Institute's Legacy Museum, laying out as it does in photos, videos, and text, the four-hundred-year history of the slavery-to-prison pipeline that has underpinned so much of our past. While I had known this history, seeing it depicted in such clear and compact form made it all the more compelling.

From these experiences I came away rejuvenated and clearer in my sense of where we have been as a country, and where we need to go—even if I am not so clear as to how we will ever get there.

· · ● ● ● ● ● ·

Reflecting

MaryBeth Ingram

I could reflect on the places and sites we visited. All powerful. I knew what I was going to see on the trip, but seeing it first-person makes it real in a way that you can never explain or transfer to someone else. Faced with the ugly history of terror put upon Black and Brown people is humbling, but it also incites such anger and grief. Anger from how in the hell did this happen? Where were the Christians? Where were the loving compassionate people of any faith or ethnicity because the White people, White Christians were anything but Christian. They forgot the very Jesus they follow. Grief that comes in tears. No longer guilt tears, they now come from grief much like Jesus cried over Jerusalem, lamenting that they did not know or recognize him and his tears on the cross from agony and pain; from deep within his experience of knowing that they (we) missed the mark, missed the opportunity to find the other way with him.

But what I want to reflect on is the behavior of the White people on the trip, myself included. Whiteness is so insidious and not once did any one of us set our privilege aside and shift power to the Black and Brown people on the pilgrimage. Like so much Whiteness, it wasn't done in meanness, but in ignorance. We could have said at the start of the week that we'd like people of color to have first choice anywhere we go, first in line, first in the pews, first to be served—first, first, first. I mentioned this to someone here at home after the trip and their reaction was "MaryBeth, not everyone wants to be first; some like to sit in the back." It's hard to disagree with that, but it misses the point.

Acknowledging there's a power and privilege imbalance is something we White people don't do; we need to notice and we need to offer our front row spots even if some still want to stay in the back row. A White person doesn't think twice about getting in line first, being the first in the door, or being closest to the exhibit. It's what we've always done—claim the best spots. I imagine a person of color may be just as acculturated to not get in line first or be the first in the door. Perhaps concerns for safety, acceptance, and inclusion come before claiming a chair or seat at the table. But those automatic responses won't be disturbed without the powerful and privileged people becoming aware of our actions and willfully changing our actions. Here's an example.

At one site, we all gathered in a room to hear a speaker. The first four rows had five chairs each, or chairs for twenty people. In those chairs were fifteen White people and five African Americans. In the very back row there were seven chairs: one White person and six African American people. I'm not naive enough to say that changing who gets to go first for five days will change racism in America, but it might change us. It might teach us what it's like not to be first in the door.

I want to relate something that happened to me in the past week at home and in traffic. This is not a reflection on the pilgrimage but a reflection on me and a learning jolt I had.

I was in heavy traffic with no end in sight. I knew if I could get into the lane to my right, I could make a turn into a neighborhood and go around the back way. It was rush hour, of course. Like most drivers, you look for any opening, even a small one. There weren't any until all of a sudden, a driver of a large SUV in the lane to my right did not pull forward when the cars in front of her moved. I put on my signal and moved over. There wasn't enough room for me to move completely over and be straight in line so my back end was still a bit in the left lane. Suddenly the SUV comes forward almost hitting my car. The window rolled down and a Black woman started to screamed at me. "You think you can just come over into this lane? What makes you think you have a right to do that?"

I responded that I had put on my turn signal and entered the lane when there was an opening in front of her car and I just wanted to be able to turn right at the next corner. She said something else I don't recall and I immediately realized this was a power and privilege struggle. I apologized and said that I would back up. She said gruffly "just go ahead" and rolled up her window. I decided not to take that privilege and I backed up. I was embarrassed, felt hurt not to be understood, and in fact, humiliated. I had been jolted into the reality that embarrassed, hurt, and humiliated is plenty common for people of color and it was high time I felt it personally.

Once again, this doesn't reflect on the pilgrimage but it reflects on the issue of setting aside privilege and shifting power. I'm not completely sure why, but I wasn't very extroverted on this trip as I usually am; I hung back. I find lately that I do this—I become quiet, more observing than interacting. Some of it may have to do with a real fear of saying the wrong thing and being *that* White woman. Some of it may simply be me at sixty-seven. Who knows?

. . . .

Alabama

Judith Rhedin

Given that it's still fresh and so much transpired, I'm trying to take it in and digest the information and some of the feelings. I know I'm standing on the shoulders of such proud folks who have gone before us and sacrificed so much. In my heart, I believe that their spirits are trying to help us to move forward and it's still not easy. We owe them so much.

I cannot even put the Lynching Memorial into words—the pain . . . as I read the many accounts along the walls about people lynched, including David Walker, his wife, and four children in 1908 in Hickman, Kentucky, because he was "accused of using inappropriate language with a White woman."

Powerful oral histories shared with us by the three women in Selma. They were young teenagers and one, only eleven; all had taken part. The young people and their determination and sacrifices left me without words listening to their experiences and the legacy that they are passing on to so many people today.

Everyone had/has a role to play. We are still marching . . .

. . . .

Pilgrimage

Ruth McMeekin Skjerseth

We had a bus
But were not "touring."
We were all
. . . Seekers, but
Perhaps not all
. . . For the same thing.

Getting a view
Closer to the inside
Than ever. For me.

Things that happened
When I was young
Remembered.
Old news.
Suddenly new
Again. Hearing from
People who were
. . . There.
Seeing.
Hearing.
Learning.

Moving among
New people.
New friends?
May take more time,
. . . Time worth taking.
. . . Hopeful.

Peeling back
New layers

Of understanding.
Making mistakes.
Accepting forgiveness.

But I'm
Still White.
Looking, peering
Down the roads
Of the future.
Choose one.
Set out. Walk.
Not alone.

. . ●●●● . .

A Journey

Carolyne Starek

On Tuesday, May 21, 2019, the *New York Times* published an article entitled "Revitalizing Montgomery as It Embraces Its Past." According to the article, the opening of the Legacy Museum and the National Memorial for Peace and Justice, often referred to as the Lynching Memorial, in April 2018 has been responsible for the influx of 400,000 more visitors to the city than during the previous year. Additionally, an increase of 107,000 hotel rooms have been rented as documented in city records. I was one of those visitors who spent five nights in Alabama. I traveled with fifty-one other pilgrims to Birmingham, Montgomery, and Selma, visiting these and other sites on the Civil Rights Trail to begin to understand what I didn't know, what the history books didn't teach, and what the White world hasn't owned.

The group was named the Ambassadors of Healing and represented folk from nine states: Texas, California, Pennsylvania, Delaware, Tennessee, New York, South Carolina, and the Washington, Maryland, and Virginia area. We were coming together as Black and White, male and female, gay and straight, young and old, able-bodied and physically challenged.

We spent the first day in Birmingham, a city with a reputation as a stronghold of segregation, enforced by laws, customs, and violence. The first stop was the Kelly Ingram Park where on May 2, 1963, more than one thousand Black students, some as young as six, left school and assembled to peacefully march to City Hall. Their parents, confined to their servitude by Whites, were told to stay away so they wouldn't lose their jobs. These young foot soldiers, members of the Children's Crusade, were hosed by fire department water cannons that shredded their clothes, beaten by police billy clubs, and attacked by police dogs that bloodied their skin. This children's action was one of the many strategies employed by the Rev. Dr. Martin Luther King Jr., and his organizers committed to nonviolence. It resulted in Birmingham having to release the jailed protesters who had filled the cells and overflowed the state fairgrounds, to integrate lunch counters, and to begin to hire Blacks for decent jobs.

In the afternoon, we toured the Civil Rights Institute and I was introduced for the first time to the legacy of the Reverend Fred L. Shuttlesworth. He established the Alabama Christian Movement for Human Rights and encouraged King and Abernathy to join him in his efforts to desegregate Birmingham. Shuttlesworth's home was bombed and he was severely beaten, but he did not back down. A larger than life statute depicting his outsized role in the civil rights movement stands at the entrance.

Then we crossed the park and watched a documentary film at the Sixteenth Avenue Baptist Church. We lingered at the site where dynamite was ignited on September 15, 1965, killing four young girls. As part of the restoration of the church building, high above the pews a magnificent stained glass window, which was donated by the Welsh people, depicts a Black Jesus with elongated outstretched arms. As a reference, perhaps to the parable of separating the sheep from the goats, Christ's right hand pushes away oppression while the left hand is open to forgiveness. Apparently, there was a worldwide response to the bombing; however, I found it curious that the Welsh people had given such a significant gift.

On the bus back to the motel, I wondered where I had been on those spring and fall days, had I, as an eighth grader in a small Northern town, watched the news, or read the paper? Why can't I remember?

During the debriefing session the first night, we were assembled in a small meeting room at the Comfort Inn where we were staying. Unfortunately, the room was not large enough to accommodate our sitting in a circle, face-to-face. Instead we were arranged in tightly packed rows with some folks choosing to stand on the perimeter. When asked introduce ourselves and to share our reflections, I was moved to speak after two other White women had shared. Both of them referred to being seventy years old and learning history they had never heard.

The weekend before, I had attended my granddaughter's graduation at the University of Virginia. The commencement speaker who addressed those students had majored in global sustainability and spoke about dissonance. They acknowledged how their coursework had prepared them to change the broken world by creating discomfort, by disagreeing with the status quo, and by disarming those in government spewing untruths. I saw the connection to our work, our equity work, and what the students were told. We were being schooled in how our American history was an inaccurate, incomplete story, and how our new awareness would gird us with energy to confront injustice, in small and large ways.

As I stood to share, I felt my voice begin to quiver. I told them I was about to mark my seventieth birthday, another milestone in my life of privilege and opportunity. But earlier in the day, I had been brought to tears. I had seen my birth year 1949 written as part of a commemorative marker to the four little girls who had been murdered. We shared a birth date, those girls and me, but our lives unfolded so differently, destinies colored by the skin we had not chosen to live in. Dr. King, in his eulogy of these angels unaware, called them "martyred heroines of a holy crusade for freedom and human dignity."[2]

After several other testimonies by Blacks and Whites reflecting on the day's experience, one of the women standing nearby said, "What are all these White people doing on my trip?" She was right in observing that about half of the group had changed the complexion of the Union of Black Episcopalians. Her question hung in the air and was met with silence and uneasy, muffled laughter, but was then repeated by another Black participant. Gayle moved on. She is a wise woman.

As the day had begun, one of her clergy colleagues prayed on the bus that we "look through the lens of love, open our ears to listen, and our hearts to understand." Perhaps Gayle knew that if, over the next four days, we interacted with each other, had meals together, stood and witnessed each other's tears together, we would really begin to see one another, the humanity that lives beneath the color of our skin. She knew, before we could understand, that going forward we, each in our own way, would expand our vision of God's beloved community, a diversity to be appreciated and not denigrated.

And so it was when we returned to our homes, one of the women who had posed the uncomfortable question wrote, "Hey, Pilgrims, now that I'm back in

---

2. Martin Luther King Jr., "Eulogy for the Martyred Children," September 18, 1963, Stanford University, *https://kinginstitute.stanford.edu/eulogy-martyred-children*.

the Apple I miss all of you. I not only miss your dialogue, but also your smiling faces in the morning. I hope you all got home safely and are renewed by our experience. I know I am. I was not expecting the racial diversity, but upon reflection, I am appreciative of the experience. We don't always get what we want, but sometimes we get what we need. (Forgive the manipulation of the Rolling Stones lyric.) Peace and much love!"

The second day of our pilgrimage we traveled to Montgomery to visit the Legacy Museum: From Enslavement to Mass Incarceration, erected on the site of a former slave warehouse. We learned that the domestic slave trade in Alabama, from 1808 until 1865, grew from a population of 40,000 to 435,000. We read that slavery was justified by an elaborate narrative of racial inferiority defended by legal, political, religious, and scientific institutions. In 1857, the year of the Dred Scott decision which denied citizenship rights to African Americans, the governor of the neighboring state of Mississippi wrote, "As a Christian people, it is the duty of the south to keep them in their present position, at any cost and at every peril."[3] We also learned that separate schools for "whites and colored children" are still mandated in the Alabama constitution, despite federal legislation. There have been two attempts to overturn this regulation, one in 2004 and another in 2012, both of which were defeated. Bryan Stevenson, the founder of the Equal Justice Initiative, the creator of the museum, author of *Just Mercy*, and the man who has almost single-handedly changed the face of Montgomery, has stated that slavery didn't end in 1865, it just evolved. As Jim Wallis has written,[4] slavery is America's original sin, and it continues to be committed in individual and institutional ways across the country, everywhere, every day.

A young family visiting from New Zealand walked along with my roommate and me through a couple of the galleries. As my friend and I gazed at a photo of a young Black boy being attacked by a police dog, the little boy asked, "Why?" The answer was incomprehensible to the boy, no more than five, not because of his age, but rather because of the incomprehensibility that anyone would be so cruel to another human being.

In the afternoon we traveled to the Peace and Justice Memorial and walked reverently among the 800 columns hanging above us representing the lynching of 4,400 persons, men, women, and children between 1877 and 1950. Replicas

---

3. Quote of William McWillie, governor of Mississippi, Legacy Museum, Equal Justice Initiative, Montgomery, Alabama.

4. Jim Wallis, *America's Original Sin: Racism, White Privilege, and the Bridge to a New America* (Grand Rapids, MI: Brazos Press, 2016).

of each memorial column lie outside the structure waiting to be claimed by each of the 800 counties that are willing to confront their truth in terrorizing their fellow human beings. I listened to an Equal Justice Initiative lawyer who had been part of a homecoming service for a column in Oxford, Mississippi. She shared that the son and the grandchildren of one of the lynching victims was present to bear witness to how the act of lynching his father had scarred his life in unimaginable ways.

The next day in Montgomery, we visited the Rosa Parks Children's Museum and got on the bus, one like the Magic School Bus, that sped us through the history that led up to the bus boycott. When the bus driver said to an exhausted Rosa Parks, "I am going to have you arrested," she responded, "You may do that. I am a protestor and not a victim." Her life was guided by righteousness, justice, and truth. The boycott lasted thirteen months and cost the city $3,000 a day, which would amount to $20,000 per day in 2019. Fundraising efforts paid for nineteen station wagons, dubbed as rolling churches, that carried 96 percent of the Blacks to work and back every day.

One of the most poignant moments I experienced while visiting the parsonage of King's Dexter Avenue Baptist Church was when the guide told us that King always sent his wife, Coretta, flowers while crusading across the country and that on his last trip he had sent her plastic flowers so she would always remember him. After what he called his epiphany, when he said he heard the Lord saying I will be with you, he marched on in strength, love, and courage, never deterred, until his assassination on April 4, 1968.

On our last day in Alabama we went to the Brown Chapel in Selma where the march across the Edmund Pettus Bridge had been planned. Two beautiful women spoke to our group. Joyce began by recalling life in the Jim Crow South. Everything was separate, but nothing was equal. She likened it to the time when you are taught to color in school. The teacher, in this case the Whites who were in charge, instructed you to stay within the lines. And that, Joyce said is what they did. When the Klan rode into her neighborhood, they were told to get down on the floor below the windows. When she was a child, less than 2 percent of the Blacks in Selma were registered to vote. Her mother was an eighth grade social studies teacher and when she went to register to vote, she was asked to recite the preamble of the constitution. She could do it because she was a student of history. But, without reason her application was rejected. When she returned to try again, this time she was told to recite the entire constitution.

Leading up to the voting rights march, which began with crossing the bridge on March 21, 1965, Diane attended mass meetings that always began with songs to help get their minds focused. They would sing, "This little light of mine, I'm gonna let it shine," and "Goin home to my Lord to be free. Before I'll be a slave, I'll be buried in my grave," and "Ain't gonna let nobody turn me around, turn me around. Ain't gonna let George Wallace turn me around. I'm gonna keep on walking, keep on talking. Marching to the freedom land."

Diane marched four times and was arrested twice. In the mass meetings they were told to be prepared to be arrested and to cover their heads, to not react when called the n-word and to persevere when struck with a cattle prod or a billy club. On Bloody Sunday, she and her brother were running with an elderly woman. When the woman couldn't keep up, she waved Diane and her brother on. When Diane looked back, she could see the woman being badly beaten by a mounted man who had been deputized to rain down terror on the marchers. She remembered that the sheriff wore a badge that said in big Black letters, "NEVER." It was to send the message that they would never get to Montgomery and would never get the right to vote. Fortunately, his was not the last word.

Joann Bland, who is featured on the NPR podcast "White Lies," told us that she was first arrested at age eight. Her grandmother had told her, "Go get your freedom," admitting to Joann that she always had wanted to sit at the lunch counter in town. After Turnaround Tuesday, the second time marchers crossed the bridge, three hundred people walked on to the capital in Montgomery, where they were met by 25,000 others, joining together in a modern-day biblical chant of "Let my people vote!" Joann also reminded us that when King crossed that bridge, he knelt down to pray. So I guess you could say that Colin Kaepernick was following in King's footsteps—both men bringing injustice to its knees.

One of the most enduring memories I have of the entire pilgrimage is that of the people who gave us tours and spoke of their lives growing up in the Deep South, many of whom were survivors of marches, protests, and violent actions. They were proud, dignified, and serene individuals and I hoped that somehow the likes of Steven Spielberg would venture south to capture their stories and preserve them for us all.

This travel log, as such, is the "what" of my story and as I live into the experience I must reflect on the "so what." I have questions, and going forward will search my heart for the answers. Why as a White person did I choose to go on the pilgrimage? Was I trying to heed the words of Atticus Finch to Scott that "you have to get inside another person's skin and crawl around in it to really get to know him."[5] I had been to the African American Museum of History and Culture in DC and saw the towering statue of Thomas Jefferson erected in front of the words that all men are created equal against a backdrop of bricks inscribed with names of his slaves. I believe I wanted to go to ground zero to see and touch and feel where our cruel history unfolded and how the brave men and women fought back. I wanted to pay homage to those who had the courage to stand up.

But, as my friend and fellow traveler reminded me, I could not feel the pain of the woman looking for the names of family members inscribed on one of the Arkansas commemorative columns at the lynching memorial. I could not feel the pride of the woman who crossed the Edmund Pettus Bridge in her father's footsteps. He had been a doctor in Washington, DC, who traveled to Selma to march with King. I could not feel the intense interest of the woman who was determined to trace her family lineage back to plantations maintained on the backs of her ancestors, like those who built the White House. But I was there standing up. Standing with them.

I attended Gayle's church in Washington, DC, on Sunday and we sang "This Little Light of Mine." I will be back this Sunday for the commemorative service acknowledging the four hundredth anniversary of the enslaved Africans arrival in Jamestown, Virginia. Four hundred years. As an Ambassador of Healing, there is much to learn and unlearn looking through the lens of love and understanding.

. . . .

5. Harper Lee, *To Kill a Mockingbird* (screenplay), December 25, 1962.

40

The Pain of Racism

ROMANS 8:22–28, NLT

Charles D. Fowler III

Lifelong Pain

Eighty-one years ago, a Charlottesville, Virginia, native's father was struck and killed by an automobile driven by a White student attending the University of Virginia. The student was driving at a high rate of speed down Main Street from the area of the rotunda at the university to the area of Vinegar Hill, a Black enclave, a distance of approximately one mile. At the time of the death, Main Street was not as it is now. In the evening, there was no parking on either side of the street. At that time, there was very little traffic and no stores or businesses. The child of the deceased was ten years old. To prevent action by the family of the deceased, the father of the driver of the vehicle hired a lawyer, who quickly offered a settlement to the widow, the young son's mother. The proposed settlement was to pay all bills due as of that day and the balance of the existing mortgage on the house. In 2019, one might ask why anyone would accept such an offer; however, consideration must be given to the status of a Black family, specifically, and Black people, in general, in Charlottesville of that time. The widow accepted the offer; however, with the death of the father, other issues suddenly became of critical importance for the future of the family. How would the bills be paid from that point on? What would happen to two brothers left without a father to advise them, guide them, and protect them and their mother over a lifetime? In a segregated society, how would the children survive in an environment steeped in the practices of slavery and the subhuman treatment of people of color? How would they receive the quality education needed for admission to a college? How would they afford it?

Because of segregation and racial bias, institutions such as the University of Virginia were not among their choices; choices the White driver of the vehicle did have. The reality was that painful days were ahead for them and others in a myriad of situations in Charlottesville in particular and in the Southern states of this country in general. Do Black lives really matter? The life and future of the White student was worth more than all of the members of the Williams family, then, and in the future. Because that is what that father was purchasing—his son's future, which the father considered more important than justice for a Black family. The fact that money was offered to secure the future of the White son is White privilege in action.

The Pain of Racism

Pain is described by *Webster's Collegiate Dictionary* as "acute mental or emotional distress or suffering, trouble, care or effort taken for the accomplishment of something."[1] It is my view, and apparently the views of others, that the level of mental and psychological pain upon many in society is as great as any that has been experienced or seen nationally in a very long time. This is pain as it relates to things felt, done, or experienced by people, one to another.

Racism is defined by the *Oxford English Dictionary* as "the belief that all members of each race possess characteristics or abilities specific to that race, especially so as to distinguish it as inferior or superior to another race or races."[2] The impact of such a feeling runs deep and is in my opinion an accurate description of what this country has come to be known for. It is what it has been since its beginnings.

Therefore, while it is true that everyone within a country or race, be it the United States or elsewhere, cannot be painted with the same brush, our country's beginnings and the long lingering practices of bigotry, oppression, and racism for four hundred years cannot be ignored. The vestiges of enslavement, family separations, and destruction still haunt our nation, no matter how much we would like to ignore them or find a way to make them go away. Blatant discriminatory practices and perpetual dehumanizing treatment of people of color are a part of the DNA of our country and are particularly and especially hurtful, even though such practices are perhaps more subtle now than in the past. These practices continue to take their toll on the minds, bodies, and spirits of those affected and are particularly hurtful when those beneath the sole of the master's proverbial boot find out that it is literally impossible to make a way out of no way. Therefore, all things being considered, the present continues to

---

1. *Merriam-Webster*, s.v. "pain," accessed June 19, 2019, *https://www.merriam-webster.com/dictionary/pain*.

2. *Oxford English Dictionary*, s.v. "racism," accessed June 19, 2019, *https://www.lexico.com/en/definition/racism*.

point to the fact that our nation, the United States of America, has not done enough to correct the ill practices of the past. And for people of color, while much has changed since our country's beginnings, we have yet to overcome the obstacles of racism that we experience on a daily basis. The bottom line seems to be, the ordinary vicissitudes of life notwithstanding, that our daily struggle appears to still have its roots deeply planted in the pain of racism.

My Beginnings

Although I was not born in Charlottesville, my mother, grandmother, and great grandmother were. Records reflect that my great grandmother's mother, Patsy Carter, was born enslaved. My father was born in Lynchburg, Virginia. I spent my early childhood in Charlottesville, from my infancy until I was eleven years old. At that time, the city of Charlottesville was a little town of between 25,000 and 28,000 people. To a sixth-grade student, very little seemed to happen that could be considered earthshaking.

Through the eyes of a child in a separate but equal education system and less than equal world outside of the public school system, all that seemed to be required of me was to go to school at the then-segregated Jefferson Elementary school during the week and to Sunday school and church on Sunday morning. In retrospect, though it is hard at this point in my life to remember accurately, Charlottesville seemed to be noted for places such as Monticello, the home of Thomas Jefferson, the Thomas Jefferson Inn (now the building where the US Government's Federal Executive Institute (FEI) is located), the University of Virginia, the University Hospital, the Keswick Country Club just outside of town, and other places perhaps of interest for those of means. I am reminded, as I think about these places, that I did not see Monticello until, at forty-two years old, I came back to Charlottesville to attend FEI for executive training. I was taken aback when I realized that the FEI was the place I remembered as the Thomas Jefferson Inn. It had once been a place where Blacks could only enter to cook, clean, and maintain the inn, which housed a great restaurant and living quarters. My father had taken me there as a child, around the side of the building to the kitchen where some of his friends were the cooks and waiters.

In Charlottesville, two major railroad lines, the Southern Railroad and the Chesapeake and Ohio Railroad, the University of Virginia, University Hospital, Monticello, and a place called Vinegar Hill, a *colored* neighborhood and business area, defined the city to me, both geographically and racially. The trains, especially, captured my attention, for the gigantic diesel engines, green and white for Southern and blue, yellow, and vermillion for C&O, were as fascinating then as they are now, for I am still a railroad buff.

As a child, The University Hospital and the University of Virginia were not well known to me, except in name only. The University Hospital was segregated and, according to records, the University of Virginia admitted its first African American student, Gregory Swanson, into the law school in 1950. "Following his successful lawsuit, a handful of Black graduate and professional students were admitted during the 1950s, though no Black undergraduates were admitted until 1955 and UVA did not fully integrate until the1960s."[3]

I was aware, even at my age, that *colored* people did not venture comfortably into the neighborhood surrounding the university unless they were going there to perform their duties as paid help for the residents. The restrictions for people of color in the university neighborhood were unwritten, but not unusual, since equal access and service were not available in many places in the town of Charlottesville; many restrictions for Black people were unwritten unless needed from White persons or the police as reminders. This included department stores, where we might be admitted with certain rules, and city transportation, where we, people of color, boarded the bus and sat or stood in the back.

Through the eyes of a child, Charlottesville appeared to be a nice place to call home. Though segregated, with Whites Only and Colored Only signs prominently posted in and around bus stations, railroad stations, water fountains, movie theaters, and department stores, to an eleven year old things seemed relatively normal, for I had nothing with which to compare a segregated society at the time. At noon, the fire house horn would blare and could be heard throughout the city. At 9 p.m., curfew was noted by the soft tolling of a bell that also could be heard throughout the city. Whatever may have transpired during the day, things seemed relatively quiet at night. What I didn't know, nor fully grasp as a child, was the importance of my father's position and activities outside of the walls of First Baptist Church.

The NAACP

My father, Charles D. Fowler Jr., was the president of the local chapter of the Charlottesville National Association for the Advancement of Colored People (NAACP) from 1953 to 1955. Daddy, at some point, was employed as

---

3. Wikepedia, s.v. "Gregory Swanson," accessed June 9, 2019, *https://en.wikipedia.org/wiki/Gregory_Swanson*.

a railway postal clerk for the Southern Railroad. He and others guarded and sorted the mail in a railway car and dropped it off along the way, holding the mailbag just outside of an open train door to be snagged by a stationary iron hook while the train was passing through various towns.

Daddy, a veteran of the Army, had a degree in business administration from Howard University but could not find employment that was comparable to his education. I do not know the exact dates of his employment with the US Postal Service because our family was in transition during his last days in Charlottesville and our move to Washington, DC. In his off hours, he trained himself in printing and subsequently opened a printing business on Preston Avenue, a major thoroughfare in Charlottesville. At some point, Daddy also obtained a license as a real estate broker and went on to enroll as a student at Howard University's Law School.

While I do not recall radical opposition to segregation in Charlottesville, the society that existed in Charlottesville was one in which persons of color did not have equal access to all of the things needed and considered necessary to be considered successful by members of the existing society. Segregation and racial discrimination were the same as they were elsewhere in certain states in the South. I am certain there was pain in being considered second-class citizens by those of the majority race; however, I do not think my father nor any of his associates ever felt they were second-class citizens, nor second class in anything else that was placed before them.

On a wall in my son's, Charles D. Fowler IV, home, is a certificate and reminder of what his grandfather Charles D. Fowler Jr. accomplished as president of the Charlottesville Chapter of the NAACP in trying to address the ills of society at that time. The citation reads in part:

> During his brief administration from December 1953 to December 1955, unprecedented advances were made by the Branch. . . . Petitions for immediate integration were filed with the City and County School Boards. University of Virginia Hospital facilities for Negroes were vastly improved and the hospital was partially integrated. . . . Our Branch was enlarged during the first year of his administration by 1300 percent, thus winning for us the national award for membership increase. Branch members numbered 60 when he took office and two years later, when he left us to study law (at Howard University), they numbered 1200. . . . His courage, his integrity, his dedication to the principle of equality for all—these will endure in our memory."

The issue of public school desegregation was a hotly debated question in Charlottesville. Not until July 26, 1955, did it become clear to the White community that Blacks in Charlottesville were going to attempt to desegregate the school system. On that date, my father announced that the NAACP would present petitions from Black parents to the school board requesting the transfer of their children to White schools. He said, "We believe it is the constitutional right to attend integrated schools. We're asking the board to abide by the decision of the Supreme Court, and do it in good faith. We are afraid if we don't do anything, it will just be waiting a long time. We waited a long time for equalization of schools. I'd like to see Charlottesville face reality. It's going to come one way or another. . . . It's certainly going to Court."[4]

However, even with all of the accolades and accomplishments, I am certain that Daddy felt the pain, as did his longtime associate and friend of many years, Mr. Eugene Williams. The two of them, along with mortician Raymond Bell, walked together in planning their strategies to address the inequalities of racism, bigotry, hatred, and injustice and "met on street corners under lights from city poles, in their suits and ties, because there were no Starbucks or McDonald's in which we could leisurely meet over coffee and a sandwich or two."[5]

While I do not recall hearing of marching and boycotting in Charlottesville, I know that Daddy and others used the legal system to press for desegregation of the public schools and general acceptance in the use of all public facilities in Charlottesville. After the Brown Decision, they specifically concentrated their efforts on the public schools.

At some point, they called on a lawyer named Thurgood Marshall, the future Justice of the US Supreme Court, to assist them in their efforts to increase the membership of the Charlottesville NAACP. According to Mr. Williams, Mr. Marshall came to Charlottesville to assist the chapter in recruiting new members. As we are acutely aware, the 1954 decision in *Brown v. Board of Education* to end the separate but [un]equal policies and segregated school systems across the country was a game changer.

When I was in the sixth grade in Charlottesville, the Black high school was the Jackson P. Burley High School and the White high school was Lane High

---

4. Dallas R. Crowe, "Desegregation of Charlottesville, Virginia Public Schools, 1954–1969: A Case Study," University of Virginia Library, January 1, 1971, *https://libraetd.lib.virginia.edu/public_view/rf55z7799*.

5. Personal interview conducted with Mr. Eugene Williams, August 5–December 1, 2019.

School. In 1959, the court ordered their integration. On November 18, 2011, markers commemorating the integration of Venable Elementary School and Lane High School were placed at each school. On the markers, the names of the Charlottesville Twelve, the first to integrate the public schools, are listed. Today, the building that was Lane is now the Albemarle County Office Building. Among the twelve students listed, two of them were my classmates at Jefferson Elementary School.

The Movies and a Father's Guidance, Love, and Protection

In Charlottesville, there were four theaters that I recall: The Paramount, the Jefferson, the Lafayette, and the University. I sat upstairs in the "colored" balcony sections of the first three named, but never sat, nor have I ever been in, the fourth theater. I recall the vivid memory of having to enter the Paramount Theater from the side street to go up the stairs with my grandmother to the balcony, because Black people were not allowed to enter the theater through the Main Street doors or sit on the ground level. I also recall the day as I sat in the balcony watching a movie that a White usher appeared and ordered all Black people to move to one side. A rope was then placed in the center from the top of the balcony to the rail overlooking the lower level; on one side of the rope sat the White clientele and on the other side sat the Black clientele. At the time, I did what I was told to do and what I saw my grandmother and others doing. What a memory, even now, of the insanity of such practices. Those on either side of the rope could physically touch each other, just a rope's width away. I also retain the memory of an occasional *empty* box or two of popcorn, *accidentally* falling from the balcony on to the heads of those who sat below.

I remember the day I asked my father if I could go to see a movie at the University Theatre and he said, "You can go up there if you wish, but they are not going to let you enter!" I did not go, but to this day, I appreciate my father being such an example in the struggle to receive equal treatment, that he impressed upon me that it was the right thing to at least want to test whether I could gain entry to a place where there was no chance of being admitted.

Unknowingly, I was a part of the struggle of a race of people with the desire to want to be a part of a movement to confront the existing conditions of being denied access, purely because of the color of my skin. It was a chance to at least think about going against a segregated society if I wished to do so. I'm certain that if I had headed to the University Theatre, my father would have been close by somewhere to ensure my safety. As I write this, I feel the pain of a father who had to explain to his son why he wouldn't be admitted to areas where White people's children felt empowered to go whenever they pleased by their so-called God-given right, even at the expense of others in a so-called free society.

Charlottesville, Virginia, August 2017

I left Charlottesville in 1957, and almost three years have passed since the violence that occurred when the White supremacist sympathizers and opponents of the Ku Klux Klan clashed in Charlottesville on August 11 and 12, 2017, at a Unite the Right rally. The confrontation resulted in the death of Heather Heyer, who was intentionally run over by an automobile driven by James Alex Fields Jr.; in the tragic course of events, nineteen other people were also injured.

In the crowd of people present during the rally were students and perhaps even faculty members at the University of Virginia, along with residents of Charlottesville and other cities as far away as California. Present were members of the far-right, which included self-identified members of the alt-right, new Confederates, new fascists, White nationalists, new Nazis, Klansmen, Blue Lives Matter, and various right-wing militias—groups that claimed that those on the other side were worthless. On the other side, probably more than a few who felt that Black lives didn't matter, or that all White people are evil and racist.

Organizers of the Unite the Right rally said they were defending a statue of Confederate General Robert E. Lee, which the city planned to remove from a public park. The rally and the death of Heather Heyer brought to mind memories of the Charlottesville I left in 1957 and some of the positive thoughts I had about the present state of society in Charlottesville were shattered with the death of Heather Heyer. The violence and loss of life caused a sadness inside of me, as if someone had placed a dark cloth over my eyes obscuring the positive changes that had occurred in Charlottesville since my departure. The rally reminded me that perhaps things had not changed as much as I thought they had. A dose of reality jolted me. The turn of events that day shattered what I can now see was a false sense of great advancement and improvement. The events of that day caused me then, as well as now, to come to grips with the reality that the pain of racism runs deep, for there are still those who would return society back to the practices of the fifties (and before) if they could.

The underlying factors of lingering and in some instances, never-ending hatred and mistreatment of others cannot be overlooked or trivialized when all it takes is the proposed removal of a bronze statue to cause those of opposite opinions to clash to the point of violence.

On August 12, 2018, Anthony Salvatore of CBS News, reported:

> A new CBS News poll conducted by YouGov finds 61 percent of Americans say that racial tensions have increased over the past year. Majorities of whites, blacks, and Hispanics feel this way, but blacks are especially likely to think so: 78 percent feel tensions have increased. . . . Seventy-three percent of African-Americans feel the president tries to put the interest of Whites ahead of minorities, and 58 percent of Hispanics feel the president tries to put Whites ahead of minority groups.[6]

In an article, "Race in America 2019," Juliana Menasce Horowitz, Anna Brown, and Kiana Cox stated, "More than 150 years after the 13th Amendment abolished slavery in the United States, most U.S. adults say the legacy of slavery continues to have an impact on the position of black people in American society today."[7]

Therefore, I am compelled to at least ask the following questions to those African Americans who feel that we as a people have *arrived*.

If some of us can now be described as the haves, those who have achieved the American Dream, then what do we say to those who continue to be the have-nots? Do we feel their pain? Are the groans we hear, the groans of not just the oppressed of our race, but the groans of people of color the world over—are they real to us?

The Bible says in Romans 8:22 (NLT) "that all creation has been groaning as in the pains of childbirth right up to the present time." All creation. Do we as African Americans living in 2020 still feel the pain of racism and segregation or is it now more of an afterthought than a constant reality of our twenty-first-century lives? Is it possible that with over seven and a half billion people on this planet called Earth, that the collective pain of others is too much for us to consider and that often times, we will block out even the worst pain, unless it is our own?

---

6. Anthony Salvatore, "Poll: One Year after Charlottesville, Majority of Americans See Racial Tensions Rise," CBS News, August 12, 2018, *https://www.cbsnews.com/news/poll-one-year-after-charlottesville-americans-see-racial-tensions-on-increase/*. The CBS News 2018 Battleground Tracker is a series of panel studies in the US. This national poll was conducted by YouGov using a nationally representative sample of 2,238 US adults between August 8–10, 2018. The margin of error based upon the entire sample is approximately 2.5 percent.

7. Juliana Menasce Horowitz, Anna Brown, and Kiana Cox, "Race in America, 2019," Pew Research Center, April 9, 2019, *https://www.pewsocialtrends.org/2019/04/09/race-in-america-2019/*.

Presently, the United States of America finds itself in a peculiar position when it comes to human rights, immigration, integration, gender discrimination, and interaction with its citizens, neighboring border countries, and neighbors around the world. Somehow, as the complexions and nationalities of those coming to the shores of this country change, there is a disconnect between our nation's actions and the words on the Stature of Liberty:

> Give me your tired, your poor, your huddled masses yearning to breathe free,
> The wretched refuse of your teeming shore. Send these, the homeless, tempest-tossed to me, I lift my lamp beside the golden door.

Today the United States faces massive problems within and without concerning race relations. Consequently, how we handle or fail to address these matters is critical because with these problems comes pain. We know that from our country's beginnings, racist and institutionalized practices that began before the founding of what would become the Unites States of America have caused great pain. That pain has emanated from August 1619 until now; from the brush arbors of slavery to the separate and [un]equal societies of just a few years ago; to the attempts to move our country back to some of the not-so-subtle racial practices of yesteryear. The question becomes, do we feel the pain and is it sufficient enough to cause us to do something about it, even if it is no more than to seize opportunities to be heard and to be present at some of the many opportunities that are going on to protest injustices?

Many of the things that we as African Americans have to face are not new. Racially bigoted incidents have once again become more frequent and more subtle. Various groups feel empowered to openly defy court orders, law enforcement officials, and anything else that goes against their positions, especially when it comes to matters involving race and equality. All of this is somewhat bizarre, when no one except the indigenous, so called *discovered* people, who were here before there were settlers or colonies or a United States, have a legitimate right to say they belong here. Consequently, what to do about the pain of racism is something that continues to be a part of our daily lives.

In retrospect, I feel that in the midst of perhaps unseen and unknown turmoil and conflict in the city of Charlottesville over the years, there was one place in which a sense of stability could be found, purpose could be defined, and positions in the colored community and society could be of importance. That place was the Church.

The Church

My memory of Charlottesville in 1957 is that there were four prominent Black churches, and that church was the place where the Lord was revered and where order, advancement, and education for young aspiring children and adults was paramount. Church was the place where direction was freely given and where such direction was seriously considered by its members. Church was where matters affecting the community in particular and society in general were central in discussions by pastors and members.

I belonged to First Baptist Church located on Main Street, directly across the street from the main terminal for Southern Railroad. Mount Zion Baptist Church, Ebenezer Baptist Church, and Zion Union Baptist Church were the other three Black churches. Even as a child, I grasped that the Black church had a role outside the walls of the church, especially in matters involving society and took that role seriously. My father was a deacon at First Baptist Church. I cannot say if pastors in Charlottesville in the fifties were social activists because I do not know; children were not privy to that information.

When speaking of the pain of racism, we must keep things in context as we consider the role of the Church in matters such as integration. It was not until April 12, 1963, five years after my departure from Charlottesville, that the activities in Birmingham, Alabama, captured the attention of the nation and the world. However, when considering the Black church in Charlottesville and other places, according to S. Jonathan Bass in *Blessed Are the Peacemakers*, "Overall [Birmingham's] black pastors provided only lukewarm support for King's campaign," and, "Wyatt Walker later estimated that fewer than 10 percent of Birmingham's black clergy participated in the movement."[8] According to Bass, at some point Dr. King said that the true measure of a Christian was a commitment to engage social concerns,[9] and he told Black ministers, "If you can't stand up with your people, you are not fit to be a preacher."[10]

On Monday, April 8, 1963, at a mass rally, the Rev. Ralph Abernathy announced that he and King were leading a group of protestors to jail during the middle of that week.[11] Later, on Wednesday, April 10, Dr. King announced that they would lead a march to the Birmingham jail on Good Friday and that he, Abernathy, and Shuttlesworth would wear denim work clothes, the

---

8. S. Jonathan Bass, *Blessed Are the Peacemakers* (Baton Rouge: Louisiana University Press, 2001), 106.

9. Bass, *Blessed Are the Peacemakers*, 106.

10. Bass, *Blessed Are the Peacemakers*, 106.

11. Bass, *Blessed Are the Peacemakers*, 107.

movement's "sacrificial uniform."[12] Dr. King said, "We are now confronted with recalcitrant forces in the Deep South that will use the courts to perpetuate the unjust and illegal systems of racial separation."[13] Abernathy told the reporters that Christ had died on the cross nearly two thousand years ago and "tomorrow we will take it up [the Cross] for our people and die if necessary." On that Thursday evening, at Sixth Avenue Baptist Church, it was the Rev. Ralph Abernathy who told reporters at a gathering, "We are going to turn this town upside down and inside out tomorrow. I'm not going to fail tomorrow and M.L. King's not going to fail tomorrow and lots more of us are not going to fail tomorrow. . . . We are going to a higher judge than Judge Jenkins."[14]

Considering the role of the Black church in the sixties, the question now is, *What is the role of churches in general and the Black church specifically in the midst of such controversies and tragedies as the Alt Right rally and has that role changed from the fifties and sixties until now?* Do our so-called Black churches and followers of the same Lord and Savior of other Christians have a higher calling as all Christian believers have, to love one another? In answering the question of a Pharisee concerning the great commandment in the law, Jesus said in Matthew 22:37–40 (KJV): "Thou shalt love the Lord thy God with all thy heart, and with all thy soul, and with all thy mind. This is the first and great commandment. And the second is like unto it. Thou shalt love thy neighbor as thyself. On these two commandments hang all the law and the prophets."

Too often, this divine instruction is misconstrued and misused, since the intent is for a much higher calling than physical love. It is indeed a divine call that we emulate the agape love of God, while knowing that even in our very best moments, when we strive to have this kind of love, the love of God in our hearts, minds, and souls, we will still fall short. No human being has the ability to love in the way that God loves all of God's creation. We are called upon, in Matthew 5:44 (KJV), to "Love your enemies, bless them that curse you, do good to them that hate you, and pray for them which despitefully use you, and persecute you." This is a monumental request that only God can place in our hearts, through the power of the Holy Spirit. So relevant to this line of thought, we might ask ourselves as well as others, in our human frailty, *Do we really feel the pain of the masses?* I submit to all who would seriously consider

---

12. Bass, *Blessed Are the Peacemakers*, 108.

13. Bass, *Blessed Are the Peacemakers*, 108.

14. Bass, *Blessed Are the Peacemakers*, 108.

this question that pain comes to all of us when we genuinely love. Yet we can be sure that reciprocal love is far better than reciprocal hatred.

It is my opinion that the Black church has done much to mitigate the pain of yesterday's separate but [un]equal society, as well as the ills of today's society in general, but for me, mitigation of pain is not the elimination of pain, nor is it the elimination of pain's source. The source of our pain in this case is a society, a world in which outright racism, overt hatred, and disregard for anything and everything is occurring more often than not, no matter where one may go.

Surely many like my father suffered extreme pain in the silence of their midnight hours, while holding on to the inspirational messages and activities of the Black church and its leaders. Their pride, perseverance, and fortitude were encouraged and supported by faith in the Word of God provided by ministers and those in leadership positions in the Church. In many instances, churches seemed somewhat smaller and more welcoming than those of today. I do not recall hearing of conversations centered on the color of a preacher's robe, the hierarchy of positions within the confines of the local church, or the size of the physical church building. I am of the opinion that it was and is the Word of God that inspired them and helped them to know that church membership and the Word of God involved more than just coming to church on Sunday morning.

The Word of God requires life-changing direction and commitment for those who are hearers of the Word. It is the hearers of the Word who ultimately become doers of the Word. It is the duty of those who would be representatives and spokespersons for the Lord to make a difference in the world. The Bible says in the book of James 2:17 (KJV), that "Even so faith, if it hath not works, is dead, being alone." That does not mean works righteousness, because we cannot work our way to heaven. Jesus Christ has already paid the price by shedding his own blood on the cross. However, if we have faith, it ought to be evidenced in our actions.

The Black church, through hearing the Word of God from pastors who believed and held on to the Word, assured their congregations that they all were indeed soldiers in God's army, not just in name, but also in action. They knew and remained faithful to the calling on their lives, to hold up the blood-stained banner. They knew that such a calling to the pulpit and membership meant doing something meaningful and not to just sit in a chair or on a bench and do nothing.

Indeed, people like as Mr. Eugene Williams, Mr. Raymond Bell, and my father were soldiers in God's army and, even with the death of his friends,

Mr. Williams has not abandoned his post. I am certain he will continue to hold up the blood-stained banner until the very end. The old hymn of the church says it best:

> We are soldiers in the army,
> We have to fight, although we have to cry.
> We have to hold up the blood-stained banner.
> We have to hold it up until we die.[15]

The records of the leadership and members of Black churches of the civil rights era speak for themselves. The record reflects that they do not appear to have availed themselves of what Dietrich Bonhoeffer would characterize as *cheap grace*.[16] For grace has always come to us with a price. The One who is the author and finisher of our faith and the source of all grace is our Lord and Savior, Jesus, the Christ, the Son of the living God, who paid it all on the cross.

We know that churches of the fifties and sixties held on to God's grace and were willing to give their all so that future generations might not have to go through what they were going through now, including the past ills and injustices. However, to keep the present-day ills in perspective, we must ask ourselves whether there has ever been a time in the world when all was well, nothing was wrong and there was no need for anyone to stand up and be counted against evil in all of its many forms? Pain and the effects of such pain on the lives of human beings did not start with the United States of America. Such pain started in the beginning, with Adam, the Garden experience, and thereafter, the growth of humankind's inhumanity to each other within all of God's creation.

The pain of today's bigotry and not-so-subtle racism is still just below the surface; however, determining what needs to be done and then getting it done is quite a challenge. The legacy, dignity, and presence of the Black church of the past still stands and is still remembered and respected for its place in the forefront of major movements that took on the responsibility to remedy the wrongs of those who would discriminate against people of color. Now, with the advent of technology and social media, perhaps there are reasons why churches seem less active and visible in the forefront of major movements to right the wrongs of this era. One need only to look at the younger generation where

---

15. James Cleveland, "We Are Soldiers of the Cross," *http://www.songlyrics.com/rev-james-cleveland/soldiers-of-the-cross-lyrics/*.

16. Dietrich Bonhoeffer, *The Cost of Discipleship* (New York: MacMillan, 1953), 37.

church attendance is not the requirement that it was in the fifties and sixties, nor is it seen today as the necessity it was fifty or sixty years ago. People of color no longer feel an absolute need to meet in the church to strategize, because freedom now exists to meet almost anywhere one wishes. This is a disconnect as older church populations hold on to the past of hymn books, sanctuaries, and pulpits and places to fellowship, while the youth hold on to social media and less of a need to be in a physical church building.

We may disagree concerning what the answers are to these questions and who is worthy of accolades and recognition. We may struggle to accurately identify those who we think have remained true to their calling; however, I think we can agree that Black church leadership and members of the fifties and sixties demonstrated that they were concerned enough corporately, as evidenced by their actions and recorded by history, that they put their concerns into action. There was a sense of urgency because while the burden of existing in a segregated society and earning an acceptable wage was hard enough, there were organizations such as the Klan, the John Birch Society, and others that were not only threatening, they were dangerous. Therefore, it would seem that we ought to be able to do so much more to make a difference and to correct the grievous wrongs that still exist in our communities today. If we give it serious, considerate thought, there is nothing to prevent us from coming up with possible strategies and solutions and then putting our concerns into action. Paul points to the attitude and way to proceed through the word in Philippians 4:13 (KJV), "I can do all things through Christ which strengthens me."

As one who put all that he had on the line, Rev. Dr. Martin Luther King Jr. speaks as loudly today as he did during his lifetime, "If a man has not discovered something for which he will die, he isn't fit to live."[17]

While some may struggle with these words, Dr. King was not suggesting that we leave home in the morning with the intent to offer ourselves as living sacrifices. He seemed to be saying that actions speak louder than words and we ought to be committed to something that is so precious to us, until we will fight for our belief at all costs. In his case it was to resist to the end, those who would keep us in bondage. Ultimately, that in which we believe can possibly cost us our lives, but the definition of a martyr is one who loses their life because of what they believe; not because they get up in the morning saying, today I am going to be a martyr.

---

17. Martin Luther King Jr., speech, Detroit, Michigan, June 23, 1963.

If we struggle with the words of Dr. King, an introspective look should cause us to at least consider who we really are and to whom we belong. Scripture reinforces that such words, actions, and examination are still relevant when we measure ourselves against the eternal standard set before us; the death of our Lord and Savior, Jesus the Christ. The humanity of Jesus speaks to us when we consider the words of the prophet Isaiah, which are described by *The New Interpreter's Bible Commentary* this way:

"This particular eschatalogical dialectic, if that is the way to describe it, has remained eschatologically open in its history of interpretation."[18] At a minimum, we hear the words of Isaiah describing the extreme sacrifice of one for many:

> He is despised and rejected of men; a man of sorrows, and acquainted with grief: and we hid as it were *our* faces from him; he was despised and we esteemed him not. Surely he hath borne our griefs, and carried our sorrows: yet we did esteem him stricken, smitten of God, and afflicted. But he was wounded for our transgressions, *he* was bruised for our iniquities: the chastisement of our peace *was* upon him; and with his stripes we are healed. (Isa. 53:3–5, KJV)

It may be worth considering whether we are doing ministry that goes beyond Sunday morning sermons. Are our Sunday morning words from on high convincing and sufficient enough by our witness to encourage us and others to want to be disciples of the Lord and agents for change, no matter who our audience of supporters as well as detractors may be?

Consider the Great Commission in the Gospel of Matthew 28:19–20 (KJV), "Go ye therefore, and teach all nations, baptizing them in the name of the Father, and of the Son, and of the Holy Ghost: Teaching them to observe all things whatsoever I have commanded you: and, lo, I am with you always, even unto the end of the world."

We are not asked to go to the Cross. Jesus did that for us. We are asked to acknowledge the one who died for us and to act like his sacrifice means something to us, so much so until we are willing to go beyond the ordinary to help alleviate the misery and pain that others feel in being marginalized and discriminated against.

If Jesus's words in Matthew are a bit much, then consider the Gospel of Mark, which simply says, "Go ye into all the world and preach the gospel to every creature" (16:15, KJV). This means to at least make an attempt to preach

---

18. *The New Interpreter's Study Bible, A Commentary in Twelve Volumes*, vol. VI (Nashville: Abingdon Press, 1994), 461.

(communicate) God's word to anyone who will listen and not just to those in whom we find comfort.

Conclusion

In preparing myself to write, I called upon my father's good friend, Mr. Eugene Williams and asked if he would be willing to spend some time with me concerning my father and Charlottesville. My father transitioned to glory in June of 1988; however, I have always known that there was a close connection between my family and the Williams family. Mr. Williams's mother and my great grandmother once lived within a few houses of each other on Dice Street. Though that portion of Dice Street no longer exists because of eminent domain exercised by the city of Charlottesville in the early 1970s, the ties between the families were never broken. Mr. Williams and my mother, Cornelia Gault, were childhood classmates.

After several phone conversations, I traveled to Charlottesville and spent a few hours with Mr. Williams. During our time together, I listened intently as he shared thoughts and information with me concerning the Charlottesville that was once my home. I am eternally grateful for the words, experience, knowledge, wisdom, and evidence of perseverance that Mr. Eugene Williams shared with me, for he is truly an example of one who has come through the fire with his integrity intact and his head bloodied but unbowed.

The Charlottesville of my youth and my brief eleven years there pale in comparison to those of my father and his counterparts and to the many classmates I left in Charlottesville when I departed permanently. Today, I have no known relatives left in Charlottesville because all of my extended family, including aunts and uncles, first and second cousins and others, have either died or moved to other places in the United States.

Still, I end this essay enlightened, fortified, and reinvigorated, as the reality of actual human experiences and the national headlines remind me that the pain of racism still dwells with many in our country, for we have not yet achieved victory. The battlegrounds and those who would deprive others of their God-given freedoms and rights as human beings who God created are alive and well. Those battlefields require the same vigilance and dedicated opposition to stem the ever-rising tide of hatred for anything or anyone who does not look like or act in a way that another human being feels they should.

Across this country, from sea to shining sea, hope still remains eternal. Even in the face of the continued pain of racism, we cannot forget that we have had the presence and impact of the Rev. Dr. Martin Luther King Jr., who was assassinated for his stance and actions concerning racism and civil rights for people of color. To say that he was disliked by many persons in this country would be an understatement; however, today the Martin Luther King Jr. Memorial is located in West Potomac Park next to the National Mall in Washington, DC. It is situated on four acres and includes the Stone of Hope, a granite statue of Dr. King. The statue is a testimony as to who he was and what he stood for.

We cannot forget that we have had a Black president, Barack Hussein Obama, who was elected and served two full terms, eight years in office. Before that, with the pain of racism very much a reality, not many of my father's time could or did envision that these two events would ever become a reality. So while racism and the pain it causes appear to be on the rise again, we can ill afford to lose hope or fail to remain faithful that we serve a God who has seen us through many dangers, toils, and snares and that it was the grace of God that has seen and will see us through.

I acknowledge Mr. Williams, for it is he who is responsible for the continuing question asked throughout this essay, "Do we feel the pain of others?" I am externally grateful and appreciative of the time he allowed me to spend with him. In our conversations about many matters involving my father and him and our families, I felt the sincerity and concern that he has for those whom he has come in contact with over a lifetime of ninety-one years. I also felt the pain that he carries with him, even in his ninety-first year. As stated in detail in the beginning of this essay, I felt the pain inside of him as he shared with me a significant loss that he suffered very early in his life. I felt the pain as he described the circumstances around that loss. A loss that is still so painful, so vivid and so devastating for him, that he can describe it as if it happened yesterday. Painful, because due to the racial ills of society at the time, justice was subverted and life-altering events subsequently occurred out of the necessity for the survival of a family left behind. The necessary acquiescence to the offer made to his mother created further pain that no monetary amount would have been sufficient enough to right the wrongs of that day, nor to replace all that he and his family lost forever, within an instant.

As I listened, his question, "Do we feel the pain of others?" became even more impactful, because I could hear the pain in his words and can only imagine, even now, how I might feel in his shoes.

On Being Discouraged and Lacking Compassion

Mr. Williams understands that, at times, we get discouraged. He says that he has learned that the first answer to anything concerning race, advancement, or dismantling of instruments that have been used against us is going to be "No!" Certainly, we want, yes, but that is not going to be the first answer that we receive. Mr. Williams feels that we cannot allow such responses to cause us to become easily discouraged.

Mr. Williams knows what the pain of racism is, and in comparing it to everyday feelings, says, "when you hurt, you scream." The continued pain of racism hurts when one considers that many Black persons living today have witnessed or heard about their parents, grandparents, and great grandparents having to put up with decades of the same old treatment and collective pain. At some point, the hurt is so painful until they scream in many different ways because the pain is overwhelming.

When we see others who appear to become disorderly in certain official settings, he suggests that before we judge them, we might want to consider that their anger and frustration in attempting to deal with the "system" while getting the same old answers and perhaps no more results than those who have gone before them, results in pain. Their pain. I submit to those who may read this, that in speaking with Mr. Williams, I am convinced that we must consider the pain of others; for even if we "walk a mile in their shoes," the shoes are still theirs, not ours. We must have compassion for others who don't handle things in the way we would handle them. Remember that the Rev. Dr. Martin Luther King Jr. encountered those in Birmingham who felt he was being too radical, but he felt people had been hurting under racism long enough. He felt it was time for him to proceed and proceed he did.

I now leave you with these thoughts. To be sure, the pain of racism is ever with us, but so are all the other troubles of this world. We have work to do, sometimes in the midst of a storm of pain, suffering, and doubt. As we consider formation at the congregational level, it is important that the elders share their stories; their stories of how they have survived racism in this country. They have a story to tell that would enrich the lives of our young people. Let us go forth with assurance, doing the work that God has given us to do.

41

Black History[1]

Rebecca Steele

I am serving as pastor of Grace Lutheran in Ft. Washington, Maryland—a remarkable, sweet, and faithful congregation that is generously letting me explore some ideas and directions with them for the sake of call and ministry, theirs and mine.

Recently, I referred to Dr. King's Birmingham campaign and the Children's Crusade in my sermons. Afterward, one person confessed that he was surprised to hear about Dr. King when it wasn't Black History Month. Another person I admire said she was a teenager in the sixties when the country was torn apart by the civil rights movement. She had heard from trusted adults that King was a troublemaker and that more recent history has treated him as a saint. She had been confused for decades and was seeking insight on how to understand him from a faith perspective. Given the sincerity of these comments, and given that we are in the season of Pentecost where we are invited to lean into spiritual growth, and given my awe of Dr. King as being one of the most profound embodiments of rigorous discipleship, I decided I would refer to Dr. King regularly in the upcoming weeks of Pentecost—not as a political point of reference, but as a teacher to show what it means to follow Jesus.

It turns out that King's collection of sermons in *Strength to Love* might as well have been written specifically as an accompaniment to the Luke lectionary cycle. Copies of *Strength to Love* were ordered for the congregation and there were reading assignments for homework each week. It would seem that as we confront the issue of race in this country and misinformation, more opportunities should be developed to bring together the writings of the saints of the civil rights struggle and the cycle of church seasons.

---

1. Editor's note: This was written in January 2019, in preparation for Black History Month.

Strength to Love Reading Schedule—Season of Pentecost			
Week	Lectionary Gospel Text	Strength to Love Reading Assignment (By Chapter)	S2L Biblical Reference
1	Luke 10:1–11, 16–20 Sent out 2 by 2	Intro	
2	Luke 10:25–37 Good Samaritan	3: On Being A Good Neighbor	Luke 10: Good Samaritan
3	Luke 10:38–42 Mary and Martha	2: Transformed Nonconformist	Romans 12: Be transformed by renewing of mind
4	Luke 11:1–13 Knock at Midnight	6: A Knock at Midnight	Luke 11: What friend, when asked for bread, will say I have nothing to set before him?
5	Luke 12:13–21 Man who was fool	7: The Man Who Was a Fool	Luke 12: Thou fool, this night thy soul shall be required of thee
6	Luke 12:32–40 Be ready	15: Pilgrimage to Nonviolence	(MLK reflects theologically on nonviolence.)
7	Luke 12:49–56 Not peace but a sword	5: Loving Your Enemies	Matthew 5: Love your enemies
8	Luke 13:10–17 Heal on Sabbath	12: Antidotes for Fear	I John 4: Perfect love casts out fear
9	Luke 14:1, 7–14 Humble selves for battle	13: The Answer to a Perplexing Question	Matthew 24: Why could we not cast out Satan?
10	Luke 14:25–33 Take up cross	1: A Tough Mind and a Tender Heart	Matthew 10: Wise as serpents, harmless as doves
11	Luke 15:1–10 Lost coin	9: Shattered Dreams	Romans 15: Paul's failure to get to Spain
12	Luke 16:1–13 Shrewd Manager	10: How Should a Christian View Communism?	Amos: Let justice roll down
13	Luke 16:19–31 Poor Lazarus	14: Paul's Letters to American Christians	(King writes in Paul's voice to the United States.)
14	Luke 17:5–10 Mustard seed	11: Our God is Able	Jude 24: To him who is able to keep you from falling

Continued

Strength to Love Reading Schedule–Season of Pentecost *Continued*

15	Luke 17:11-19 One returns to give thanks	4: Love in Action	Luke 23: Forgive them, they know not what they do
16	Luke 18:1-8 Persistent widow and judge	8: The Death of Evil upon the Seashore	Exodus 14: Israel saw the Egyptians dead on the shore
17	Luke 18:9-14 Piety of the Pharisee, and tax collector	Preface by Coretta Scott King	

42

The Browning of Theological Education

Frank A. Thomas

One of the critical facts facing seminaries and divinity schools everywhere in the twenty-first century is, by all credible projections, theological education will be "browning" for the foreseeable future, meaning increasing numbers of women and people of color will be seeking theological education. With this future, it is incumbent for women and people of color to ensure that the education we receive meets our needs and experience. Theological education is expensive and all too many students will be taking on life-altering debt. Therefore, it is important that we get a good return on that investment in that we can find places of employment when we graduate and that racism (and sexism) will not continue to place barriers to our gainful employment.

We must also take responsibility to ensure that our teachers are in partnership with us concerning our academic learning and spiritual formation, represented in culturally competent administrations and faculty, as well as course and curriculum design. In the late 1960s, African American students protested about the need for education relevant to the Black experience and helped shape Black studies classes, curricula, and programs all over the country. We must make sure our voices are heard today and speak up for our needs in theological education. The bottom line is if we do not speak up and advocate for culturally competent and relevant theological education, it will not happen.

Faculty who design curricula and teach courses have a special responsibility in this new era of theological education. It is critically important that all who teach, particularly faculty of color and women, speak up on behalf of an increasingly diverse student body. In many instances, faculty members have spoken up and fostered the beginnings of significant change; however, the burden of a greater intentionality is required to see the change that must occur. Further, we all must involve ourselves in the push for much more diverse leadership in deanships and presidencies connected to and supporting theological and accrediting institutions, boards of trustees, and granting and funding institutions. In addition to these, we must also develop new, fresh, creative, and dynamic programs that speak to diversity, not only at the master of divinity and doctor of ministry degree levels, but also, at the PhD level—for example, the formation of the very first PhD Program in African American Preaching and Sacred Rhetoric at Christian Theological Seminary. I await the first PhD program in Black Theology, Womanist Theology, and much more. We must find complimentary programs that will train and equip faculty who will teach this increasingly diverse student body. If we do not vision and speak, no one will vision and speak for us. We will move the Church from the ground up because those we graduate will not be content with the Church of old.

Reflection Questions

1. Were your Sunday (or Sabbath) school materials diverse and culturally based?

2. If you have children and they attend Sunday (or Sabbath) school, are the materials diverse and culturally based?

3. If you attend adult Bible study, were you encouraged to consider the stories and events through the lens of cultures other than your own?

4. If you have attended seminary, did you take courses that lifted up the African American experience in the country and the Church?

5. If you are non-White and African American courses were offered at your seminary or divinity school, did you take any of those courses? Why or why not?

6. If you are African American and African American courses were offered at your seminary or divinity school, did you take any of those courses? Why or why not?

7. Regardless of your race, would you consider participating in a program that offered Black preaching and sacred rhetoric? Why or why not?

8. If your seminary offered courses in the Black theological experience, were they required or elective courses?

9. If you attended or attend seminary, does your institution offer immersions or travel that focuses on the Black experience in this country? If yes, have you participated in one? Why or why not?

10. Have you ever considered researching your family's involvement in the civil rights struggle or the continued struggle for human rights and sharing that story as part of the formation process with your congregation?

Contributors

Paul Roberts Abernathy is a progressive free-thinker and retired Episcopal priest, formerly the rector of St. Mark's Capitol Hill, in Washington, DC.

Claudia Marion Allen is an activist, a writer, speaker, and teacher for justice. She is passionate about activating the activist in all of us. She is a member of the Seventh-day Adventist Church.

Jennifer Amuzie is a millennial activist and Episcopalian who attends Calvary Episcopal Church in Washington, DC.

Jennifer Baskerville-Burrows is Episcopalian and in 2016 became the first African American woman elected diocesan bishop in the history of the Episcopal Church. She serves as the eleventh bishop to the Episcopal Diocese of Indianapolis.

Antonio J. Baxter is a late millennial, an MDiv student at Wesley Theological Seminary, and a candidate for the vocational diaconate in the Episcopal Diocese of Washington. He attends Calvary Episcopal Church in Washington, DC.

Nathan D. Baxter is an Episcopalian, the retired bishop of the Diocese of Central Pennsylvania, and the former dean of the Washington National Cathedral.

Tempie D. Beaman* is a rostered minister of word and service in the Evangelical Lutheran Church in America (ELCA) and a graduate of Pacific Lutheran Theological Seminary in Berkeley, California.

Walter Brownridge is an Episcopal/Anglican priest and serves at Christ Church, Grosse Pointe, Michigan.

Mariann Edgar Budde was elected ninth bishop of the Episcopal Diocese of Washington in 2011. She is the first woman to be consecrated diocesan bishop in the history of the diocese.

Kevin Burdet is a millennial and attended Calvary Episcopal Church in Washington, DC, before making a move to Seattle, Washington, in early 2019.

Staci L. Burkey* is a GenXer and an atheist.

Nicole D. is a millennial who is seeking.

Kelly Brown Douglas is an Episcopal priest and currently serves as the dean of the Episcopal Divinity School at Union and the canon theologian for Washington National Cathedral.

Laura Evans* is an Episcopalian and attends St. James Episcopal Church in Austin, Texas.

Gayle Fisher-Stewart* is an Episcopal priest and currently serves as the interim rector of the historic St. Luke's Episcopal Church in Washington, DC.

Marlene Eudora Forrest* is a priest in the Episcopal Church and currently serves as Priest-In-Charge at St. Philip's Episcopal Church in Richmond, Virginia.

Charles D. Fowler III is an ordained deacon and serves at Hemingway Memorial AME Church in District Heights, Maryland.

Wilda C. Gafney is an Episcopal priest and professor of Hebrew Bible at Brite Divinity School in Fort Worth, Texas.

Morgan G. Harding* is a millennial who is Church-averse and is waiting to see whether the Church lives into its call to follow Jesus.

James C. Harrington,* a civil rights lawyer of forty-six years, is an Episcopal priest and serves at Proyecto Santiago Missional Community, St. James Episcopal Church in Austin, Texas.

Vincent Powell Harris is an Episcopal priest (ret.) in the Episcopal Diocese of Washington. He is committed to keeping alive the history of the Episcopal Church as it intersects with race.

MaryBeth Ingram* is an Episcopalian and attends St. Matthews Episcopal Church in Westerville, Ohio.

Peter Jarrett-Schell is an Episcopal priest and serves as the rector of Calvary Episcopal Church in Washington, DC, where he lives with his wife and son.

F. Willis Johnson is a spiritual entrepreneur, ordained elder, and church planter in the West Ohio Conference of the United Methodist Church.

Mike Kinman is a GenXer, an Episcopal priest, and serves as rector at All Saints Episcopal Church, Pasadena, California.

Ginny Klein* is Episcopalian and attends Ascension Episcopal Church in Silver Spring, Maryland.

Steve Lawler is an Episcopal priest and recently retired from St. Stephen's and the Vine in Ferguson, Missouri. He currently serves as founding director for the Walker Leadership Institute, Webster Groves, Missouri.

Charles Michael Livingston Jr is a millennial who was raised Episcopalian.

Monai Lowe is a millennial currently working as a pharmacist in Washington, DC. Her denomination is Baptist.

Sandra T. Montes was born in Perú and grew up in Guatemala and Texas. An Episcopalian, she is also a musician, writer, and speaker and blesses the Church by speaking out to help the Church "become wider and not Whiter."

Deniray Mueller* is Episcopalian, an ordained vocational deacon, and serves as legislative liaison in the Episcopal Diocese of Southern Ohio.

Rebecca S. Myers* is an Episcopal priest and currently serves as rector of the Episcopal Church of the Nativity and St. Stephen's, Newport, Pennsylvania.

Kevin C. Pinckney is an Episcopalian and attends St. Andrew's Episcopal Church in College Park, Maryland.

Judith Rhedin* is an Episcopalian and attends St. James Episcopal Church in Austin, Texas.

Gene Robinson is the first openly gay and partnered priest to be elected bishop in historic Christianity, becoming the ninth bishop of the Episcopal Diocese of New Hampshire in 2003. Now retired, he worships at St. Thomas Episcopal Church in Washington, DC.

Glenice Robinson-Como is an Episcopal priest and formerly served as canon pastor at Christ Church Cathedral in Houston, Texas. She is currently the rector of All Saints Episcopal Church, Stafford, Texas.

Cara Rockhill is an Episcopal priest and recovering defense attorney, who is somewhere between a millennial and GenXer, currently serving at St. Andrew's Church in Marblehead, Massachusetts.

Jamie Samilio is an Episcopal priest and gay woman who serves at the Episcopal Church of the Holy Cross in the Diocese of Virginia.

Ruth McMeekin Skjerseth* is Episcopalian and attends the Church of the Epiphany in Herndon, Virginia.

Carolyne Starek* is Episcopalian and attends St. Columba's Episcopal Church in Washington, DC.

Rebecca Steele is ordained in the Evangelical Lutheran Church in America and is pastor of the Grace Lutheran Church in Ft. Washington, Maryland.

Rob Stephens is an ordained minister in the United Church of Christ and serves as national political director for Repairers of the Breach and co-director of the June 20, 2020, Moral March on Washington with the Poor People's Campaign: A National Call for Moral Revival.

Frank A. Thomas is an ordained minister and currently serves as the director of the PhD program in African American Preaching and Sacred Rhetoric and is the Nettie Sweeney and Hugh Th. Miller Professor of Homiletics at Christian Theological Seminary, Indianapolis, Indiana.

Kwasi Thornell was ordained an Episcopal priest in 1972. He has always pushed the envelope of what it is to be Black and Episcopalian. He is retired and is committed to assisting churches and other groups understand and end the disease of Alzheimer's.

Shayna J. Watson* is a GenXer, an Episcopal priest, and currently serves as the canon pastor and diversity officer at St. Stephen's Episcopal Cathedral and School in the Episcopal Diocese of Central Pennsylvania

Alissa Williams serves as managing editor of SpectrumMagazine.org, an independent Seventh-day Adventist publication. She is a millennial and lifelong lay member of the Adventist Church, and seeks to use her platform to highlight the fundamental truth that social justice is the gospel message.

* Participated in the May 2019 Pilgrimage to Alabama.